D1617157

Postsocial History

Postsocial History

An Introduction

Miguel A. Cabrera
Translated by Marie McMahon

LEXINGTON BOOKS
Lanham • *Boulder* • *New York* • *Toronto* • *Oxford*

LEXINGTON BOOKS

Published in the United States of America
by Lexington Books
An imprint of The Rowman & Littlefield Publishing Group, Inc.
4501 Forbes Boulevard, Suite 200, Lanham, Maryland 20706

PO Box 317
Oxford
OX2 9RU, UK

British Library Cataloguing in Publication Information Available

Library of Congress Cataloging-in-Publication Data

Cabrera, M. A.
    Postsocial history : an introduction / Miguel A. Cabrera ; translated by
Marie McMahon.
        p. cm.
    Includes bibliographical references and index.
    ISBN 0-7391-0683-X (cloth : alk. paper)
    1. Social history—Historiography. 2. Culture. I. Title.

    HN28.C26 2004
    306'.09—dc22   2003018520

Printed in the United States of America

Contents

Foreword

The title of Miguel Cabrera's book serves admirably to define a definite movement in historical writing. If, as he writes, the historians he describes have different intellectual trajectories and come from different traditions, so that they might not always see what they have in common as more important than what separates them, nonetheless their work has a definite identity, despite the evident differences. The term of his title, postsocial, catches well this identity, in terms of the search for a form of thinking and writing about the world that seeks to extend beyond the old understandings of the social, but yet at the same time retains that term "social" as a sign that to disown it entirely is to leave behind essential dimensions of understanding. Therefore, the term points forward without losing sight of the past, which for historians is no bad thing. It is a good name.

What the name stands for, elaborated in great detail by the author, is the attempt to move beyond established understandings of the social, evident in history, especially social history, and the social sciences more widely. As he shows, far from being a mere legacy of the past, these approaches are still extremely powerful. Such understandings, to put it briefly, tend to conceive of society in static, mechanical terms—the idea of society as a framework or structure is emblematic—and as unproblematically given in the nature of things as a "real," autonomous entity, exerting its own pressures and influences upon other domains of life regarded as separate from it, chiefly "culture." What the book also helps us to recognize is the rather analogous move in what has been called "the new cultural history," despite its deep genuflection to the supposed autonomy of culture and representation. Here "society" and the "social" are frequently smuggling by the backdoor, or else old-fashioned revisionism comes back in, simply denying any role to the social at all in its emphasis upon a voluntary acting human agent, or upon a voluntary action of representation itself. What is particularly interesting about the book is its success in nailing down this usually unacknowledged intellectual conservatism of the new cultural history.

The way forward, then, would seem to involve some idea of the social, yet to radically rethink this idea. The book is a contribution to this rethinking, one that has the very great merit of being not only about social theory, but also about what historians do, what they write, the arguments that they have. I can think of very few works that mediate the relationship between theoretical concerns and the practical writing of history, and this is decidedly one of them. It is therefore extremely timely in its appearance. Its timeliness also relates to the widespread rethinking of the idea of the social going on across a very big range of disciplines. This book is a contribution to that gathering debate, a unique and particularly interesting one, unique in the sense that it is relatively unusual for historians to theorize their own practice.

This rethinking of the social is pursued in terms of the agenda of the book: the author considers the "discursive" construction of social reality, unpacking the term and separating it from its solely linguistic associations; he then considers the constitution of interests and identities and explores the concept of social action. Central to all these concerns is his desire to avoid traditional theoretical interpretations of the world as neatly divided into various kinds of twos: society and culture, the objective and the subjective, the material and representation, and other familiar spirits of the past. In his desire to circumvent the failures of these old dualistic interpretations, this old dichotomous rendering of the world, he is at one with attempts to look at the social world anew. What in particular he brings to this new look is a relational understanding of the production of meaning in the historical past, the term "relational" referring to the necessity to situate systems of meaning within particular settings of the social but without losing sight of the recognition that meanings are always made discursively. While he does not explicitly develop here those new understandings of the social with which his project is in deep sympathy, nonetheless the agenda of the book creates the conditions in which historical writing can be linked again to new sorts of social and cultural theory. In particular, they can be linked to what we might call postsocial theory, in short the social being understood as in these new guises something fluid, mobile, practical, and about as unlike the old idea of the framework as might be imagined.

This new sort of social also involves the material, so that alongside the dualisms mentioned already would be those of society and nature, and the human and the nonhuman. Although the book tends to emphasize the creation of meaning among human actors, and therefore to emphasize representation rather than objects or things, it is part of the rainbow alliance of the postsocial, which would embrace words and things together as part of one world. In particular, science studies has much to teach cultural history here, and goes far to augment postsocial history. Which is to say that everywhere traditional understandings of what the limitations of our inherited, traditional vocabularies still directs me to call the social order are breaking down, when the social and cultural, and the economic and political, are no longer distinct, and distinctly useful theoretical demarcations of the world, and when we must embrace the operations of language and the physical workings of the world together in similar kinds of explanations. This book is an important contribution to this work of the postsocial, and therefore to the critical but constructive scrutiny of tradition.

Patrick Joyce
Department of History
University of Manchester
July 2003

Acknowledgments

I want to express my deepest gratitude for the crucial collaboration and inestimable support of those individuals who made the writing and publication of this book possible. Gabrielle M. Spiegel read the manuscript and provided highly suggestive commentary, and with enormous generosity dedicated her precious time and remarkable talent to my efforts. Her invaluable backing helped bring about the publication of this book. Equally generous with his comments, Jay M. Smith gave extremely valuable and disinterested assistance. The observations of John R. Hall on an early draft were extremely useful and an especially significant contribution at that critical moment. For some time now I have had the incredible privilege to count on the constant encouragement of Patrick Joyce, who urged me to put my ideas on paper and actually gave me the opportunity to present them for the first time in a public forum. For many years now, I have enjoyed the huge personal benefit his perspicacious remarks, overall understanding, and tireless support sustain. Without the enthusiasm and material support of my unflagging friend and intellectual sounding board, Marie McMahon, this book would never have seen the light of day. Finally, I owe special appreciation to a group of colleagues at the University of La Laguna who have strived to provide me with an amicable and propitious environment, one always favorable to agreeable discussion and, more and more, to passionate and fruitful debate. My sincere thanks to each and every one of them. They are Inmaculada Blasco, Joaquín Carreras, Blanca Divassón, Jesús de Felipe, Victorio Heredero, José M. López-Molina, Jorge Sánchez, Álvaro Santana, and Javier Soler.

Introduction

This is a book in historiography addressing theoretical developments in the field of historical studies over the past two decades. During these years, a time of notably intense historiographical debate, an incremental critical rethinking of the main theoretical assumptions previously underpinning historical explanation has occurred and in the process a new theory of society has begun to take shape among historians. Such, at least, is the conclusion I draw from my examination of recent historiographical developments. They evince a new theoretical outlook essentially different from predecessors; one that involves a qualitatively distinct way of understanding how society works, of explaining individuals' consciousness and actions, and of conceiving of the genesis, nature, and reproduction of social relations and institutions. This theoretical shift is giving rise to a new change of historical paradigm, a change that seems as far-reaching as that brought about, in its time, by the emergence and spreading of the so-called social history. Now, like then, much of previous historiographical common sense is collapsing around us, and many inherited historical interpretations, including the most firmly settled ones, are being revised, substantially rectified, or simply abandoned and replaced by others. Although still in its early stages, this historiographical mutation is already visible even to the least attentive observer, and its marks can be felt in many fields of study, be they recently created ones, such as gender history, or those of a longer-standing tradition, like labor history or the history of liberal revolutions. This book has been written, therefore, for the purpose of putting forward the terms in which this new historiographical rendering of social theory is being carried out, assessing its practical implications for historical analysis, and offering a preliminary as well as summary account of the new theory of society just now emerging.[1]

The last two decades have also witnessed an extensive, lively, and highly valuable debate on the nature of historical knowledge. Indeed, much recent historiographical discussion has focused on the epistemological status of historical writing, and the amount and richness of the literature generated are almost impossible for any one reader to tackle. However, although acknowledging the great importance and stimulating challenges of this particular arena of historiographical debate, I do no more than heed its significant existence here. On this occasion, I am more concerned with and exclusively driven by the practical purpose of addressing the more immediate problems of historical explanation that historians face daily.

The origin of the new kind of history and its theory of society is to be found in the decline of social history and, specifically, in the crisis of the theoretical dichotomous and objectivist model which grounds social history. A growing and resolute doubt among historians has been cast on the premise, so deeply rooted in the history profession, that human societies are composed of an objective sphere (identified in general with the socio-economic instance) holding causal primacy and of a subjective or cultural sphere deriving from the former. And, therefore, that, in other words, individuals' consciousness and practice are causally determined by their social conditions of existence. As I describe more thoroughly in chapter 1, social historians have been forced, almost from the beginning, to come up with different ad hoc conceptual supplements in order to respond to the anomalies and explanatory shortcomings of their theoretical model and, as well, in order to make new social phenomena and situations (of both the past and the present) intelligible. This is what triggered a pronounced internal evolution in the paradigm of social history, an evolution that still continues today. From a certain moment in time, however, a significant minority of historians began to suggest that in order to surmount such anomalies and shortcomings, it was not enough to reformulate the central tenet of social history. Instead, facing what proved to be increasingly sterile as a tool of historical analysis, it was necessary to put this tenet itself under critical scrutiny. At the same time, these historians began to react against the secular dilemma between materialism and idealism, between objectivism and subjectivism, or between social explanation and intentional explanation in which historical scholarship had been trapped for decades, as this too was found to be another serious hindrance to potential exploration of new explanatory possibilities. Thus, efforts within social history to make the causal connection between social structure and subjective action more flexible, complex, and contingent eventually led, over time, to casting doubts on the existence of not only such a causal connection, but of the two instances involved in it as well. The outcome of this critical reaction has been the emergence of a new picture of social life, one that appears to be governed by a different causal logic, and to which I will turn my attention from chapter 2 onward.

Of course, if one enlarges the scope of the problematic under examination, the decline of social history and the ongoing theoretical reorientation in the field of historical studies are quickly recognized as only a part of a far more encompassing process of cultural, scientific, and intellectual change, commonly termed the *crisis of modernity*. In fact, recent vicissitudes over historical writing and the intensity, patterns, and terms of the historiographical debate in the last few years are only fully intelligible if viewed within this larger frame. In a certain sense then, the emergence of the new conception of society is no more than an outstanding chunk of this general process of change and, therefore, it could be said that this book is actually dealing with the effects of the impact of the crisis of modernity on the field of history. That does not mean, however, that the new form of history is just a reflection or a mere effect of so-called postmodern philosophy and that historians, as is sometimes exhorted, should therefore feel obliged to confront the present situation in defensive terms against this presumed external enemy threatening history and endangering its very survival.[2] Such a diagnosis seems mistaken, since historians have not been simply passive receivers, but, on the contrary, active participants, and because history—and the social sciences in general—is indeed a major protagonist in scenarios concerned with future conceptions of the world, society, or political practice. This is why taking up a defensive stance seems short-sighted and, quite frankly, debilitating, since it shuns active engagement in debate and thus reduces the chances for overcoming the historiographical impasse the decline of social history purports.

The reasons why the crisis of modernity has affected history so deeply are easy to identify. Since historical science and the conceptual frameworks with which it has worked were forged within—or rather, are essential components of—a modern social worldview, the crisis of modernity is bound to provoke a collapse of established historiographical paradigms and a *denaturalization* of the analytical concepts of both social and traditional history. The crisis of the modern worldview has brought forth an awareness that these concepts, and the theories of society they underpin, are not mere representations or labels of social phenomena or processes that really exist but, rather, historically specific forms of making social reality something intelligible or meaningful. Historians were previously unaware because they themselves remained part and parcel of and worked within the modern conceptual universe. Thus, the crisis of modernity has triggered a sort of conceptual disenchantment and a loss of theoretical innocence that seem to be irreversible. For as Patrick Joyce

shrewdly notes, once innocence is lost, it cannot be regained.[3] Once concepts have lost their representational status and, consequently, their theoretical aura, central notions of social analysis such as individual, society,
class, nation, revolution, or politics can no longer be used in the same
sense, with the same epistemological certainty, or with the same analytical function as before.

But this is not all. Apart from the collapse of a particular body of concepts, the crisis of modernity has also entailed a correlative collapse of the
very epistemological foundations they rested upon. If modern categories
are not representations of an objective social reality, but rather effects of a
certain meaningful arrangement of such a reality, then their practical efficacy—that is, their power to guide social action for so long—cannot be attributed to the fact that they reflect either human nature or objective laws
of social life. It should be attributed to the capacity of the categories themselves to generate and become embodied in social practices, relations, and
institutions. If this has really been the case, then historical scholarship
must immediately assume its implications for the study of society. The
first of which is that the historical formation of concepts not only becomes
a primordial subject of inquiry, but, even more importantly, it constitutes
the very foundation of social theory.[4]

Thus, the theory of society that is currently taking shape within historical studies has come to rest on new assumptions. It assumes individuals
are not autonomous subjects (as they are for traditional history) and calls
into question the view of social reality as an objective entity possessing
the power to *causally* determine the meaningful practice of individuals (as
social history claims). If the latter were the case, then the concepts that
people use to apprehend and make sense of their social world and to
arrange their practice would be cultural or ideological reflections of such
a world. However, as both the crisis of modernity and historical inquiry
itself are making clear, such concepts are not mere representations of the
real working and development of human societies, but rather specific
ways of conceiving of them. To speak so is to say the following: language
is not simply a means of communication but a pattern of meanings, and
therefore does not limit itself to naming real phenomena but actively constructs them as meaningful entities, that is, as objective ones. The meanings that people confer on social context and their place in it, as well as
the ways in which they define themselves as agents, are always dependent on the conceptual lens through which such a context is apprehended,
and not on the context itself. Ideas, forms of consciousness, or identities
are neither rational or intellectual creations nor expressions of the social
sphere, but the results of an operation of meaningful construction of reality. What this implies, as a theoretical corollary, is a new concept of social
action, different from that of both intentional and social explanatory mod-

els. Human practices are neither rational actions nor socially determined ones, but the effect of the mediation of a certain way of conceptually constructing social situations and relations. Previous theoretical approaches had explained human action in terms of either the free-will decision of agents or the determination of social circumstances. With the advent of the new theoretical paradigm, human action has instead come to be explained in terms of the meanings that agents confer on social context when they apply the conceptual pattern prevailing in each juncture. Thus, the old dual theoretical scheme (reality/ideas) has been left behind and replaced with a triadic scheme (reality/language/ideas) in which language is a specific domain of social life that works as an active mediation in making the meanings that underlie practice.

So far, I have expressed myself, in reference to both the present-day state of social history and the emergence of a new theory of society, with a certainty that many readers probably find not only excessive but even groundless as well. Is the crisis of social history really so profound as to allow the claim that we are witnessing a new change of paradigm? After all, idealist historians have never ceased to criticize the tenets of social history and in recent years this criticism has even intensified and so-called revisionism is particularly vigorous at the moment. Can one really insist, moreover, in claiming that the ongoing historiographical debate is more than just another episode in the old quarrel between materialist and idealist history? That it has gone beyond the boundaries of that quarrel and laid the foundations of a new kind of history opposed to both social and intentional explanation? Since these are crucial issues in any diagnosis of the present-day state of historical studies, I do try to be somewhat more precise about the exact sense in which my words should be taken before actually turning to my more confident claims. First of all, this diagnosis of recent theoretical developments in the field of historical studies is not being put forward for the first time here. On the contrary, it has been not only previously held, more or less explicitly, by many authors, but has even been a subject of reflection and discussion for some time for a significant portion of the history profession. To cite just one example, Geoff Eley has maintained that the crisis of social history is fostering the opening up of an "imaginative and epistemological space" from which unusual forms of historical analysis are emerging. He even goes so far as to identify the ongoing theoretical shift as an irreversible move from a history based on the notion of social causality to another based on the notion of "discourse."[5] It is true, though, that the new theory of society remains widely unheeded and that its presence is not always immediately perceptible to the observer, as its features are not as clearly defined as those of social history or of traditional history. In fact, most of the authors who have dealt with recent developments in historical studies either view these as merely a somewhat more sophisticated prolongation of social history or they even encompass them in a somewhat voracious revisionist return to idealism or subjectivism. One has to keep in mind that the frontiers of the new form of history are still in flux and its theoretical framework riddled with ambiguities or gaps, and lacking clear contours. On the terrain of research practice, in particular, the break with preceding forms of history is partial and hesitant and the dividing line between them is often blurred, and on most occasions, the components of the new conception of society appear mixed up with those of previous conceptions. Such hybridity thwarts easy recognition of elements that are in open conflict with long-existent paradigms and that just might allow us to get around impasses into a new historiographical and theoretical territory.

Furthermore, the new theory of society often lies only latent in the works of the very authors bringing its emergence forth, and many historians who have actually contributed to current historiographical change seem to ignore any significant discontinuity between their theoretical outlook and that of social or new cultural history. And I have to admit that I suspect most of the authors whose works I consider conducive to the emergence of a new theory of society would probably feel misrecognized, think my reading of their writings tendentious or excessively forced, and dismiss the conclusions I draw as groundless or overstepping their actual positions. I should also point out that there is no particular historical work or individual author fully embodying the new kind of history, and anyone looking for an explicit account, a sort of handbook, will search in vain since, as far as I know, no such a work exists. Finally, although a few labels, some better than others, have been in circulation and do unequivocally point to this new kind of historical paradigm, so far no name enjoys anything like widespread acceptance.

However, none of the above, no matter how problematic, is meant to suggest that the new theory of society is a nonentity or that it is merely a passing mirage. It only means, as I have already said, that this theory is emerging, that it is still in initial stages of formation. A close historiographical examination reveals not only profound and extensive erosion in the explicative model of social history, but the crystallization of a potential alternative to it as well. Thus, albeit still embryonic, there is enough stuff there to announce a new theory of society available to history scholarship. Despite the weaknesses and concomitant objections heeded above, there is before us such an accumulation of fresh elements in the field of historical studies that, taken into account as a weighty whole and assembled as if they were pieces of a puzzle, strongly indicate, in my opinion, a new historiographical landscape. As well as they shape a new theoretical framework for analyzing and explaining historical processes and social phenomena. This series of elements includes everything from symptoms of dissatisfaction, intuitions, and suggestions for critical reconsiderations to completely new concepts and empirical assertions and from theoretical reflections, controversies, and localized rebellions to reinterpretations of historical phenomena and expressly alternative proposals. Many examples of these are to be found in this book.

The crucial point, from a historiographical perspective, is that the appearance of this set of elements—scattered in a multitude of works by various authors—has set up minimum conditions for going beyond the limits of preceding paradigms and for overcoming, as well, that choking secular dilemma between objectivism and subjectivism, allowing, thus, an alternative to social history that is not a return to the theoretical horizon of idealist history. In my opinion, the authors tackled and drawn upon here have, intentionally or not, led the discipline of history into unexplored territory and sketched the contours of a new agenda for historical research. Authors whose works contain elements that transcend the limits of preceding paradigms include historians like Keith M. Baker, Patrick Joyce, Zachary Lockman, Mary Poovey, Joan W. Scott, William H. Sewell, or James Vernon and historical sociologists like Richard Biernacki, Anne Kane, or Margaret R. Somers. Until a better term is available, I refer to the new kind of history their works produce as *Postsocial History*.[6]

The central body of this book is intended to give an account of the main features and theoretical assumptions of postsocial history. Although for the reasons explained above, on many occasions I can only offer general outlines or fleeting sketches, and, on others, I merely point out the gaps that only future developments can fill. Just the same, my presentation of the new historiographical paradigm may give the impression of being too schematic, abrupt, and lacking nuance and of giving short shrift to the complexities and modulations of social life. Such a brief work cannot pretend to fully explore or exhaust each and every implication or all the related issues. My purpose in writing this work is to highlight only the major theoretical premises of the emerging conception of history and to underline, as well, contrasts with preceding paradigms, all in order to foster reflective attention to current historiographical change and thus, hopefully, propitiate more effective discussion of it. If, eventually, the path cleared by postsocial historians proves fruitful for social analysis, there will be time enough to embody what is just a conceptual skeleton here, with future flesh, blood, and pulse. It would be useless to deny, likewise, that, as any historiographical book, this also involves an undertaking of theoretical elaboration, even if only minimally. The simple fact of identifying, selecting, and connecting a set of fragments that have, until now, remained scattered and not always expressly related implies per se an act of theoretical construction. Moreover, at certain times, I inevitably have to refer to some of the still unexplored implications of the decline of social history and the simultaneous resistance to the tendency to take refuge in traditional history. And in doing so, some of the trends already present in the terrain of historical practice will be carried to their logical conclusions. In any case, I try to keep the task of theoretical elaboration to the minimum necessary to guarantee a coherent exposition. And I also try to carry out such an undertaking with maximum caution, that is, staying within the limits authorized and permitted by the actual state of historical scholarship.

1

The Background:
From Social History
to the New Cultural History

I

In order to properly understand the concerns of postsocial historians and appraise the significance of the new theoretical approach, one must bear in mind the previous historiographical stage from which they stem. Thus, before proceeding to bring the main features of the emerging paradigm into sharper focus, I briefly recapitulate the internal evolution of social history in this chapter.

At the beginning of the 1960s, social history was already a well-established and prestigious academic endeavor in such pioneering countries as France and the United Kingdom and a blossoming one elsewhere. Although traditional history maintained its hegemony in quantitative terms, the new historiographical paradigm took root, gained ground, and grew into the most dynamic and innovative area of the discipline. At that time, two major schools or traditions—historical materialism and the *Annales* School—predominated, even though many social historians do not fall into either one or the other. The external manifestation of this reorientation of the discipline toward social history was a gradual move away from high politics, the star of traditional history's gaze, and a shift in analytical interest toward social and economic phenomena. However, such fresh concentration on socioeconomic matters actually ensued the adoption of a new theory of society by social historians. In open conflict with the subjectivism and factualism of traditional history, social historians brandished an objectivist theory of society based on the notion of social causality that triggered a marked transition from an explanatory paradigm founded on the concept of *subject* to one founded on the concept of *society*. In traditional history, subjectivity is underived, understood as a preconstituted center on which social practice rests, and historical agents are thus considered individuals possessing an autonomous rational conscience whose actions are fully explained by the explicit intentions that motivate them. From this viewpoint, society is an entity that is qualitatively no different from the sum of the individuals who compose it and, therefore, conscious intentions enjoy the rank of causes and, to an even greater extent, constitute the very grounds of social science. Social analysis consists primarily of an undertaking of comprehension or interpretation for the purpose of reenacting the thoughts and mental universe of social agents. In sharp contrast, social history disallows subjectivity in the sense of rational creation. To speak of subjectivity in social history can only refer to a reflection or expression of the social context in which human beings are placed. The causes of actions have nothing to do with autonomous individual agency, and given the social nature of the causes of actions, human beings may even remain unaware of them. The notion of *social subject* within a dichotomous and objectivist scheme, one granting primordial causality to social factors not individual agency in the production of meanings, has ruled a substantial share of historical research for decades and remains in force today even though important internal modifications have loosened the causal link.

This and the next paragraph continue to outline significant features of the social history paradigm before turning to a necessary examination of those modifications. The basic theoretical premise of social history is that the socioeconomic sphere constitutes an *objective structure*, in the double sense that it has an irreducible autonomy, including an internal mechanism of operation and change, and that it is the bearer of intrinsic meanings. Individuals' subjectivity—and the cultural realm in general—is, for social historians, no more than a representation or expression of their social being and, therefore, meaningful actions are causally determined by the material conditions of existence and by the position people occupy in social relations. The structural nature of economic conditions and the social relations rooted in them are also what mold the social edifice as a whole. On some occasions, this structural quality is also attributed to other factors, as occurs in some phases of the *Annales* school with demographic fluctuations and geography, but the theoretical principle remains the same: in all cases, society is conceived as a systemic unit made up of a series of vertically arranged strata and governed by a causal hierarchy that guarantees a basic fit between the upper and lower strata. The familiar distinctions between base and superstructure, between structure and action, or, in the annalist case, between levels or temporalities are due to this dualistic scheme. Such a theoretical scheme justifies the ambition to write a *total history*, that is to say, a history that approaches the different realms of social life as pieces of a whole whose intelligibility comes from just one of them.

The causal mechanism through which the socioeconomic sphere exercises its determination over the cultural or subjective sphere is understood by social history in the following terms. In general, the different positions that individuals occupy in the economic terrain translate into social divisions that, in turn, crystallize in forms of consciousness, identities, systems of beliefs, and values, and in legal bodies or political institutions. Specifically, the relations established in the socioeconomic sphere define the objective interests of individuals and, therefore, the actions these individuals take are due to a more or less conscious purpose of satisfying such interests. It is this social anchoring of interests that enables the distinction to be made between on the one hand objectively adequate behaviors and, on the other, deviate and anomalous behaviors that are the fruit of a false consciousness, that is, behaviors originating in an ideologically distorted image of reality.

Of course, this brief and selective characterization of social history's theory of society slights its rich complexity and heterogeneity but that is not my purpose nor a necessary task since numerous studies provide excellent and thorough discussions. Here I only break down the objectivist or materialist paradigm of social history into its basic components in order to highlight those most relevant to subsequent discussion and critical reconsideration from the 1980s onward. And in order to approach the critical rethinking of the last twenty years in a fully effective way, one is obliged to begin with those modifications, mentioned above, of the paradigm from within, that is, to begin to talk about what was an extremely significant internal evolution within social history itself. Since social historians operate within a dichotomous framework, this evolution has consisted of a gradual loosening or flexibilization of the causal link between social context and consciousness, that is, a partial rectification of the previous objectivist unilaterality allowing a *relative* autonomy to the cultural (or political) sphere and granting individuals an active role in the production of meanings. This evolution includes a reconceptualization of social relations with assistance of notions like the Thompsonian one of experience or the Chartierian one of representation. The result of this subjectivist or "culturalist" turn in social history was the appearance of what is called *sociocultural* or *new cultural history* which brings into relief a theory of society that profoundly reformulates the dichotomous and objectivist paradigm of classical social history, although without actually transcending it. Thus, before considering the terms of the crisis suffered by this paradigm and calibrating the implications this spells for social analysis, there is a need to look at this internal evolution of social history, as this is the starting point from which postsocial history will begin to emerge.[1]

Even in the 1960s and more so from the 1970s, the explanatory model of social history experiences regular critical review requiring appreciable transformation. At the same time and as part and parcel of such critique, social historians (both historical materialists and annalists) took a growing interest in studying culture. This shift in orientation, marking a transition from classical social history to sociocultural history (or as Roger Chartier, a protagonist in this reorientation, likes to say, from the social history of culture to the cultural history of the social), bespoke a growing dissatisfaction concerning the theoretical pattern of classical social history. As Joyce Appleby, Lynn Hunt, and Margaret Jacob write, it was the "disenchantment" with explaining everything in economic and social terms that drove many historians to reconsider the nature and the role of culture, defined as society's repertoire of interpretative mechanisms and value systems. Of course, this emphasis on culture was accompanied from the beginning by the conviction that the cultural was not a simple function of the material but that, instead, "people's beliefs and ritual activities *interacted* with their socioeconomic expectations,"[2] and that, therefore, one should look at the effects of this interaction for an explanation of the conduct of individuals and, in general, of the way society works. As Lynn Hunt herself had already said in a previous publication, by focusing increasingly on culture, these historians started to challenge "the virtually commonsensical assumption that there is a clear hierarchy of explanation in history (that is, in all social reality), running from biology and topography through demography and economics up to social structure and finally to politics and its poor cousins, cultural and intellectual life."[3]

For this reason, as Raphael Samuel has noticed with ironic shrewdness, historians started to spend more and more time on subjects that an earlier generation of scholars would have reserved for rents, prices, and wage rates. That is to say, they transferred their attention from social structures to cultural practices, from "objective" reality "to the categories in and through which it was perceived, from collective consciousness to cognitive codes, from social being to the symbolic order."[4] Another feature of this theoretical reorientation was a cooling of relations with sociology and the embrace of anthropology from which historians began to cull methods, subjects, vocabulary, and concepts. While sociology had provided some of the conceptual and methodological instruments for studying social and economic structures, the preferential subject of classical social history, anthropology, became a point of reference and a crucial supporting discipline when untangling the terms of the contribution of cultural practices to the configuration of social relations started to preoccupy historians. Also, as must be recalled, this opening up to culture immediately led to heated theoretical and methodological contention centering on issues related to the *fragmentation* of history. The causal link between socioeconomic base and cultural superstructure seemed less than crystal clear when blurred with all the dust rising from the "inherently centrifugal tendency"[5] afflicting the discipline. Pervasive worries about fragmentation, or the so-called crumbling of historical studies, an omnipresent object of debate, sunk some into profound disquietude and provoked a serious "disciplinary crisis,"[6] because such excessive thematic dispersion undermined potential elaboration of integrating syntheses.[7]

What, for our purposes, warrants underscoring in reference to this particular conflagration, almost extinguished nowadays, is the fact that the notions of fragmentation and crumbling do not refer only, or even primarily, to thematic dispersion in historical research, in which case a merely formal description of the state of the discipline would suffice. These notions refer to far greater concerns, namely to a loss of theoretical cohesion following that "subjectivist" reformulation of the dichotomous and objectivist model, and specifically, to the theoretically disintegrating effects ensuing from progressive autonomization of the cultural sphere. We have before us, then, notions social historians brandished to call attention to the increasing debilitation of social causality and to deplore concomitant disinclination to draw up a total history, one that thinks of society in function of the existence of a basic instance containing, implicitly, the social totality. As Lynn Hunt says, in reference to the *Annales* School, "the topics seemed to proliferate endlessly without provoking any new thinking about the structures or relationships within this admittedly vague notion of 'total history.'" Such topics, she adds, appeared to multiply like "building blocks of a construction without plan or clear shape."[8] Moreover, the widening of scholarly interest toward the cultural sphere operates as an accelerating factor on the theoretical transformation itself. With the diversification and extension of fields of study and the delimitation of particular parcels of research and as attention is drawn, more and more, to subjective practices, a theoretical model based on a restrictive notion of social causality proves increasingly uncomfortable to operate. In fact, the appearance of historiographical orientations like microhistory and the history of everyday life actually bespeak this. What this new orientation holds is the following: that precisely when social practices are analyzed in their individual or group specificity, the chain of objective determination appears to be refracted by the capacity of individuals to take decisions and adopt life strategies that are not immediately inferable from their social position and by the capacity of the cultural sphere, in general, to influence and recreate socioeconomic conditions.

Thus, the critical reformulation of classical social history carried out by sociocultural historians lies, in essence, in rethinking and redefining the causal link among the different components of society. Whereas for social history the connection between social structure and conscious action was one of single-minded determination of the latter by the former, for the new cultural history, the relation between the two is one of reciprocal or dialectic interaction. This new theoretical approach preserves intact the previous dichotomous split and continues to give causal primacy to social context, but it attributes an active function in the constitution of identity and in the configuration of practice and social relations to the subjective or cultural sphere. Indeed, new cultural history is the result of a process of historiographical rethinking in which the historians involved have been permanently led by an ambition—if not an obsession—to overcome the opposition between objectivism and subjectivism, between social physics and social phenomenology, between physicalism and psychologism.[9] Although, to be more precise, what these historians have pursued is a point of equilibrium, a harmonious combination between the two, between constriction of the social and the autonomy of consciousness.

Objectivism explains social life in terms of conditions of existence independent of agents, while subjectivism explains social life by appealing to the ideas and beliefs of the agents themselves. New cultural historians challenge both explanations as one-sided views incapable of grasping the dual character of social phenomena: subjectivism for ignoring external constraints on actions, the social dimension of "subjects," and objectivism for failing to heed the constitutive effect representations have on social reality itself. Certainly, the argument goes on, social life is materially conditioned, but material conditions do not affect conduct directly or mechanically; they affect conduct through the cultural dispositions and experiences of individuals. For these historians social life, in fact, only exists in and through symbolically mediated actions. In this sense, the structural properties of social systems are both the means and the outcome of meaningful practices since the action not only reproduces the structure but also creates it at the same time. Only a theory of society, conclude the new cultural historians, based on the interaction between material attributes and symbolic properties, between the pressure of reality and the generative capacity of culture, between external coercion and individual initiative, is capable of explaining the workings and changes of human societies.

From this theoretical perspective, consciousness is not a passive reflection of social conditions, but the result of an active unveiling of their properties. Meanings are an attribute of reality, but they only acquire life and thus become historical factors when they are activated by social practice and culturally formulated by agents. The production of meanings takes place in the space of crossing, tension, or negotiation between social structure and representations. For new cultural history, the social sets up the possibilities of consciousness (and, in this sense, it is objective), but the specific historical constitution of identities occurs in the subjective domain. And the same could be said of interests. As in social history, these remain objective in nature, but according to new cultural history interests only manifest themselves and are translated into action when subjects discern or recognize them in the course of practice. This implies not only that interests do not attain to consciousness by themselves, but through individuals' cultural dispositions, but also that the fit between interests and behaviors neither occurs spontaneously nor is inexorable. Instead, it is dependent upon the existence of an adequate space of experience. In other words, that, unlike social history for which the relationship between structure and action is unmediated, new cultural history maintains that there is a *symbolic mediation* between the two.

In this framework, culture is no longer viewed as an epiphenomenon, as a functional derivation of social conditions or as a mere receptacle of ideas. Rather, culture becomes *practice*, that is, a dynamic instance that supplies the generating principles of distinctive practices and that, in consequence, is a coproducing factor of social relations. In new cultural history, culture retains its subjective character, but it overflows the limits within which social history had confined it and pervades society as a whole, even those areas previously considered to be the exclusive domain of objectivity and governed by an autonomous and impersonal mechanism. The ideal pervades the material or, to be more precise, the ideal and the material penetrate each other, as all practices, including economic ones, are constituted by meaningful actions and, therefore, are dependent upon the representations that individuals have of the world.[10]

What gives culture its relative autonomy and its capacity to mediate between social positions and individuals' decision making is the fact that reality is always understood through established cultural traditions. Social and economic changes do not impact on inert raw human material or a blank mind, but on individuals who have cultural values and an accumulated symbolic heritage. Cultural dispositions comprise a cognitive structure generated by previous experiences, and it is through this inherited symbolic device that individuals meaningfully apprehend any new reality, although, at the same time, the encounter between cultural tradition and new social situations is always resolved in a progressive *adjustment* of consciousness to the new objective context. This is, for example, the relationship that Edward P. Thompson establishes between Industrial Revolution and radical tradition, in which the latter operates as an available vocabulary, as a means through which interests, previously existing in the sphere of relations of production, are expressed. Thus, on the one hand, socioeconomic changes do not act upon raw human material, but upon social groups subjectively forged by radicalism, that is, upon freeborn Englishmen. That is

why, according to Thompson, the making of class is both a social and an economic phenomenon and a cultural and political act, and it is essential to
make a careful distinction between class situation and class formation.[11] But,
on the other hand, the radical vocabulary is the means of transmission of the
new social context, as class makes its way through radical ideology until it
emerges in the consciousness, causing the cultural sphere to end up submit-
ting and adjusting to the transformation of the social structure itself.

In short, what new cultural historians claim is that although social relations are implicit in objective conditions, they are not fully accomplished
until they become explicit in the realm of representations. Social relations
are not established once and for all, but remain open and subjected to con-
tinual recreation by members of the community. An this is why, for social
identities to be constituted and become historical agents, it is not enough
for them to exist in the level of socioeconomic structure (a requisite that sociocultural historians, of course, never dispense with), but they must acquire conscious life through an act of awareness or self-identification in
which their members recognize the interests entailed in their social position
and start to act in accordance with them. Although identity properties are
socially intrinsic, identities are historically specific and, therefore, they are
not social essences, but cultural or subjective accomplishments. Social position is undoubtedly an objective potentiality of unit, a probable identity, but
this potentiality may or may not crystallize in subject, as it is in the course
of social practice, that is always meaningful, where individuals establish
ties and trace the contours of identity which convert them into agents. It is
in the course of meaningful practice where the *objective sense* of social conditions is transmuted into *lived sense*. This could explain the importance of
so-called theory effect, as it is applying a specific system of classificatory
categories that potential identities transform into real identities and social
groupings become historical subjects. This is the reason why new cultural
historians openly challenge the explanatory value of the concept of false
consciousness, with which social history referred to the disturbing effect of
ideological factors that temporarily impeded the accomplishment of identities. Because if identity is a symbolic entity and not a social essence, then
consciousness cannot be either true or false, but simply what it is.[12] Furthermore, it should be remembered here that for new cultural historians,
objective conditions are not limited to relations of production or location in
social structure. They also include all forms of differentiation, such as gender, race, generation, or community, as well as resources (be they material
or cultural) that subjects have at their disposal in the course of action.

From this point of view, the social being is the *perceived being*, as it is on
the latter and not on the former, where individuals' actions and identity
are immediately grounded. This is why, for new cultural historians, historical analysis must pay attention not only to individuals' real position,

but also to the way it is perceived, since both reality and its perception constitute an indivisible whole. Such constitutes a theoretical tenet that obviously forces historians to partially restore the comprehensive or interpretative method of traditional history, once relegated to the dustbin by social history. Because if action does, indeed, refer in the immediate term to perceived being, then, apart from heeding the social conditions of existence, it is essential to reconstruct the conceptions, intentions, and mental universe of subjects as the only way to grasp the effects of symbolic mediation on their practice. This is the conception of society that new cultural historians apply, for example, as I have just indicated, to the study of classes. Although class exists socially, its making as a historical agent occurs in the realm of subjectivity. The only class is the actualized class, made conscious and mobilized by a struggle of classifications that is specifically symbolic. Unlike social history (for which class is a subject regardless of the class awareness of its members), new cultural history establishes a clear separation between social class and actual class, and grants explanatory primacy to the latter. This is why, for instance, in recent years, more and more attention has been paid to the concept of people in labor history, as this, and not class, was the perceived being during much of the nineteenth century and, therefore, the one that operated as the definer of the identity and the organizer of the practice of the individuals involved.[13]

And the same could be said, to offer another example, of this history's understanding of political power. For new cultural history, power relations are not an epiphenomenon of social divisions. On the contrary, since representations work as mechanisms for the fabrication of respect and submission, political domination does not depend exclusively on social position, but also on the struggle to impose a certain definition of social properties, that is, on the credit accorded to the representations that individuals or groups offer of themselves and of others (in sum, on perceived being). As Roger Chartier argues, power does not only involve economic and social relations of force, but also symbolic relations of force. Political domination depends on the process "by which the dominated accept or reject the identities imposed on them with a view to ensuring and perpetuating their subjection," and, therefore, conflicts between groups are struggles between representations, in which the stakes are always the capacity of groups or individuals to ensure recognition of their identity.[14] Of course, the fact that power is not a mere projection of objective social properties, but a symbolic appropriation of them, does not mean that power relations are an intersubjective convention, without any correlation with social divisions. The only thing this means is that the struggle to impose a particular image of the world and base some given relations of domination on it, is a historic process that goes beyond the limits of social structure and requires a meaningful participation of individuals. This is precisely the fact that makes it possible for the dominated to resist, as they take advantage of the symbolic dimension of power to attempt to impose alternative representations. Furthermore, it implies that the forms of dependence themselves provide resources which are creatively appropriated by the dominated to have an influence on the activity of their superiors. And thus, for instance, according to Chartier himself, in the case of gender, although representations of female inferiority are inscribed in the thoughts of women themselves, that does not exclude the possibility of deviations and manipulations that can transform representations that have been forged to ensure subordination and submission into instruments of resistance and affirmation of identity.[15]

As a result, new cultural history brings with it a new concept of social action. If, as I have indicated, the causal flow that comes from the objective is in permanent interaction with another one that comes from subjectivity, then action refers, in the last analysis, to social structure, but, in the first analysis, it refers to meaningful experience (what gives social action a high degree of contingency). For new cultural historians, social position predisposes individuals to behave in a certain way, and they *tend* to do so, but it does not prescribe their conduct. Between social position and action there is a *space of indetermination* whose existence implies that although individuals are constrained by social conditions they have not chosen, social processes are the outcome of the choices that individuals themselves make. In their social practice, individuals have a broad margin of freedom for designing or implementing their living strategies, for making an inventive use of social norms, and, in general, for recreating received meanings and reshaping social conditions of existence. In the same way, the individual is never completely wiped out by the collective, since membership of a group does not prevent the existence of personal trajectories. As Giovanni Levi says, "no normative system is de facto sufficiently structured as to eliminate all possibility of conscious choice, of manipulation or interpretation of the rules, of negotiation."[16]

II

It is not surprising, therefore, that the first impression one gets when approaching new cultural history is that of a broad and resolute move to rehabilitate human agency. New cultural historians intend to rescue individuals from the ostracism and structural subsumption to which social history had condemned them, confer on agents an active role in shaping social practices, and take human agency as the starting point for historical inquiry. That picture, however, has to be completed and balanced to avoid the one-sided understandings into which both commentators and detractors of the new cultural history often fall. The dauntless insistence of new cultural historians to prevent social structure from drowning subjects never reaches the point of forcing them to dispense with social causality, to stop granting this an explanatory primacy, and to confer absolute autonomy on the cultural or political sphere with respect to social base. Although new cultural history submits the dichotomous and objectivist model to severe criticism and gives it a profound reformulation, it never abandons it. It never stops taking for granted that society and individual, structure and action, or simply reality and ideas are the primary components of historical processes and that, in consequence, the explanation of actions lies in the relation between them. As Patrick Joyce has remarked on the subject, "however 'culturalist' this theory became, the basic idea remained that class and politics were rooted in the realities of material life."[17] And it is not surprising to hear certain social historians confidently claiming the opening up of the discipline toward culture, emotions, and the symbolic to be no more than *complementary* to the socioeconomic studies prevailing in the previous phase.[18]

New cultural historians do distance themselves from objectivism (which reduces actions to structures), but also from symbolic interactionism (which reduces structure to actions), which is why they are so dead set against any attempt to restore the concept of natural subject and the comprehensive history inherent to it. If one has to properly characterize the new cultural history's theory of society, one would say that it is based on a *weak* or second grade social causalism, whereby action refers causally to experience and to representations of that world, but these, in turn, refer to the world itself. That is, that social reality is apprehended and transmuted into action through the cultural resources available, but this reality imposes structural or meaningful limits that subjects cannot go beyond. New cultural history grants subjectivity and individual creativity their own space to deploy, but it continues to claim that the cognitive categories through which individuals grasp and meaningfully arrange social reality are an *internalization*, even if a symbolic one, of such a reality. And, therefore, as I have pointed out, the power of these categories to generate social practices depends, in the last analysis, on their *theoretical efficacy*, that is, on how they fit the properties and intrinsic laws of social reality itself. Thus, if one were to apply the Peter Schöttler's classificatory criteria, one would say that new cultural historians reject the notion of *mentalité*, typical of social history, but remain faithful to the notion of ideology, including its connotation of a distorted image of reality.[19]

As Roger Chartier himself states, it is true that representations are "matrices that shape the practices out of which the social world itself is constructed" and that "the patterns from which classificatory and perceptual systems arise" are veritable "social institutions," but such matrices and patterns, in turn, *incorporate*, "in form of collective representations," "the divisions of social organization."[20] All of which means that the principles of vision and division and the organizing categories of social life are the product of a structure of differences that is objective. The cultural construction of the social is certainly a specific ingredient of historical processes, but this construction is socially rooted and constrained by the resources available to individuals by reason of their social position. Subjects perform an active grasping of their world and, in this sense, they construct it, but this grasping is always done under structural coercion. In fact, symbolic classificatory systems are effective in structuring society because they themselves, in turn, have been previously structured by society itself. This implies, as I have remarked, that the meanings that are made explicit and acquire historical existence in the cultural realm are already implicit in the domain of the social and that the fact that the objective has to be actualized in and through the cultural only affects the particular historical form that identities adopt, but not their nature, which is always objective. From this point of view, social relations are something created and constructed by agents, but not in a social vacuum, as subjectivists believe, but within a social space that distributes individuals and determines their representations and decisions. People apprehend the social space from a certain perspective, but one depending on the place they occupy in the social space itself. This is exactly what is meant by symbolic mediation and is the exact sense in which the claim that actions have the power for recreating social conditions needs to be understood.

In this theoretical model, there is not a simple or straightforward, immediately sociological, equation between social attributes and cultural dispositions, but social position imposes its constrictions on subjective creativity. That is, that the social base does not determine practices, but it does establish the conditions of their possibility. Agents are free to invent, do, think, or act, but only *within* the limits of these conditions and in accordance with the resources their social position provides them with. Culture has infinite freedom to generate, but a freedom constrained by historically specific social conditions. This explains why culture always tends to engender ideas and behaviors that are reasonable within a given system of objective regularities and that creativity is limited in its diversity and only relatively—not completely—unpredictable. According to this weak or symbolically mediated objectivism, identities are actualized—as I have repeated—in the subjective sphere, but that does not mean that they are socially arbitrary entities. Forms of consciousness cannot be deduced from social structure, but there is a bond of affinity or suitability between the two that becomes evident in the fact that ideas emerge and become embodied in certain social groups and not in others. And thus, for instance, Lynn Hunt argues heatedly, with respect to the French

Revolution, that a permanent "above" and "below" does not exist in causal terms. There is rather an interaction between ideas and reality, between intentions and circumstances, and between collective practices and social context. Hunt even claims that, in certain situations, the subjective (or political) sphere can become temporarily independent of its social base. Nonetheless, the claim that there is no relationship of determination does not imply that there is not a "fit or affinity" between social position and conduct, since certain ideas are "embraced more enthusiastically in some places and by some groups than in other places and groups." Which leads her to conclude that although "revolutionary politics cannot be deduced from the social identity of revolutionaries, then neither can it be divorced from it: the Revolution was made by people, and some people were more attracted than others to the politics of revolution."[21]

Adopting this theoretical outlook has obviously affected the profile of the object of historical studies and has forced a redefinition of the terms, methodological procedures, and conceptual tools of historical inquiry. Having ceased to take for granted that the study of social context per se provides the essential in the explanation of actions, the investigative gaze has shifted increasingly from the social and economic sphere to that of experience and representations, from the systems of positions to living situations, from collective norms to singular strategies. Once one reaches the horizon of new cultural history, research in history, as Hans Medick states, "is faced with a fundamental methodological conundrum, namely, how to comprehend and present the dual constitution of historical processes, the simultaneity of given and produced relations, the complex mutual interdependence between encompassing structures and the concrete practice of 'subjects,' between circumstances of life, relations of production and authority on the one hand, and the experiences and modes of behavior of those affected on the other."[22] From here on, practices (and not structure) are the starting point of social analysis, as practices are the space in which the meaningful interweaving between social coercion and individual initiative takes place. Inquiry has to start from manifest attitudes, experiences, feelings, and behaviors, since the conceptualization agents make of reality and their ensuing actions and resulting ways of life are the immediate framework of actions and the place where social relations shape themselves. This is the reason why new cultural historians devote more and more time to the study of the specific logic of the cultural, and attach, as well, such great importance to the cultural objects or devices that, in their opinion, take an active part in shaping identities and in moulding conducts. This is the case, for instance, of Judith Walkowitz and melodrama (in her study on sexual policy in Victorian Britain) or that of Michael Sonenscher and theatre, in his account of the constitution of the identity and practice of the sans-culottes.[23]

In short, historians are obliged to add a subjectivist moment, in which they must examine how and to what extent representations keep up or modify social conditions (as it is subjects who convert meaning into positive ingredients of social life), to the objectivist moment, in which representations are placed in causal relationship with the social conditions that are their foundation. Given that social reality itself is also a subject of perception, any historical inquiry must take into account both reality and its perception, as visions of the world not only form part of the world, but they also actively contribute to its construction. This is the meaning of the familiar Chartierian assertion that the world is a representation, or what the Thompsonian equation between class and class consciousness implies.

Thus, if I had to summarize what has been said so far—and do so in up-to-date terminology—I would say that the historiographical developments described here entailed a passage from a conception of language as exclusively mimetic to a conception of language as not only mimetic but generative as well. From this point of view, although ideas and symbolic practices are a product of social conditions, they, in turn, operate on these conditions, reinforcing, reshaping, and giving cohesion to interests, identities, and social divisions. The theoretical assumption here, to use the precision and elegance of Carroll Smith-Rosenberg, implies society is the result of "the dialectic between language as social mirror and language as social agent."[24] This characterization of language as a mixed entity is the most advanced point that new cultural history reaches in its move away from the original core of social history. In any case, it is a formulation that reaffirms and proceeds along a path started some time ago by theories of language like the Bakhtinian one, rescued and revitalized, precisely, by new cultural historians or by authors, like Raymond Williams, who are close to them.[25] In recent years, this return to Bakhtin has not only intensified, but the Russian author has become a primordial resting point for those historians that are opposed to anyone who challenges the dichotomous theoretical model.

Of course, as is well known, in the process of disengagement from classical social history and invigoration of human agency, some historians have taken a further step. They have gone beyond the limits of the materialist paradigm, have abandoned all trace of social causality, and have granted absolute autonomy, once again, to human subjectivity and culture (as well as to politics). In other words, they have restored the concept of rational subject and the intentional explanation of actions it implies. Even though their proposals often appear enriched with a more sophisticated intersubjective, instead of merely individual, view of cultural universes, they have basically reverted to the theoretical horizon of traditional or presocial history. Such restoration converts these subjectivists into mere revisionist historians.[26] I am not, however, going to deal with this particular historiographical episode, the so-called revisionism already referred to in this essay, since it hardly leads to any significant novelty or theoretical innovation.

The theoretical developments described so far have affected to the same extent both historical materialism and the *Annales* School, the two main trends of social history. Historical materialist historians underwent a similar process of moving away from objectivism, and of gradually attributing an active role to subjectivity and culture in the shaping of identities and social practices. In its case too, this was a response to the existence of gaps between social position and consciousness, or, to be more precise, between what social theory prescribed as natural behavior and the actual conduct of people, a particularly disturbing fact in a leading field like labor history, one that had been profusely used as a terrain for empirically verifying such social theory. To attempt to overcome and, at the same time, to explain these gaps, some Marxist historians, in tune with all the other social historians, resorted more and more to the notion of subjective or symbolic mediation, as they began to adopt a mixed notion of language and started to grant a growing relative autonomy to culture and politics. The *Annales* tradition has followed a similar trajectory. The historians of its fourth generation have reacted against a history of *mentalités* based on the notion of "third level." Against its one-sided objectivism and its serial and quantitative methodology, unable to provide an account of individual production of meanings, Annalist new cultural historians uphold the creative nature of subjectivity, the relative sovereignty of the cultural, and the capacity of individuals to generate social ties and implement living strategies that transcend structural coercions. In the Annalist field, this conception of society reaches its summit in the work, both theory and applied research, of authors like Roger Chartier or Bernard Lepetit.[27]

But apart from triggering an internal evolution in established traditions, new cultural history has generated new kinds of historical practice, now familiar characters of the current historiographical landscape. In applying the new theory of society, historians have been pressed not only to analyze historical processes in terms of interaction between structure and action, but to reduce, as well, the scale of observation in order to grasp more fully such interaction in its specific operation. In fact, the new theory of society demands, as a prime requisite, that the space corresponding to structural determination in historical processes be delimited as precisely as possible from the space that corresponds to the freedom of subjects to design and put into practice their particular strategies of action. With the explicit purpose of getting a grip on the play of forces between the structural and the subjective in their specificity, two of the most characteristic modalities of sociocultural history were born, Microhistory and *Alltagsgeschichte* or German history of everyday life.

Microhistory emerged with the aim of grasping the interrelationship between social structure and action, between systems of norms and personal strategies in their concrete individual and daily historical expression, in order to unravel the contribution of action and personal strategies to the making of social relations. Paraphrasing Natalie Z. Davies, one could say that it aims to scrutinize and poke around in the small, often invisible, interactions between structural constraint and individual singularity in an effort to reconstruct the *dynamic of experience*.[28] In order to attain this goal, it is necessary to reduce the scale of observation and to carry out an intensive study of historical sources. Only in this way it is possible to examine closely the process of formation of consciousness, that is, the way in which people, although inscribed in social and normative structures, create the meanings that underlie and guide their actions. That is why, on the one hand, microhistorians focus their attention on contradictions within normative systems and on the fragmentation and plurality of the points of view that make societies fluid and open and cause them to change through slight and constant choices that operate in the interstices of the complex incoherencies of every system. And why, on the other hand, microhistorians shift their investigative gaze from socioeconomic processes, state institutions, and social elites toward inventive uses and resources deployed by traditionally anonymous individuals, small groups, or communities. As Giovanni Levi states, if one looks for a more realistic description of human behavior, one must recognize the relative freedom beyond, although not outside, the constraints of prescriptive and oppressive normative systems. From this point of view, "all social action is seen to be the result of an individual's constant negotiation, manipulation, choices and decisions in the face of a normative reality which, though pervasive, nevertheless offers many possibilities for personal interpretations and freedoms." The crucial issue is, therefore, to define the margins of individuals' freedom, the extent and nature of free will within the general structure of human society.[29]

Something similar could be said of *Alltagsgeschichte*, born in reaction to what is called German historical social science. The purpose of *Alltagsgeschichte*, according to the claims of its theorists and practitioners, is to analyze the concrete forms in which individuals, actively and creatively, appropriate their social conditions and transform them into practice. As Alf Lüdtke argues, the location of individuals and groups is determined by the systems of relations of production, but these do not explain by themselves the "particular activity" and the "way of life," since the conditions for action are something given and, at the same time, a product of the action itself.[30] What historical analysis has, thus, to capture is the play of differences between social situation and conduct, the way in which social actors interpret, press on, or reject the former, because, as historians of this school like to say, paraphrasing the well-known maxim of Karl

Marx—"men" make history in given circumstances, but they make it! It is this purpose of reconstructing the forms of practice in which individuals appropriate their social conditions that has led *Alltagsgeschichte*, as Geoff Eley writes, to shift the historian's agenda from impersonal social processes to the experiences of human actors. Although, as Eley warns, this is not "to supplant but to specify and enrich the understanding of structural processes of social change." In this case too, the ambition of historians is simply to overcome any dichotomy opposing objective and subjective factors.[31] As a result, *Alltagsgeschichte*, like Microhistory, focuses on small units, in which the density of living situations and contexts of action can be made visible, and on the actions of the ordinary people and the "nameless" multitudes, who had remained largely anonymous in history.

III

However, as I have stressed, my main purpose in this first chapter is not to offer an account of theoretical developments in the discipline of history over the last century or to characterize the preceding forms of history in order to be able to appreciate with greater clarity its contrast with postsocial history. This chapter has been written with the aim of highlighting the theoretical patterns and the conceptual logic that have governed such developments. And in this respect, the conclusion seems obvious: in all this time, the historiographical debate has consisted of and adopted the form of a permanent tension or confrontation between objectivism and subjectivism, between materialism and idealism, between social coercion and individual freedom. In both the quarrel between social history and traditional-revisionist history and the internal evolution of social history itself, it has been this tension or confrontation that has governed the process of theoretical renewal in historical studies. And the predominance of this dichotomous conceptual framework has had a double consequence. On the one hand, it has meant that any weakening of one of the terms of the binomial could only lead to the other one being strengthened and vice versa, thus subjecting historians to a kind of vicious circle or perennial pendulum-like movement from which escape is impossible. On the other hand, it has implied the fencing off of a field of disciplinary concerns and the definition of a certain range of relevant problems. In particular, it has implied that any theoretical reflection and any empirical inquiry have to be aimed at determining what the exact relationship is between the two components of that binomial, that is, at determining the degree of dependency of consciousness and actions with respect to social context. The answers to this question given by historians range, as we have seen, from those who grant an absolute autonomy to subjectivity, to those who consider it an expression of the social sphere, and those who advocate some kind of combination of the two stances.

In recent years, however, the historiographical debate seems to have entered a new phase. The reason is that some historians have ceased to pose discussion and to tackle analysis in the conventional dichotomous terms and they have started, for the first time, to try to avoid altogether the dilemma between social explanation and intentional explanation in which historical analysis had been secularly trapped. A feeling of disenchantment seems to have driven such historians. Despite the profound theoretical reformulation carried out by new cultural history and its notable degree of conceptual sophistication, the shortcomings and anomalies of the classical social paradigm have not been resolved. Thus, instead of continuing to combine and recombine the same ingredients, as they had been doing up to this point, these historians began, in practice, to question social structure or human agency as primary components of historical processes and, therefore, that the explanation of action lies in the relation, of whatever type this may be, between both instances. On the contrary, these are not primary instances, but both are derived ones and, therefore, they cannot be taken as a foundation for social theory. Thus, it is not a case of reducing the domains of social causality and widening those of rational action (or vice versa), but of attributing to individuals' practice and to resulting social relations a very different origin and nature. The consequence of this has been the emergence of a new view of society, one *equally* opposed to that of social-new cultural history and to that of traditional history, making it possible, at the present time, the coexistence of *three*, instead of only two, historiographical paradigms in conflict. Which means that reverting back to subjectivism (be it partially or completely) is not the only possible alternative to social history, as there is another, quite different option.

If my diagnosis is correct and if the aforementioned dilemma between materialism and idealism is really being overcome by historical scholarship, *in practice*, then there does not seem to be any compelling reason to place the frontier of historiographical debate in the preceding phase, to restrict, in other words, the critical review of social history to it or to entrench oneself theoretically to that previous boundary.[32] Instead of a final goal, new cultural history has only been an especially fruitful phase in the relentless search for an answer to the question of why people behave as they do. In the end, one could say, paraphrasing Jon Lawrence and Miles Taylor, that the emerging theory of society of postsocial history is really no more than a novel attempt to resolve the *same* "problems" that the debates surrounding E. P. Thompson's *The Poverty of Theory* had already tried to resolve.[33]

2

✛

Beyond the
Cultural Turn: Discourse
and Postsocial History

I

After this necessary preamble, I can now proceed to unfold the concrete terms in which the dichotomous and objectivist model has been significantly rethought in the last two decades and, thereafter, I can begin to put forward the basic assumptions of the new theory of society just now emanating from that recent rumination. I start with a general presentation of the theoretical framework of postsocial history. More detailed description of its major components, with illustrative examples from relevant works, follows.

Immediately evident when first examining historiographical developments since the 1980s, and especially those from the 1990s, is an increasing and marked decline of the concept of *objective reality* and, consequently, of that of social causality as well. Such a decline is indeed the very triggering factor and theoretical diving force of these developments. Thus, when reading recent historical studies in which authors address, some more explicitly than others, what is, for many members of the history profession, troublingly resilient dilemma, it is easy to notice a growing and resolute calling into question of the assumption that social reality is a structure, in the sense that it possesses intrinsic meanings, and that, thus, social conditions of existence project themselves, in the form of representations, on individuals' consciousness and determine their behavior. When these particular scholars undertake such scrutiny they carry out their explorations with the more or less express purpose of finding an alternative to social history. And, for them, a successful one would also be

able to effectively sidestep any recourse to the idealist explanatory model
and to its notion of rational subject.

The basic idea that has been making headway is that, as historical
scholarship is showing, social sphere is not an objective or structural entity, and, therefore, there is no causal connection between individuals' social position and their meaningful practice. On the contrary, this scholarship is showing that the meanings that individuals confer on social
context and the place they occupy in it, and depending on which they organize, orient, and make sense of their practice, have a very distinct
source and are constituted by a historical process essentially different
from the one assumed by social historians. A process that had not been
noted or heeded until a short while ago and one that is impossible to
grasp, comprehend, or analyze with a dichotomous theoretical scheme,
and whose existence forces us to provide a new explanation for the actions of historical agents and the shaping of social relations and institutions. Thus, just as critical questioning of the concept of individual or rational subject led, in its time, to the decline of traditional history and laid
the foundations of social history, the erosion of the concept of social structure is giving rise to the current emergence of postsocial history and, with
it, of a picture of society that is not only more complex, dynamic, and mul-
tirelational, but also and more importantly, one governed by a different
causal logic.

The main reason why these historians call the objective character of social reality into doubt is because the incorporation of social reality into
consciousness always occurs through *conceptualization* of that reality.
Which means that social context only starts to condition the conduct of individuals once they have conceptualized it, or made it meaningful in
some way, but never before. And, therefore, social conditions become
structural and start to work as a causal factor of practice once they have
reached some kind of meaningful existence, and not merely because of
their material existence. At first glance, this statement may not appear to
contain anything that cannot be found in new cultural history. As we
know, new cultural historians had already rebelled against the tenet of
classical social history that actions are socially determined regardless of
any awareness agents may have of it, and they had gone on to maintain
that social position is only translated into action once its meaning is culturally and experientially discerned by individuals in the course of practice. On just such presumed affinity rests, precisely, the call for conciliation between new cultural history and postsocial history.

However, as soon as one takes the historiographical examination further, it becomes clear that postsocial historians have gone beyond their
new cultural counterparts, reaching a point in their rethinking of the objectivist paradigm that new cultural historians, still immersed in a di-

chotomous outlook, could hardly obtain. Although saying, like new cultural history, social context only becomes a causal factor of historical processes once it has been conceptualized, postsocial history actually redefines the very genealogy and nature of the categories by means of which this conceptualization is carried out. Any impression of affinity is only an apparent one. Once postsocial history undertakes such redefinition, a pronounced discontinuity between new cultural history and a postsocial one becomes patent. We are talking about two very different kinds of history. Once that redefinition has been done, the conceptualization of social reality can no longer be considered as an act of consciousness or of experiential discernment of the intrinsic properties (meanings, interests, identities) of such a reality, but, rather, as an act of a completely different nature.

Let us not forget that, for both social and new cultural history, categories, concepts, or cognitive patterns of perception used by individuals to apprehend and meaningfully arrange social reality, are a reflection, representation, or internalization of social reality itself. Either because these categories are mere labels of real social phenomena (such as society, class, sex, property, works, public sphere, or market) or because they are cultural, ideological, or symbolic expressions of social context or divisions (like those of individual, natural rights, freedom, sexuality, nation, bourgeoisie, proletariat, or social revolution). Be that as it may, the essential point is that, in both cases, categories are considered a means of transmitting the attributes of a previously existing social objectivity and that action grounded on these categories is socially determined.

It is on this point, precisely, that a profound and far-reaching theoretical shift has come about over the past two decades. During these years, the assumption that has gradually taken shape in the field of historical scholarship is that the body of categories through which individuals grasp and meaningfully arrange social reality and organize their practice is not a subjective reflection of an objective social structure, but a *specific social realm*. It is a particular domain with its own historical logic. The concepts individuals apply to their social environment are not mere mental reproductions of it nor do the categories or principles on which individuals base their practice have their origin in the social sphere (of course, they are not purely rational, intellectual creations of some underived, ahistorical, and autonomous subject either). On the contrary, according to postsocial historians, the concepts and categories that form the base of practice and of social relations constitute a complex relational network that is neither objective nor subjective and whose origin, in causal terms, is different from and external to the two instances (real referent and subjectivity) that they put into relation. In the same way, conceptual or categorial changes are not simply the consequence of changes in social context but happen through a specific mechanism of reproduction. In sum, and as Margaret R. Somers cogently says, these categories are neither internalized values nor exteriorized interests but constitute, instead, an independent relational structure that develops and changes on the basis of its own internal rules and processes and, as well, in historical interaction with other domains of social life.[1]

In recent efforts to name this historical realm and its specific historical logic, scholars have coined, or borrowed from other disciplines, various terms, seeming, in some cases, to strew their work with odd new words. But, with sufficient usage, many have now become much more familiar to us and can even be quite useful. Unlike most, the term *discourse* was already well established and has been employed in ways that allow, even animate, its current appropriation. Most, as indicated, are more recent, and some are less familiar because of the sense in which they are presently employed, for example, terms like meta-narrative, master-narrative, or even just narrative. On other occasions, authors have turned to primarily descriptive labels, such as categorial/conceptual matrix, body, network, code, set, or framework. Here, in this work on recent developments in historiography, all these terms are taken to be synonymous and used indistinctly. I am, though, inclined to favor discourse. Steady, serious rumination has accompanied its long existence, and such rooted chewing provides valuable insight when facing difficult questions about the production of meaning. No matter the issue of terminological diversity, all these various terms refer to an always already extant system of rules of signification that actively mediates between people and social reality and creates the space in which both objects and subjects are forged in any historical situation. Such is impossible to grasp with the standard dual scheme, which actually denies it.

It would seem quite logical to proceed to unfold at this point the historical reasons and evidence that have led postsocial history to formulate its theoretical premise about the origin and historical specificity of concepts and categories. I have preferred, however, for reasons of practical priority, to leave this to one side for the moment and to continue, instead, with preliminary exploration of the implications this premise has for social theory and for historical analysis. In any case, those who wish to do so can change the sequence and read the last section of this chapter first.

II

In a purely descriptive sense, the term discourse refers to the coherent body of categories, concepts, and principles by means of which individuals apprehend and conceptualize reality (and, in particular, social reality) and through which they implement their practice in a given historical situation. A discourse is a conceptual grid of visibility, specification, and classification by means of which individuals endow social contexts with meaning and confer sense on their relations with them, through which they conceive and define themselves as subjects and agents, and by which, consequently, they regulate and guide their social practice.[2] But, as I have pointed out, what makes the concept of discourse, in relatively recent decades, one of the most far-reaching theoretical and analytical innovations in the field of historical study and the social sciences is the subsequent claim that such a categorial body constitutes a specific social realm. This being so—that discourses are really not social representations or rational creations—allows at least two more claims. First, that discourse historically operates as a veritable *system of meanings*, in the sense that it is not a means of transmitting the meanings of reality but, rather, an active component of the process of constituting those meanings. Or what amounts to the same thing, the meanings reality acquires when conceptualized are not previously inscribed in or determined by reality itself, but depend on the categorial body that people bring into play in each case. Second, that if discourse is neither a means through which social sphere exercises its determination, nor is it an instrument in the hands of rational subjects, then discourse operates, in the configuration of historical processes, as an independent variable (and it must be taken as such in historical inquiry). This twofold claim is certainly crucial—a cornerstone—to the emerging theory of society and the new historiographical paradigm.

Thus, a discourse is, as Joan W. Scott asserts, a specific structure of statements, terms, and categories, historically, socially, and institutionally established, that operates as a veritable meaning-constituting system through which meanings are constructed and cultural practices organized, and through which people represent and understand their world, including who they are and how they relate to others.[3] It is in the "social discourse," as James Vernon writes, where events (both real and imaginary) are endowed with a significance and coherence they would otherwise lack and, therefore, it is such a discourse that enables subjects to make moral sense of the world and imagine themselves as agents within it.[4] For Margaret R. Somers, a meta-narrative is a "causal emplotment" providing the conceptual framework and sequence that give significance to independent instances and translate mere events into episodes. By making a selective appropriation of the unlimited series of social events, this conceptual network determines how these events are processed and what criteria will be used to prioritize and render meaning to them.[5]

If one also adds that every discourse specifically contains or involves a *social imaginary* or a general conception of society, it implies that discourses have the power to provide the structuring principles of social relations and institutions, to project in practices, and to become embodied in identities. Thus, along with discourse, the notion of social imaginary has become one of the central pieces in the ongoing reconstruction of social theory, appearing more and more in works of both theoretical elaboration and empirical research. The term *social imaginary* refers to the set of assumptions or principles concerning the working and changes of human society through which people make sense of social events, conceive and delimit themselves as subjects, and design and justify their practice. This is the notion that one can find, for example, in one of the most salient contributions to the issue, authored by philosopher and social theorist Charles Taylor.[6]

Although focused on its modern variant, Taylor's paper outlines the main features of social imaginary and, above all, unfolds its performative and normative effects on social life. According to Taylor, social imaginary is not a set of ideas but the background that enables them. Social imaginary is, therefore, what enables, through making sense of them, the practices of a society as well (91). Or in Joyce's words, social imaginary does not refer to particular representations or actions but to the foundational assumptions about what counts as an adequate representation or practice in the first place; it is a notion that can be used to describe the most basic conceptual conditions of possibility for a society's operation.[7] From this point of view, social imaginary is the understanding background existing well before people begin to think about their world and, therefore, is what establishes the context of action and makes practices possible. Insofar as it provides people with a theory of society or conceptual framework for understanding and analyzing social phenomena, social imaginary also provides them with their expectations, prefiguring, thus, their practices (91–93). As Taylor emphasizes, in his effort to explain what he is trying to get at with the term, social imaginary is something much broader and deeper than the intellectual schemes people may entertain when thinking about social reality in a disengaged mode. He has in mind, instead, the ways in which people imagine their social existence, how they fit together with others, how things go on between them and their fellows, and their expectations, ones usually met and the deeper normative notions and images underlying expectations. For every social imaginary incorporates a sense of the *normal* expectations that we have of one another, the kind of common understanding which enables us to carry out the collective practices that make up our social life. That is, it incorporates some sense of how we all fit together in carrying out common practice. From this point of view, social imaginary is not only that common understanding that makes common practices possible, but a widely shared sense of legitimacy as well. It is, as Taylor stresses, both factual and "normative," since it provides us not only a sense of how things usually go, but also an idea of how they ought to go, of what missteps would invalidate the practice (106–108).

Thus, in adopting and applying the concept of discourse (or social imaginary), postsocial scholars, one might say, give an account of the fact that people experience the world, establish relations among themselves, and undertake their actions, always from within a categorial matrix that they cannot transcend and that effectively influences their living activities. Or, as Trevor Purvis and Alan Hunt argue, the concept of discourse attempts to grasp the fact that people live and experience always within a discourse, in the sense that this imposes a framework that limits what can be experienced or the meaning that experience can encompass, and thereby influences—allowing or impeding—what can be said and done.[8] An example of discourse, one that has become a cliché, is the so-called modern discourse, whose grid of categories, over the last two centuries, has worked to generate much social, political, cultural, scientific, and ethical practice, first in the West and later in the rest of the world. Somers describes its liberal variant ("Anglo-American citizenship theory") as a genuine relational matrix of epistemological assumptions with a capacity to establish rules for including and excluding evidence, modes of structuring of temporal and spatial patterns, or criteria for what counts as public or private domains. It has, thus, the capacity to shape the conduct of individuals and their social and political relations.[9] Discourses, then, constitute structured configurations of relationships among concepts, connected to each other by virtue of sharing the same conceptual network. And subsequent implications include the following two. First, every concept can be deciphered only in terms of its "place" in relation to other concepts in its web[10] (and not in terms of its link with a real referent). Second, the activation of a concept, for the purpose of endowing either reality or social practice with sense, mobilizes the whole categorial network to which it belongs. And, therefore, the latter must be taken into account as a capital explanatory factor of individuals' meaningful reactions to social environment and, in particular, to changes in this.[11]

Thus, the appearance and adoption of the concept of discourse have meant that a sharp distinction and a clear separation have been drawn between *concept* and *meaning*, with the consequent location of the two in different social spaces. That is, the distinction and separation (both theoretical and empirical) between, on the one hand, the categories through which individuals apprehend and make sense of social reality and, on the other, the meanings and forms of consciousness (interpretations, ideas, beliefs, value systems) that result from this operation. Of the two, *only* meanings should be considered subjective entities, in the sense that agents are not only aware, fully, of their existence but handle them at will in the course of their practice and social interactions. This is not the case of concepts, as these come to people fully formed by a given discourse or social imaginary of whose existence and mediation they are usually unaware. Concepts not only impose on and transcend subjects themselves, but lie beyond their intentional control. Let me illustrate such a distinction with a trivial example. The concepts of freedom, equality, individual, citizenship, and class are one thing, and the ideas of freedom, equality, individuality, citizenship, or class that people forge as a consequence of these concepts being brought into play are something quite different. From which, in turn, it follows that if people can aspire to be free and equal and if they feel like rational individuals or citizens with rights or identify themselves as members of a class, it is because the respective concepts already existed. Using somewhat more technical and recently resonant terms, one can say postsocial history has, in essence, adopted a new concept of *language*. Or to be more thorough, postsocial history has distinguished operationally between the conventional notion of language as a *means of communication* and the notion of language as a *pattern of meanings*, and has based its theory of society on the latter and not on the former exclusively. This distinction—between language as mere vocabulary or nomenclature to designate events, things, or ideas and language as an active generator of the meanings with which such events, things, or ideas are endowed—constitutes the major theoretical driving force of the ongoing reorientation in historical studies. The greater or lesser acceptance of this distinction has recently become a real touchstone for characterizing and classifying historians and, eventually, social scientists in general.

Of course, this distinction is not to be found in the two previous historiographical paradigms, nor, given their grounding in a dichotomous view of society, is it one that either paradigm could have been made. For both, there is no such fundamental difference between categories and meanings because, since they do not recognize the former as specific instances, both are encompassed within the parcel of subjective entities. Whether they are rational creations or social reflections, concepts and ideas or categories and words are the same thing, and they have a similar nature and function. Until the concept of discourse emerged, historical scholarship had only made use of a notion of language as vocabulary or means of communication. For idealist or traditional history, language is a subjective or intersubjective creation and a means of transmitting thoughts, as well as an instrument through which subjects deploy their actions in the world. In more modern variants of idealist history, like so-called contextualism, language is conceived as a cultural resource, as a menu of available concepts that subjects use and handle at will, conferring whatever meanings they wish on them. Contextualists accept that individuals always think and act within conceptual or linguistic universes but, with their continued attachment to the notion of rational subject or intentional agent, contextualists rule out the capacity for concepts themselves to impose on their users and, thus, to play an active role in the production of meanings. For contextualists, as David Harlan states, the individual is a creative agent self-consciously manipulating a "polyvalent" language system. And, thus, for example, a writer stands *outside* and *before* that system, confronting it as a set of verbal possibilities to be manipulated and exploited in order to realize his or her intentions. And the resulting text is, as for J. A. G. Pocock, an expression of the author's consciousness, untouched by any trace of meaningful construction.[12] For materialist history, language is a means of communication too, not of a rational subject but of a social subject and, therefore, it is the means by which social contexts and divisions are translated into subjectivity and action. Finally, as we know, new cultural history grants language a generative function, but only as a symbolic means, not as a pattern of meanings. For new cultural history, meanings continue to have an existence prior to and independent of concepts, which do nothing more than provide such meanings with a verbal form.

Unlike previous types of history, based on an instrumental and *constatative* notion of language, postsocial history is grounded on a constitutive or *performative* notion, one in which language does not just transmit thoughts or reflect the meanings of social context, but actually takes part in the constitution of both. Indeed, as postsocial authors argue, the only way to overcome the explanatory shortcomings of the dichotomous framework is to cease conceiving of language as only vocabulary and to start treating language as a pattern of meanings—one that takes an active part in constituting the objects people talk about and the subjects who translate such meanings into action. As Joan W. Scott likes to repeat, language is not just words or utterances, but whole ways of thinking, of understanding how the world operates and what one's place is in it. To continue, Scott warns, to use the term language only in the sense of vocabulary or words, is to reduce it to literal utterances, to just another datum to collect, and to lose, then, all notion of how meaning is constructed.[13]

The advent of the concept of language as a categorial pattern, different from language as a means of communication, vocabulary or factual label, has primarily led to the formulation of a *new theory of production of meanings* (and, therefore, of the making of consciousness.) As I have already pointed out, recent historical scholarship is making clear that, given the specific nature of categories for conceptualizing social reality, the meanings that individuals grant to social phenomena (including their location in socioeconomic relations) are not attributes that these possess and that language merely designates, transmits, or makes conscious. Rather, they are attributes that social phenomena acquire when a certain discursive pattern of meaning is applied to them. Meanings (and the forms of subjectivity they give rise to) are not representations or expressions of their social referents, but, instead, the effects of discursive mediation itself. What a social event, situation, or location means for a historical agent (and that induces it to act in a certain manner) is not something that depends on or follows from that event, situation, or location, as if each possessed a sort of essential being. What each may mean depends, instead, on the categorial network through which each has been conceptualized or made meaningful.

For postsocial paradigm, the meanings of social reality are constituted through an operation of *differentiation* (and not one of reflection, as social historians claim). Which is to say, basically, that if every new social phenomenon is always grasped through a preexisting conceptual framework, then the meaning with which that phenomenon is endowed is born out of the differential relation or contrast between existing concepts. If every social phenomenon is always apprehended and made intelligible in terms of preceding meaningful phenomena, then its meaning stems from a reorganization, updating, adaptation, or widening of a previously existing network of meanings to include and make room for the new phenomenon.[14] Meanings, as in social history, continue to have a link with the social context that is their referent, but it is no longer a representational or objective link, but a merely material one. And that is why postsocial historians have ceased to conceive of consciousness as an expression, of whatever kind, of social position, since consciousness does not arise from an act of awareness or experiential discernment of objective meanings, but, on the contrary, from an operation of differential construction of such a position.

Meanings have lost their former condition of subjective expressions to become historically shifting sets of relationships that are *contingently stabilized* in a point of historical time.[15] Since social referents cannot fix their meanings, as these are dependent upon discursive conditions, meanings are always in a state of precarious equilibrium and threatened by the watchful presence of other meanings, ready to invade their territory and expel them from it, to make them disappear. As Keith M. Baker states, meanings are "always implicitly at risk."[16] Because, as new categorial frameworks emerge, the same real phenomena, sometimes suddenly, take on new meanings and lose or see their former meanings altered, and they cease to be interpreted, enunciated, characterized, or classified as had been done up until that new moment. It is here, and not in changes in the social context of perception nor in developments of human thought, where one should look for an answer to John E. Toews's thoughtful and crucial question "why certain meanings arise, persist, and collapse at particular times and in specific socio-cultural situations."[17]

This new theory of the production of meanings is having far-reaching repercussions on the historical study of society, and some of these have already been pointed out or suggested earlier in this book. Such a theory involves a complete rethinking of standard notions of objectivity and subjectivity, as well as an urging to adopt a new concept of action, different from both the intentional and the social or structural ones. Concerning objectivity, the new theory essentially implies that objectivity is not coterminous or coextensive with reality. That is, social objects are not implicit in the social facts or phenomena that are their material support or referent, but are constituted as such in the very process of discursive conceptualization of social phenomena. If meanings are not representations of social objects whose attributes have merely been labeled, then social objects emerge from discursive mediation itself, and through a process of differentiation from other objects. From this point of view, only social phenomena have a previous existence, but not the objects they give rise to. The latter can emerge (turning such phenomena into relevant factors of social practice) or not emerge at all, or they can adopt the most diverse physiognomies, all depending on discursive conditions. And thus, for example, race, place of birth, homosexuality, tongue, class, poverty, hunger, madness, social inequalities, or economic crises, although they irrefutably exist as real phenomena, only become objects (and start to mold behavior) once they have been endowed with meaning within a certain discursive regime and depending on the meaning they have acquired. And, of course, if every being, as something different from mere existence, is constituted within a discourse, then this implies, as Ernesto Laclau and Chantal Mouffe point out, that it is not possible to differentiate the discursive, in terms of being, from any other area of social reality.[18] Thus, postsocial history does not limit itself to historicizing objects. It does not advocate a sort of historical relativism, according to which the *same* object is perceived in different ways depending on the historical moment in time. If such were so, postsocial history would be nothing new compared with social history. Instead, what postsocial history carries out is a deep rethinking of the very nature of objects, which have ceased to be social and have become discursive.

The same has happened with the notion of subjectivity. By virtue of the new theory of production of meanings, individuals' subjectivity cannot continue to be regarded either as a rational autonomous realm or as a reflection of social context. Subjectivity (including identity) is rather a depository of the meanings with which individuals endow social world and their place in it, by applying a certain discursive framework or social imaginary. By moving subjectivity away from both rational action and social structure, postsocial history is, thus, calling into question and leaving behind the concept of culture as well as that of ideology. Even though the term culture can have many different senses, some of which even come close to the concept of discourse, in its prevailing historiographical use, culture has usually been conceived as a subjective sphere, whether rational or representational.[19] As for ideology as false consciousness, it must also be eradicated from historical scholarship, since it implies the existence of a social being that, although possibly veiled or activated symbolically, is discernable in the final instance, and has the capacity to become embodied in consciousness and to project itself in action. As Anson Rabinbach argues, if language is what "naturalizes" social reality and, thus, provides individuals with the certainty necessary to undertake their actions, then one must put aside from social analysis any notion of ideology, with its purpose of illuminating the real social truth mystified by the veil of class interest. As Rabinbach himself says, the problem of false consciousness has given way to the problem of how representation is organized and, therefore, the point is no longer to "unmask" ideological falsity with the white light of truth, but to analyze the "unnatural" and linguistic process of construction of consciousness itself.[20]

The collapse in standard notions of objectivity and subjectivity has led to and paralleled the decline of the dichotomous theoretical model as a tool, in any of its forms, of social analysis. The replacement of the reality-consciousness dualism with the reality-discourse-consciousness triad starts that decline but, above all, it is with the incorporation of this third factor into historical analysis. With the latter, objects and subjects (structure and agency) lose their previous condition of primary components of social processes and become, instead, derived, secondary entities. Both social structure and cultural dispositions have turned out to be effects of the same process of meaningful construction of social reality.[21] In particular, the concepts of base and superstructure have collapsed and, along with them, the picture of society as a systemic totality that is implicit in an objective social base, and of which the superstructure is a reflection or function. This is the very reason why the secular and absorbing debate on the degree of autonomy of the cultural (or political) realm with respect to social context has become obsolete. The purpose of historical research has markedly changed, from determining the degree of fit between the two instances (as if there were a causal connection between them), to trying to unravel the specific process of discursive mediation through which the social has given rise to the cultural.

Finally, the concept of discourse and the resulting theory of production of meanings have brought about a new concept of social action. Social practice and behavior have ceased to be explained in terms either of human agency or of social determination (or of some kind of combination of the two), and it have begun to be explained in completely different terms. If forms of consciousness are not subjective reflections of social context, but effects of a meaningful construction of it, then actions grounded on those effects are not determined by social context itself but depend, instead, on the specific way in which it has been discursively conceptualized. And, therefore, it is in discursive or conceptual mediation itself where the causes of such actions are to be found. Any action is, doubtlessly and as social history maintains, a response to pressure or requirements of social context, but it is a response that is *discursively mediated*, not a structurally determined one. As Patrick Joyce sums it up: to identify one thing in terms of another is always to reinterpret and remake, to being anew, indeed to "constitute" or "prefigure" the world, but, and furthermore, if something new is always addressed in terms of something old, then it "means that 'agency' is built into the nature of language."[22] From which it follows, in turn, that if actions are not a structural effect or function, but effects of the historical deployment of discourse, then the practical efficacy of actions does not have a theoretical base, but, rather, a rhetorical one. Such an efficacy does not depend on the greater or lesser agreement between consciousness and reality, but on the degree of influence or historical prevalence of the underlying discursive regime. And thus, for example, many struggles of labor movement were effective for decades not because they reflected a sort of natural trend of capitalist society, but because people involved were imbued with the categories, tenets, and expectations of modern social imaginary, thinking of and facing such struggles as, specifically, a revolutionary threat.

With all that said, I can now proceed to sum up the central premise of the theory of society that has been taking shape in the field of historical studies over the last couple of decades. This premise says that in any historical situation, there is a specific categorial matrix or pattern of meanings through which individuals enter into meaningful relation with their social environment, and through which they implement and confer sense on its practice. That matrix or pattern takes an active part in the making of the meanings with which social environment and location are endowed, and thereby its mediation actively contributes to the shaping of consciousness and identity, and really works as a causal foundation for actions and social relations and institutions. From this perspective, discursive mediation is not only an essential component, but also a capital explanatory variable of social processes.

However, as the theoretical status granted to reality by the emerging theory of society has become one of the main issues of controversy and critique, it would be wise to avoid precipitated conclusions and disabling misunderstandings and to be a little more precise about the exact role that postsocial history confers on social reality in the shaping of consciousness, practice, and social relations. As should be already clear, postsocial history is antiobjectivist, not antirealist. What it calls into question is not the existence of social reality, but the claim that this is objective, in the basic sense already stated that it possesses intrinsic meanings and, by virtue of this, has the capacity to determine the meaningful actions of individuals. In other words, one can hold that a real phenomenon or situation is objective only if it involves or is able to give rise to, even if only potentially, a certain response, belief, attitude, or action, if it is able to generate a meaningful behavior and not just a merely material, physical, or bodily reaction. If such is not the case, then real phenomena cannot be considered objective entities, but only real ones. Thus, despite the insistence of some critics on charging postsocial history with the rather absurd and incomprehensible charge of wanting to delete any distinction between fact and fiction, what postsocial historians do is simply distinguish between *fact* and *object*. That is, they make a distinction between real and meaningful phenomena and claim that the latter is not a causal effect of the former but an effect of the interaction between real fact and a certain categorial pattern. The discursive character of objects does not affect the real existence of the phenomena from which objects are produced, because being real is one thing, but being objective is something else. The real is given by mere existence, objectivity by the possession of a meaning.[23]

Countless examples could be given here to illustrate the difference between social fact and object, as well as the constructing operation that mediates between the two. One very significant example, close in time, appearing quite suddenly, and still quite fresh in my mind is child abuse, highlighted and studied by authors like Ian Hacking. And as Hacking himself stresses, child abuse is a clear example of object construction before our very eyes. Even though child abuse, as a social fact or practice, has always existed, it was only objectified as such and endowed with the meaning it presently carries just recently.[24] As he explains so well, the objectivization of child abuse (as a relevant and morally negative fact) has not been the result of the discovery of a horrible fact, but of applying to this a series of analytical and value categories. These categories converted some events, previously unheeded or repressed, into abuse. These categories themselves caused the meaningful experience of events, even if similar to those beforehand, to begin to be very different (254). Thus, it is patent that in this case we are not dealing with an object that is discovered or of which we become aware, but simply with an event that, from a certain moment on, is objectified as morally and legally condemnable. This does not mean, insists Hacking, that child abuse is not a *real* fact. But, he argues, it is the case that, in 1960 nobody took into consideration what, in 1990 is taken to be child abuse. Or, if you prefer, many of the practices now considered child abuse were not understood as such three decades ago (257). That is why, concludes Hacking, child abuse is not one fixed thing, it is not a truth "out there," which it is our task to discover and use, but it is instead a historically specific object (259).

Consequently, postsocial history does not deny the empirically obvious fact that between social context and consciousness there is always a connection and that every action is socially conditioned. What postsocial history does deny is that this connection is one of meaningful determination and that such conditioning has a structural character. It disagrees that a certain social position or context implies, even if only potentially or as a mere tendency, a certain response, attitude, or behavior by individuals involved, and that therefore there are socially natural conducts and deviate or anomalous ones. This even holds true, as I will discuss later, for those situations, typical of modern societies, in which agents themselves explicitly regard social position as the causal foundation of their actions. On the contrary, as I have repeated, what determines the behavior of individuals is the meaning that such a social position has acquired when made meaningful through the categories of modern social imaginary.

Thus, it is not that postsocial history dispenses with social context (the way traditional history and its revisionist revival do) or minimizes its importance for explaining the practice and subjectivity of agents. What postsocial history does is to state that social context makes its contribution to the making of practice, not as an objective or structural instance, but simply as a material referent or support. For although social conditions undoubtedly impose limits on the meanings that can be created about and conferred upon them and, thereby, restrict the actions that individuals can undertake, they are purely material limits (physical, spatial, of resources), not structural limits. Social conditions provide individuals with the material means of their actions, but not with the categories or meanings on which these actions are founded (as these have a different origin). In other words, social context can determine the purely material actions of individuals, but not their meaningful actions, that is, those that entail or mobilize some kind of meaning or system of meanings, actions involving, for instance, a conscious decision, a set of beliefs, an assessment of surrounding reality, or certain expectations. To use a trivial example, the shortage of economic resources undoubtedly imposes restrictions on the consumption of goods. But, not only this shortage can be conceived in different ways (divine punishment, natural order of things, social injustice) and bring about very different attitudes and responses, it can also be associated with the most varied consumer practices, from those that give priority to satisfying basic physiological needs, to those that give importance to public ostentation, all dependent upon the prevailing social imaginary in each case.

This is why postsocial historians think that the main theoretical shortcoming in social history lies in the fact that it takes for granted that any

constraint of social context is structural in character and that social position prefigures, prescribes, or dictates, to some extent, the meaningful actions of individuals. However, argue these historians, one thing is that all
actions are inscribed in circumstances that are not of our choice and
whose consequences are beyond the control of agents, but actions being a
causal effect of circumstances themselves is something quite different. At
least, the latter should not be inferred from the former, because, as Patrick
Joyce argues, following Geoff Eley, the fact that actions are always inscribed in social contexts which are essential to their meaning does not
imply that there is an underlying structure to which meanings and actions
can be referred as expressions or effects.[25] On the contrary, according to
postsocial historians, what must be explained, in each case, is why some
particular social circumstances have generated certain forms of conduct,
instead of taking for granted that there is a natural connection of causality between social circumstances and conduct. Or, rather, what must be
explained is how and why this connection has been constituted and acquired such a condition of naturalness. The usual rejoinder of new cultural historians—we should retain some notion of social structure if we
want to explain the unconscious causes and the unintended consequences
of actions—becomes irrelevant once social objectivity has ceased to be an
inherent attribute to become a discursively acquired property. Although
actions may be conditioned by unknown factors (an economic crisis, a demographic fluctuation, a distant event, etc.), these always exercise their
influence not by themselves but through the specific conceptualization or
meaningful apprehension that agents themselves make of their material
effects.

The new theory of production of meanings and the consequent doubt-
ing of the notion of social structure and social causality are at the root, for
example, of the reinterpretation of relevant historical phenomena like the
labor movement or the liberal revolutions tackled by some historians
since the 1980s. Although I will return to this later on, the main conclusion
one draws from this ongoing reinterpretation is, precisely, that the forms
of consciousness, identity, and practice that make up both historical phenomena cannot continue to be considered expressions or effects of socioeconomic conditions or changes but, rather, meaningful constructions of
them. In the case of the labor movement, for example, this would have
emerged as a consequence of the interaction between the liberal-radical
discursive matrix and the social, economic, and political situation of the
early decades of the nineteenth century.

As William H. Sewell argues, in his critical reading of Edward P.
Thompson, the working-class consciousness did not causally emerge
from social and economic transformations or changes in living and working conditions of the workers. Rather, it emerged from an operation of

meaningful arrangement of the new social and political environment through the basic categories or assumptions of liberal-radical discourse. In his words, the working-class or class-conscious "discourse" do not arise purely "as a reflection of and reflection on the exploitation of workers in capitalist productive relations," but is "a transformation of preexisting discourses." Liberal-radical discourse contained notions that by interacting with the new socioeconomic situation and by being "transformed," in the terrain of practice and of political agitation, generated the new working-class identity in the 1830s. And if the labor movement and workers' consciousness were not an effect, in causal terms, of social and economic transformations, but of the conceptualization of them through the liberal-radical discursive pattern, then one must search for the origin of the new form of identity and for the explanation of practice in the mediation of the latter (liberal-radical discursive pattern). Or, as Sewell himself says, "the fact that class discourse is a transformation of previously existing discourses has important theoretical implications: it means that to explain the emergence of class discourse, we must understand the nature, the structure and the potential contradictions of the previously existing discourses of which it is a transformation."[26] Such a conceptual pattern (invigorated and institutionalized by the French Revolution) constitutes "a complex and fully articulated linguistic world, complete with standard rhetorical figures, characteristic debates and dilemmas, silences and unquestioned assumptions," and it sets the terms in which people started to conceive of society and their place in it, and in which "public claims of all sorts could be couched—a language of individual citizens, natural rights, popular sovereignty and the social contract."[27]

In the case of the French Revolution, authors such as Keith M. Baker emphasize the constitutive role of discourse. According to Baker, as social explanation has weakened—an explanation that conceived political action as a reflection of objective social interests, and thought of the Revolution as the embodiment of the social, economic, and ideological rise of middle class—it has become necessary to pay attention to the categories within which revolutionary practice was forged. Either categories that already operated as organizing elements of the absolutist political system itself or categories created from these (by confirming, reformulating, or denying them, it does not matter), the fact is that their active mediation constitutes the crucial explanatory factor of the revolutionary process. For it is through these categories that individuals draw up a diagnosis of their situation, classify themselves as subjects, and elaborate a program of alternatives with which to resolve the revolutionary crisis and set up a new political, legal, and institutional order. As Baker argues, the weakening of the assumption that the Revolution is the expression of social interests has compelled historians to look at the political dynamics of the Old Regime and at the process through which revolutionary principles and practices were created in the context of an absolute monarchy. The conceptual space in which the French Revolution was forged and the structure of meanings in relationship to which the quite disparate actions of 1789 took on coherence and political force, did, indeed, come from the Old Regime. As has been suggested, this happens even if the genealogy of the new categories was negative, in the sense that the new social imaginary was built out of its contrast with the previous one. Even when earlier discursive patterns seem to have been swept away and entirely transformed, their traces, Baker writes, remain to give meaning to the new. And thus, for example, when the revolutionaries coined the term old regime to refer to the social and political order they were repudiating, they were, indeed, acknowledging that the new order could be defined only in contradistinction to what had gone earlier. As Baker concludes, it could be said that, indeed, "the Old Regime invented, structured and limited the Revolution, even as the revolutionaries invented—the better to destroy—the Old Regime."[28]

III

As promised, I now return to the issue left in suspense at the beginning of this chapter. Here, I try to clarify the exact sense of the claim that organizing and regulating categories of social life constitute a specific historical realm, and to explain through which historical process discourses are constituted and reproduced over time, as well as their relationship with social settings and changes. This issue still requires deep, detailed historical investigation and should be undertaken as soon as possible. So far, postsocial authors have devoted their efforts more to synchronic analyses of the constitutive effects of discourses than to carrying out diachronic analyses of the genesis and mechanisms of change of discourses themselves.[29] Nonetheless, in my opinion, sufficient stuff is already available for giving a preliminary outline of a *theory of the historical formation of concepts* (to paraphrase Somers's expression). The formulation of such a theory is an essential requisite for providing postsocial history with a sufficiently solid foundation. Because, if it is not reliably demonstrated that the founding categories of social practice constitute a specific social realm and have a particular historical logic, the entire postsocial paradigm could collapse and all its efforts of theoretical rethinking proved ultimately fruitless. And if such were the case, the basic assumptions of previous paradigms would remain intact and in force, thus dampening hopes for the viability of any alternative explanatory model. In fact, the lack of a more precise explanation of the genesis of categories not only diminishes consistency and innovative power in many of the works contributing to the new theory of history, but it also leaves the door open to previous interpretations of the historical phenomena these works study. Just such a lack has also allowed these works to be considered merely revisionist proposals. Thus, if the rejection of the social explanation of categories is not accompanied by a clearly formulated alternative, there is a serious risk of simply turning subjectivity into an autonomous domain and reducing the whole theoretical undertaking to a mere restoration of the idealist paradigm.[30] This circumstance should not, though, distract us from the fact that the dividing line and the contrast between idealist revisionism and postsocial history are salient enough to stave off any confusion between them.

The starting point of postsocial history's argument concerning the historical formation of discourses is the observation that any new social situation or event is always apprehended and conceptualized or objectified by means of the categories inherited from the previous situation, what implies social reality does not, on its own or from scratch, generate the concepts applied to it but does do so in interaction with a preexisting categorial system. Of course, on this occasion too, one may think that this statement does not contain anything new, since the idea that social changes are made meaningful through inherited concepts enjoys a long-standing endorsement, not only in history but also in the social sciences in general. To mention just one example, from years ago, Marshall Sahlins sustained Franz Boas's principle that the seeing eye is the organ of tradition, all experiences of the world and all appropriations of events are always done in terms of a priori thinking and that, therefore, the insertion of events in a preexisting category allows such events intelligibility. This implies, according to Sahlins, that the present, whatever it really is, is always recognized as a past.[31]

However, the argument of postsocial history goes further. In addition to heeding the role of categorial inheritance in interacting with social reality, as others have also done and do, postsocial history maintains that in the interaction between social reality and inherited categorial matrix, the latter and not the former, plays the active role. Inherited categorial matrix is what establishes conditions of possibility for the concepts such a reality generates. Inherited categorial bodies impose conceptualization rules to which new social situations must submit and through which they necessarily have to attain their conscious existence. What individuals do, when facing and conceptualizing an ever-changing and always-new social reality, is not just internalize it and label it, but incorporate it into, and impose it upon the prevailing conceptual pattern in each case. Contrary to what has been supposed for so long, new social situations or phenomena do not contain, are not the bearers, nor do they constitute the causal source of the concepts that people apply to them. These concepts are, rather, the result of a *naturalizing* process, that is, of the incorporation of such situations and phenomena into a familiar language or framework of intelligibility. To be more precise, new categories are not reflections of social changes, but the result of an operation of differentiation, that is, of the play of differences or relationship of contrasts between the preexisting categories. Here too, it could be said that inherited language is not simply, as new cultural history believes, the channel or means of communication through which social changes attain to consciousness. It is not merely the verbal form or cultural clothing that the social being adopts. Language is indeed the space in which the social being is constituted as such. Consciousness reacts to new phenomena not from scratch or a condition of tabula rasa but according to and in the terms of its own conceptual structure. Therefore, even if it is the referent that empirically activates the emergence of new concepts, these are really born from the opening up of a new space in the preexisting categorial/conceptual network. In this process, social reality undoubtedly works as a material referent of concepts, but not as an objective referent, because concepts are no more than the outcome of the conceptual readjustment, transformation, reorganization, or reconfiguration to which the old discourse is subjected for the purpose of integrating the new phenomena and endowing them with sense. Thus, while every discourse is materially connected to the social conditions that give them life, it is, however, only *causally* linked to the mediation of the preceding discourse.[32]

The fact that any connection between concept and social reality is differential, rather than referential, and that every meta-narrative is always engendered out of and within another meta-narrative (a subsequent outcome of the deployment of the conceptual potentialities of the previous), implies that discourses are *intertextual* entities and not representational or rational ones. But, above all, given that any new concept or discourse is a reconfiguration of another (other) previous one(s), even when the latter is (are) denied, and the fact that every discourse potentially contains the discourse that will have to replace it, are what enables us to claim that the categories that organize social practice do indeed constitute a specific social realm. Such categories are links in an unbroken *conceptual chain* that is not subjected causally to either social reality or to rational action or creativity. The existence of this internal mechanism of linking and reproduction, governed by its own rules of transformation, is what enables discourses, as I have said, to work as an independent historical variable in the making of social processes.

The genealogical process I have just sketched is the one that, for example, can be observed in the case of the modern discourse. The emergence of this discourse was not an effect of new socioeconomic conditions (the

rise of capitalism and middle class) but of the interaction of those particular conditions with extant discursive legacy and the consequent conceptual trans-valuation of just such a legacy, a process usually known or referred to as "secularization."[33] The process of conceptual transformation
of providential discourse into modern discourse has been insightfully un-
raveled, in recent times, by authors like Mary Poovey and David Bell,
who have studied the emergence of two of the central modern categories
out of the previous conceptual horizon. Poovey's work recovers the genealogy of the modern category of society and its developments from the
early modern period until the nineteenth century. Bell has done the same
with the category of nation, whose appearance is found in the weakening
of the religious view of society from the early eighteenth century.[34] Even
though it is not exactly a succession from one discourse to another, but between discursive variants, the same relationship of intertextuality seems
to underlie, as William H. Sewell shows, the emergence of socialism and
its concept of labor. According to Sewell, such a concept is a logical development and a reelaboration of certain Enlightenment concepts, summarized in Diderot's idea of man as a natural being who brings order and
utility to nature by transforming it. These concepts, when applied,
through the mediation of authors like the Abbé Sieyès, to political and social life, will have the effect of setting useful labor as a criterion for belonging to the nation—turning it into an association of productive citizens
who live under a body of common laws—and property—understood as
legitimate fruit of work—as a requisite for exercising citizenship. What
socialism will do is develop this conceptual substrate and advocate that
the base of political representation should be work itself, and not its indirect embodiment, property, thus establishing an equation between citizenship and labor that, from 1830, was to be the foundation of socialist
program and practice.[35]

Although, to be exact, it must be specified, as Sewell himself does, that
this discursive mutation is not only an intellectual development of a certain conceptual logic but the outcome of the interaction between that inherited categorial substrate and the new social and political circumstances
as well. In Sewell's words, the emergence of socialism out of the reelaboration or extension of Enlightenment concepts was a social and political
development as much as a logical one, as the intellectual innovations that
culminated in socialism were formulated in response to changing social
experiences in general and the struggles and vicissitudes of political life in
particular (278). It must be pointed out, in addition, that since these social
and political conditions were generated by the historical deployment of
the Enlightenment discourse itself, both the new concept of labor and the
practice that it entailed were, in turn, a response to the actual effects of applying Enlightenment ideas to the details of social and political life (280).

What has been said thus far answers, at least implicitly, the question of why discourses change, decline, and disappear and what responsibility the social context has in this. But, an even closer look at the issue is warranted. Although discourses usually enjoy a long life, no discourse remains fixed, absolutely stable, but is always in movement, in flux, churned by perennial reconfiguration. This, as I have said, is due to the fact that individuals are forced to permanently produce ad hoc conceptual supplements with which to make sense of an ever-changing social reality. New factual incorporation has an impact on and alters the initial conceptual structure. As a result, discursive formations develop and undergo internal mutations, and when these reach the point of modifying the basic conceptual core of the discourse, the discourse itself loses practical efficacy. Thus disabled, people discard it and supplant it with another discourse. A *discursive rupture* occurs. To be more precise, what happens exactly is that discourse, in its various vicissitudes, gives rise to the discursive framework that is going to challenge its hegemony and to eventually supersede it.

Discursive changes, then, are neither the fruit of human cultural creativity nor the causal effect of social transformations. The former would be true if individuals were autonomous rational subjects, but not if a process of discursive mediation shapes subjectivity itself. If subjects are constituted as such within a certain categorial matrix, they are not its overseers handling this matrix at will, but they do mobilize, develop, and deploy its meaningful possibilities in practice. And, therefore, although discourses are transformed through the use that individuals make of their terms, this does not mean that individuals themselves transform discourses. The purely formal fact that individuals make use of categories and translate them into practice should not be confused with the actual mechanism of categorial transformation. Although discourse is renewed in speech, this, in its turn, is a result of projecting the rules of signification of the discourse itself. The origin of discursive changes seems to be found in the aforementioned interaction between inherited categories and new social phenomena (although, as I have stressed, it does not mean that there is a causal connection between the two). New social situations do not bring in a new discourse, but they do prompt differential mutation in the preceding one. Although changes in the social context destabilize discourses, they do not do so per se, but differentially incorporating themselves into the discourse itself. That is, they modify discourse insofar as and once they have been objectified or endowed with a meaningful existence. Furthermore, the scope and features of such a modification are not implicit in the changes themselves, but depend on the objects which they give rise to. In other words, a new social phenomenon forces a greater or lesser discursive shift or crisis not on its own, by its own features, but in terms of the significance people grant it within prevailing discourse. Thus, for example, the collapse of socialist regimes has triggered a deep rethinking of modern social imaginary, and specifically its notion of rational emancipation. But it would probably be an irrelevant event—one without any impact—if viewed from another discursive perspective lacking any such a notion. Once again, that means discourses are not challenged or destabilized by reality, by events in the world, but by another discourse, or, more exactly, as Ernesto Laclau and Chantal Mouffe say, by the infinitude of the fields of discursivity. It is not the impact of reality that undermines the historical prevalence of a discourse (its efficacy as a guide for social practice) but the emergence of *another* discourse. As Laclau and Mouffe argue, the relational logic of discourse is limited from an "exterior," but this "exterior" is not an "extra-discursive" one. Such an exterior is constituted by other discourses, and "it is the discursive nature of this exterior which creates the conditions of vulnerability of every discourse, as nothing finally protects it against the deformation and destabilization of its system of differences by other discursive articulations which act from outside it."[36]

Margaret R. Somers, in a similar way, maintains the following: since meta-narratives are schemata of rules and procedures that have become naturalized, they cannot be destabilized by empirical evidence in itself, but only the emergence of another meta-narrative can challenge its classificatory rules of inclusion-exclusion. The historical survival of a meta-narrative does not depend on the extent to which it fits social reality, as if the latter were an objective entity of which meta-narrative is a cultural or ideological reflection. It depends on the rhetorical efficacy that stems from the fact that there is no rival meta-narrative able to dispute its hegemony. As Somers herself puts it, the survival and practical efficacy of a meta-narrative depends on its integrity, logic, and rhetorical pervasiveness, not on its empirical verification. Something that applies, she argues, to "Anglo-American citizenship theory." It has operated for over three hundred years regardless of any direct correspondence to its empirical referent, and the durable validity of "Anglo-American citizenship theory" has been due to its internal coherence, not to some appropriate fit between it and empirical world.[37] This is just the reason why discursive changes should not be understood in terms of epistemological progress, that is, of a growing theoretical or representational fit with reality, but rather in terms of intertextual adjustment. These changes do not imply that the aforementioned conceptual chain has been broken or that discursive mediation had been taken over, enabling reality to become more transparent and to finally reveal itself to subjects the way it really is. What happens is simply that reality goes on to be made meaningful through another discourse (or discursive variant) and, therefore, the space once occupied by discarded discourse is not filled up with reality itself, as social history supposes, but is now occupied by another discourse. This is what happened in the transition to modernity and this is what appears to be happening at the moment on the occasion of the crisis of the modern discourse.

To say discourse is a differential entity and that it reproduces intertextually does not mean to say that it constitutes a sort of self-referential instance, outside of social practice and immune to the impact of reality. Discourse is not, of course, a social phenomenon in the standard objectivist sense—reflecting an underlying social structure—but it is so in the empirical sense that it is a historically specific entity that is forged and transformed within social practice. Although inherited discourse is imposed on individuals as an unavoidable cognitive matrix, the practical deployment individuals make of discourse modifies it, generating new categories and getting rid of others until such superscription, we might say becomes, ultimately, another discourse. In postsocial history, the origin of the systems of meaning which order culture and practice is not found, as is the case of structuralism, in a pregiven and unconscious structure embedded in the human mind, but in the permanent meaningful interaction between individuals and their world. And, therefore, discourse is not regarded as a natural, synchronous, or static entity, but is seen, instead, as a diachronic, dynamic, and discontinuous phenomenon. For me, authors, like Christine Stansell for example, are wrong when they charge the new theory of society with considering language "a fixed—sometimes frozen—structure, with its independent laws and imperatives," as "a system above and beyond human endeavor" whose changes are the result of an "internal dynamic."[38] This does not in any way seem to be the conception of language that is emerging from the crisis of social history and that supports the postsocial paradigm. The claim that discourse works as an independent historical variable does not imply, in any way, that social causality has been replaced by a sort of linguistic or semiotic determinism. It only implies that discourse, since it is causally ungoverned by any of the domains it puts into relation, plays a constitutive (and not merely instrumental) role in the shaping of practice and social relations. As I have said, over and over, for postsocial history, the meanings and forms of consciousness that underlie different modalities of practice are not generated by discourse, but by *discursive mediation*, that is, by the interaction between real referent and categorial matrix and, therefore, mutual collaboration between the two is essential for bringing forth meanings and consciousness.

3

The Discursive
Construction of Social Reality

I

With the general theoretical framework of postsocial history now outlined, I can deliver on my promise to carefully describe the essential
constitutive pieces of the new historiographical paradigm and illustrate
them appropriately. The already stated premise, that every meaningful relationship between individuals and social context—every experience of
the world—is always mediated by a certain categorial matrix or discourse,
implies the following: the meanings individuals confer on their context are
not an intrinsic property of it but, instead, a property that context acquires
in the process of discursive mediation itself. The meanings, relevance, or
practical implications individuals confer on facts, events, or social situations, encountered in the course of their everyday life, depend on the categorial framework or social imaginary through which they are conceptualized in each case, and not on the facts, events, or situations themselves.
Said in more technical terms, such a premise implies that objectivity is a
property that social referents acquire by virtue of applying a certain discursive pattern of meaning, rather than an attribute that they possess and
that language transmits and consciousness reflects. From this point of
view, social reality has lost its former structural status and has become, instead, a mere conglomerate of events without any meaning of its own, as
well as lacking any capacity to autonomously establish meaningful or
cause-effect relationships between these events. Thus, the distinction between concept and meaning has led to the other, equally crucial distinction, the one that must be established between (social) phenomenon and

(social) object (although one could really say that each distinction implies the other). From now on, social phenomena and social objects are no longer considered to be ontologically equivalent and indistinguishable entities, as they were regarded in the paradigm of social history. Instead, they have become entities that are not only qualitatively different, but also contingently connected, in the sense that a social phenomenon can possess different meanings—that is, give rise to diverse objects—depending on the discursive regime in which it is inserted.

As for the link between social phenomena and social objects (or simply between social circumstances and forms of consciousness), what postsocial history maintains is that even though referents exist independently of language and meanings cannot be created without their collaboration, *referentiality* (that is, the rules of signification) is a power of language, not of referents. Therefore, the central meanings of social reality cannot be thought of only in terms of their relation to referents, since what renders this relation possible is not the referent itself, but that third historical variable that is discourse. Of course, as David Mayfield well notes, the fact that language is non-referential does not mean that there is not a material link between the name and the thing named. It only means that the authority behind the link, the very materiality of the connection, is not determined by the phenomenality of the thing named, but by an external power, the power of the categories through which it is named.[1] If I may draw the simile, I would say that, in the process of producing objects, reality provides the raw material (the "bricks") with which objects are built, but it is discourse that supplies the "plans" (or parameters of signification) in accordance with which the building is erected. This is what allows Joan W. Scott to argue the following: once it becomes clear that there is a deep connection between how social relations are made meaningful and how they are implemented (and even though individuals may not be aware of it, that action, therefore, always takes place within a discursive frame), every opposition between concept and practice, language and reality ceases to make sense and disappears.[2]

In effect, according to postsocial history, it is discourse—and not an alleged social structure—that, on bounding a certain space of enunciation, sets the historical conditions of emergence for objects. Discursive categories, not social conditions, are what fence off a certain real area as open or ripe for objectifying, specify identification criteria (social, material, or whatever kind) to be applied, and thus shape objects as conscious entities. In our relationship with the world, objects are never given to us as if they were existential entities. They are always given to us within discursive configurations,[3] for what language does is not name objects nor bring them to light, but truly create them, actually bring objects themselves into existence by deploying a certain classificatory system. It is by applying this system (with its criteria of inclusion, exclusion, or relevance) that people convert the surrounding facts into meaningful episodes, the merely sensitive into significant. Given their historical specificity and logic, discourses possess, as Scott argues, an authority, a kind of axiomatic or hegemonic status that allows them to establish a regime of naturalness, of "common sense," or of "truth" that is difficult to dislodge and that individuals cannot avoid in their relationship with reality.[4] In consequence, what the concepts or definition criteria that people apply to social reality or themselves do is not to merely label but to prestructure them in a cognitive way, thus determining not only what is seen (in the sense of heeded), but, above all, how it is seen. Discourse provides individuals with an epistemological scheme that, as Margaret R. Somers says, makes possible not only seeing some things and not others, but also seeing those seen in a certain way.[5] This explains why postsocial historians conclude any notion of social causality (and even less, one of human rationality) is unable to give a proper account of the shaping of historical objects and identities, that is, of the ways in which people perceive and assess social reality, including their place in it, and conceive of themselves as subjects and agents.

Postsocial history denies (in terms that sound a strong Foucauldian ring) that *natural objects* exist. This is because social phenomena do not have one or another degree or kind of meaningful relevance outside the discursive regime into which they are incorporated. And, therefore, social objects are neither something discovered or experientially discerned nor something individuals become aware of, but, instead, social objects come to life as a result of a certain way of seeing or some kind of taking heed of the social world. And thus, for example, madness, homosexuality, prostitution, or poverty—to continue in a Foucauldian vein—are not objects that have forever existed and toward which each society adopts a different attitude (repression, tolerance, indifference, government intervention, legal regulation, etc.). On the contrary, even though the real phenomena that underpin them previously existed, objects as such did not emerge until that time when categories like mental illness, sexuality, or social question were applied to them. It is these categories that dictate that some phenomena, previously granted another meaning or none at all, become relevant components of social physiognomy or defining features of individuals' identity, and generate, thus, the corresponding behavioral patterns. In the case of homosexuality, for instance, historical scholarship shows that it only exists as an object from the moment in which the appearance of the category of sexuality makes sexual practices or preferences a relevant criterion of individualization or for defining personality.[6] And the same could be said for gender in general since, in Scott's words, this is not a sociological difference between women and men but a meaning system that constructs that difference.[7]

The questioning of the notion of natural objects is one of the main themes in Mary Poovey's works. What Poovey essentially holds is that real facts or phenomena always become historical entities as a result of applying certain "protocols for knowing" or codification rules to them, a process she graphically refers to as disaggregation. These protocols, by defining an "epistemological field," draw new boundaries and thus transform "what once seemed to be an undifferentiated continuum of practices and ideas" into new representations of social reality. It is this arrangement of reality that allows objects to emerge and become factors of social life. This is the way in which new domains come to appear, specifically the social domain itself, for example, settled as such in modern society. This disaggregation of the social, by early nineteenth century, as a specific domain of reality is what leads to not only a reconceptualization of poverty, but to addressing and understanding social relations as a whole in a new, quite different way—specifically as a domain open to scientific knowledge and political regulation.[8] Poovey has continued her endeavor to analyze the disaggregation of facts and objects, questioning the truth status of the former and studying how the very notion of fact itself has acquired its modern connotations of objective entity. Her main conclusion concerning the latter is that it was the result of the settlement of a new epistemological field, one that converted numbers (and therefore statistics) into transparent and impartial means of representing reality. By according such a representational quality to numbers, modern epistemology converted numerical representations into privileged means for creating social objects.[9]

The fact that meanings—and therefore objects—are not implicit in their social referents, but are constituted in the process of discursive arrangement or conceptual diasggregation, is what enables postsocial historians to claim that social reality or context is a discursive or linguistic *construction*. Obviously, this does not mean that discourse constructs social reality in a literal sense, as a set of phenomena and material relations. It builds social reality as a *meaningful entity*. That is, it constructs, through its mediation, the image, idea, or consciousness that individuals have of it, and according to which they act. The operation of discursive or meaningful construction of society will be referred to here with the concept of *articulation*, a term historians now use with greater and greater frequency. This concept has been erected in frank opposition to concepts of reflection, representation, or expression, and has the express purpose of denoting the constitutive function of language in the shaping of objects, subjects, and practices and of stressing the rhetorical character of any relationship between individuals and their social enviroment.[10]

II

In the endeavor to profoundly rethink the connection between object and referent, between social world and its subjective picture, the critical attention of postsocial historians to the concept of *experience* has been theoretically crucial. Because if social phenomena do not bear inherent meanings and objects are, indeed, born of an operation of discursive construction, then we have to completely rethink the way in which individuals forge their experience of the social world, as well as the nature of experience itself.

In the classical materialist paradigm, worth recalling here, the concept of experience involves the existence of a social structure that imposes its meanings on subjects and generates these as such—which is why the term *experience* also designates the means through which such a structure attains to consciousness. And thus, for example, a long-lived experience of unequal relations, according to this paradigm, helps those who are subordinate to become people conscious of their specific interests or identity bonds. In new cultural history, the concept of experience refers to the historical realm resulting from the interplay between social conditions and cultural dispositions of agents. For new cultural historians and also worthy of recall, experience is not simply the outcome of social circumstances directly impressing themselves on minds, but the result of culturally approaching and actively making sense of the social world. Or to be more exact, experience is the result of deciphering the meanings of such a world in terms of the cultural devices historically available to people. Experience is not a passive reception of the world, but a subjectively recreated picture of it. This is, for example, as it is well known, what experience means for E. P. Thompson. According to Thompson, workers do not merely experience their working conditions as exploitation, but they go on to *feel* exploited in terms of their moral values and political tenets, specifically the natural rights ideology. Once again, in both social and new cultural history, however, social reality itself defines what people are to experience.

With the advent of postsocial history, the former concept of experience, in any of the aforementioned senses, lacks viability, proving useless as an analytical tool. With discursive mediation experience—understood generically as a meaningful apprehension of reality—is neither something given nor something having causal foundation in reality itself. Instead, every experience of the world is an effect of articulating that world and, in consequence, what people do is not experience their social conditions of existence, the contention of social history, but construct them meaningfully. If it is language, and not referent, that establishes the rules of signification and if, therefore, we have a world because we have a language that gives it meaning (and does not merely name it), then experience is not something individuals just have. Rather, discursive mediation itself supplies individuals with their experience by endowing their environment with meaning and, thus, transforming brute facts into objects. In other words, if it is discourse that provides reality with its objective face, then it also forges the experience that individuals have of that reality. As Geoff Eley argues, what constitutes the basic categories of understanding, and therefore the social, cultural, and political environment in which people act and think, is not the experience of the social, but particular discursive formations whose emergence and elaboration can be carefully and historically reconstructed.[11] Therefore, once this very "collapse of the immediacy of the *given*" has taken place, historians can no longer continue to consider experience as something "unproblematically available."[12] On the contrary, it becomes necessary to unravel the discursive operation by which experience itself has been configured as such.

Thus, criticism of the concept of experience not only appears as one of the primary driving forces of the current theoretical shift in historical studies, but it also constitutes one of the main supports of the emerging theory of society. In their search for a more satisfactory explanation of the behavior of historical actors and the connection between this behavior and social context, postsocial historians have been compelled to devote a great deal of their efforts, both empirical inquiry and theoretical elaboration, to this matter. This is the case of Joan Scott, whose critical rethinking of the concept of experience deserves close attention. The depth, energy, and influence of her thoughts on experience establish a landmark in the ongoing process of historiographical remaking of social theory.[13]

Scott's arguments are grounded on a double assumption. First of all, reality is not constituted by "transparent objects" of which consciousness would be a representation obtained through experience. Secondly, and consequently, language and experience are so inextricably interwoven that they cannot be separated. There is, she insists, no social experience apart from language and, therefore, they cannot be analyzed separately. Not only is life constituted of language as much as it is of social facts (like work, childbirth, strategies of subsistence, or political rallies), but more importantly, as she underscores, it is language that makes these facts intelligible: "'Language' not only enables social practice; it is social practice." Actions, organizations, institutions, or behaviors, she continues, are "at once concepts *and* practices and need to be analyzed simultaneously as such." And this is why, Scott concludes, it is absurd to posit, as Christine Stansell does, an antithesis between "rhetorical text" and "social experience." Such a stance reduces language to words or to written documents, thus seriously impoverishing the theoretical framework of history.[14]

Scott's serious efforts to get a handle on the concept of experience critically point to historians of gender or homosexuality in particular. While resuscitating their objects of study from the dead silence of previous historical scholarship, most ignore an equally great need, if not sine qua non critical corollary, to call that previous scholarship itself into question—to ask after its conceptual foundations and their possible relation to, or even concomitant connection with, such silencing, and to also ponder over both past exclusions and present-day inclusions of certain people. Historians, seeking to enlarge the picture and to amend an incomplete vision of society, still continue to base their analysis "on the authority of experience" and to conceive this—and therefore, consciousness and identity—as an expression of social reality (776). Such, according to Scott, explains why the results of this kind of history are so contradictory: on the one hand, they contribute to the renewal of the discipline but, on the other, they consolidate established assumptions. On the other hand, this history, about the lives of those omitted or overlooked in accounts of the past, has undoubtedly produced a wealth of new evidence about these previously ignored others and has also drawn attention to dimensions of human life and activity usually deemed unworthy to even mention in conventional histories. Furthermore, it has occasioned "a crisis for orthodox history by multiplying not only stories but subjects and by insisting that histories are written from fundamentally different—indeed irreconcilable—perspectives or standpoints, none of which is complete or completely 'true.'" Thus, these histories have certainly provided evidence of a world replete with alternative values and practices, one that does indeed puncture hegemonic constructions of social worlds, be they the superiority of white men, the coherence and unity of selves, the naturalness of heterosexual monogamy, or the inevitability of scientific progress and economic development (776).

But, on the other hand—and this is the essential point—this challenge to normative history has been done within the framework of a conventional historical understanding of evidence and experience (that Scott names "positivism"), one in which evidence by itself imposes on consciousness. This is why Scott concludes that documenting the experience of others in this way has been at once a highly successful and limiting strategy for historians of difference. "It has been successful because it remains so comfortably within the disciplinary framework of history, working according to rules that permit calling old narratives into question when new evidence is discovered." It has been limiting because it continues to depend on "a referential notion of evidence which denies that it is anything but a reflection of the real" (776). And it is, precisely, this notion of referentiality, "this kind of appeal to experience as uncontestable evidence and as an originary point of explanation—as a foundation on which analysis is based—that seriously weakens the critical thrust of histories of

difference." By remaining within the epistemological framework of "orthodox history, these studies lose the possibility of examining those assumptions and practices that excluded considerations of difference in the
first place" (777). That is, they lose the possibility of critically examining the
theoretical assumptions that propitiated exclusion of these objects of study
and, therefore, of contributing to the theoretical renovation of history. Histories documenting, for example, the "hidden" world of homosexuality
give testimony to the lives of those suffering silence, bringing to light the
history of their suppression and exploitation. But, the very project of making experience visible precludes critical examination of the working of the
categories of representation themselves (homosexual/heterosexual,
man/woman, black/white), and, as well, of the form in which these categories operate and of their notions of subject, origin, and cause (778).

In fact, argues Scott, the main fault of this kind of history is that it
takes the identities of those whose experience is being documented as
self-evident, and thus naturalizes their difference. By localizing resistance
outside its discursive construction and de-contextualizing it, as well as taking experience as the origin of knowledge, all issues concerning the constructed nature of experience, of how subjects are constituted as different
in the first place, and of how one's vision is structured by discourse, are left
aside, unheeded (777). As a consequence, "the evidence of experience then
becomes evidence for the fact of difference, rather than a way of exploring
how difference is established, how it operates, how and in what ways it
constitutes subjects who see and act in the world" (777). And, therefore,
this "evidence of experience, whether conceived through a metaphor of
visibility or in any other way that takes meaning as transparent," assumes
that the aforementioned oppositions are natural objects and that the facts
of history speak by themselves (778). In the case of the history of homosexuality, for example, this appears as the result of desire, as a natural force
operating outside or in opposition to social regulation, that is, as a repressed desire, an experience denied, silenced by a society that legislates
heterosexuality as the only normal practice. According to this view, when
this kind of homosexual desire cannot be repressed, "because experience is
there," it invents institutions to accommodate itself, institutions that are
unacknowledged, but not invisible. And, therefore, when they are seen,
they threaten order and ultimately overcome repression. Thus, emancipation appears as a teleological story in which desire ultimately overcomes
social control and becomes visible and, therefore, history is reduced to a
chronology that makes experience visible, but in which categories (desire,
homosexuality, heterosexuality, femininity, masculinity, or sex) appear as
labels of ahistorical and socially objective entities (778).

Moreover, by conceiving objects and practices this way, history excludes, or at least understates, not only the historically variable interrela-

tionship between the meanings "homosexual" and "heterosexual" and the constitutive force each has for the other (as they both define each other, specifying their negative limits), but also the contested and changing nature of the terrain that they simultaneously occupy (778–79). Thus, by reducing historical inquiry to a project of making experience visible, one can appreciate the alternative conducts and repressive actions, but one cannot comprehend the framework of (historically contingent) patterns of sexuality within which these conducts and actions are inscribed. That is, one can discover that these conducts and actions exist, but not how they have been constructed and which logic they follow (779). A similar conception of experience and the connection between reality and consciousness can also be observed, according to Scott, in the history of gender. In this case too, the relationship between thought and experience is represented as transparent and, therefore, the lived experience of women is seen as leading directly to resistance to oppression, that is, to feminism. In other words, that conscious identity and the possibility of politics "is said to rest on, to follow from, a pre-existing women's experience" (786–87), which leaves the objectivist and teleological framework of social-new cultural history untouched. That explains Scott's criticism of Laura Lee Downs. For Scott, the weakness of Downs's argument lies, precisely, in an analysis of the situation of women that limits itself to applying the categories of difference as if these were transparent expressions of reality and experience, without pausing to analyze the process by which such categories have been constituted and have actively participated in the making of feminine identity. However, experience of the world is not transparent, but discursive, and, therefore, meanings and actions based on experience are not anchored in reality, but in the very process of discursive construction of that experience. One cannot, as Downs does, structure the argument in terms of opposition between language and experience, ideas and reality, texts and contexts, the textual and the social, as if this dichotomous division were a self-evident fact that needs no justification. On the contrary, this opposition is no more than the effect of a "both exclusionary and productive" operation of textual constitution, that is, of a certain discursive pattern of selection.[15]

Once she has laid down the historicity and discursivity of experience, and after advocating, as a logical conclusion, the main object of historical analysis be the discursive mechanisms that articulate objects and identities, Scott proceeds to a closer criticism of the concept of experience, specifically its new cultural Thompsonian variant. Scott admits, on this point, that, in the case of historians more open to interpretive history, to the cultural determinations of conduct, and the influence of unconscious motivations, the concept of experience takes on more varied and elusive connotations. However, by continuing to assume that experience is something that people have, these historians never ask themselves how the identity of subjects is produced. In the specific case of E. P. Thompson, experience is the mediating element between social structure and consciousness, between the individual and the structural, so that this historian, in particular, separates "the affective and the symbolic from the economic and the rational" (784–85). Nonetheless, Thompson continues to consider experience shaped, in the final analysis, by production relations and, consequently, he takes the positions of men and women and their different relationships to politics "as reflections of material and social arrangements" and as part of the "experience" of capitalism. Instead of asking how certain experiences are constituted, Thompson defines experience as something cumulative and homogenizing, providing the common ground on which class-consciousness is built (785). That is why, for him, class is, in the end, an identity rooted in structural relations (785–86).

However, as Scott argues in her exchange with Bryan D. Palmer on the same issue, one cannot claim, as Palmer does, that the experience of class struggle is directly knowable except to those with a false consciousness, or perhaps none at all.[16] Such cannot be claimed given that there is no opposition between discourse and class struggle; "class struggle is produced in discourse," the latter understood, of course, not as utterances or words, but as whole ways of thinking and understanding how society works.[17] Indeed, to claim that social groups possess particular forms of consciousness is no more than a descriptive obviousness if one does not immediately add that it is the discursive framework that enables these groups to articulate their interests, give meaning to their actions, and construct their identity as social agents. In the case of the labor movement, this means, as Scott insists, that concepts like class are required *before* individuals can identify themselves as members of such a group, and *before* they can act collectively as such.[18] From which it follows, as I will discuss later on, that nineteenth-century workers did not act as they did because they belonged to the working class (however one understands this), but because they were immersed in a discursive universe that conferred a given meaning on that belonging. It is not a question of workers discerning the meaning of their social position in the course of the class struggle, and acting in accordance with it (and when they do not, it is because they are prey to false consciousness). What really happens is that these workers ascribe a certain meaning to this position and go on to act in accordance with it. This is what explains the statement of postsocial history that the working class is not an objective entity (and much less an ontological one), but a discursive construction. Because it is the modern discourse, and not the production relations (more exactly, it is the meaningful interaction between the two), that forges the subjective conviction that the proletariat is a class destined to carry out social change.

Thus and according to Scott, when historizing homosexuality, gender, or class, these historians are essentially masking "the necessarily discursive" character of experience (787). Since experience is not the fruit of the impact of reality on the subjectivity of individuals, it can be neither the causal foundation of consciousness nor what defines interests, fixes identity, or dictates conscious action. On the contrary, what we usually call experience is no more than the result of discursively apprehending reality. And that is just why social conditions, by themselves, cannot prescribe conducts; they only do so when they are thought of, regarded, or classified as relevant—endowed with or deprived of relevance, silent or significant, in sum, *articulated*, through a given pattern of meaning or social imaginary. From this perspective, the fact that every consciousness appears linked to a historical context does not mean the latter has generated the former through experience. On the contrary, as Scott says, experience itself "is a linguistic event (it doesn't happen outside established meanings)" (793). From this something fundamental ensues, namely, that experience cannot be the origin of our explanation, nor the authoritative (because seen or felt) evidence that grounds what is known, but, rather, it is experience itself that *we have to explain* (780 and 797). What, in each case, we have to explain is why individuals experience social conditions in one way and not in another way.

Thus, the critical rethinking of the objectivist concept of experience involves a radical reorientation of historical analysis. From now on, the aim is no longer to reenact experience nor, starting from it, to explain the origin of meanings and to establish the causes of actions, but, on the contrary, the aim is to analyze how experience itself is constructed starting from the discursive articulation of reality. Or, as Scott herself encourages, from now on we have "to attend to the historical processes that, through discourse, position subjects and produce their experiences," because "it is not individuals who have experiences, but subjects who are constituted through experience" (779). It is in categories like class, worker, citizen, and even man and woman, and in their historical constitution as organizers of social practice—and not in an alleged foundational experience—where we should seek an explanation for the conscious behavior of individuals.[19] A problematization of experience helps to recognize the need or obligation to proceed with a critical scrutiny of all explanatory categories, usually taken for granted and, thus, unexamined, including of course the category of "experience" itself (780).

From a postsocial theoretical outlook, therefore, the essential point, as Patrick Joyce well emphasizes, is that experience cannot be the (explanatory) foundation of anything. And thus, as Joyce himself argues, unlike the standard assumption, it was not the "experience of poverty" or the experience of "existential uncertainty and insecurity" that dictated, in Great

Britain in the first half of the nineteenth century, the conscious practice of the individuals who referred their actions to them. Nor does the "cultural activity" of these individuals express a "need for order, boundary and control" determined by a "pre-existing experience." On the contrary, both meanings and corresponding practices do not derive from an originating experience of poverty and insecurity, but from the way people articulate such an experience. As Joyce concludes, given that the very handling of reality inevitably spells constructing it, the meanings of poverty and insecurity "are made and not found."[20] And, consequently, there is no causal connection between the experience of discontent and consciousness, because language is not simply "the neutral medium" of experience, which converts the unconscious into consciousness, but, rather, it is language itself that articulates experience and, thus, generates consciousness.[21]

A similar argument is the one adduced by Zachary Lockman concerning the Egyptian labor movement.[22] According to Lockman, instead of using "experience" as a way of directly linking objective circumstances with specific forms of worker consciousness, we need to look at the discursive field within which there were available to workers several different (though interacting) ways of comprehending (or perhaps more precisely, structuring) their circumstances, their experiences, and themselves. Which forces us to also admit the possibility that a single reality can generate different forms of experience (and identity), depending on the categorial matrix in force. Among these ways of comprehending, Lockman adds, "may have been some that posited class (in whatever exact sense) as a meaningful category, but also others that did not, including craft identities, gender identities, and relations, kinship ties, loyalties to neighborhood, and what might be called popular-Islamic conceptions of justice and equity."

III

The work of Laclau and Mouffe provides us with a vivid example of articulation or discursive construction of an object and experience, the one of the modern transformation of social subordination into oppression.[23] According to these authors, the basic question to be answered, in this respect, is why, in certain circumstances, social subordination goes on to be conceived as oppression by individuals. That is why, in certain historical situations, the *fact* social subordination is converted into the *object* oppression and, consequently, becomes the base of an antagonism and generates corresponding practices of resistance. And this is because, as Laclau and Mouffe remark, oppression is not implicit in social subordination, nor, therefore, can the struggle against subordination be the result of the situation of subordination itself, as if it were inevitable or natural. Unlike what shallow observation may suggest, social subordination and oppression are not continuous planes, nor is there any causal continuity between the two. Even though, of course, social subordination is a necessary condition for oppression to come to life, it is not a *sufficient* condition. And, therefore, not only should we maintain both instances separate analytically, but also, in each case, clarify just what converts a relationship of subordination into a relation of oppression.

According to Laclau and Mouffe, what makes social subordination turn into oppression on given occasions is the existence of certain discursive conditions, that is, that social subordination is made meaningful through a specific body of categories. These are specifically modern categories like equality, natural rights, or freedom. From this perspective, oppression is not the natural expression of social subordination, but only one of the forms, historically and discursively particular, in which social subordination has been objectified. Or, to express it in simpler terms, the fact that individuals conceive of, feel, or experience their social subordination as a situation of oppression does not depend on the existence of such a subordination or its material effects. It depends, rather, on being conceptualized through a given pattern of meaning. It is only then that social subordination becomes the defining criterion of interests and identities, establishes the reasons and terms of resistance, and becomes intolerable.

Once this point has been reached, the problem is to explain how relations of oppression (relations of subordination which are transformed into sites of antagonism) are constituted out of relations of subordination (in which an agent is subjected to the decision of another one). This is because, as indicated, a relation of subordination is not, in and of itself, an antagonistic relation (153–54). As Laclau and Mouffe argue, "'serf,' 'slave' and so on, do not designate in themselves antagonistic positions; it is only in the terms of a different discursive formation, such as 'the rights inherent to every human being' that the differential positivity of these categories can be subverted and the subordination constructed as oppression. This means that there is no relation of oppression without the presence of a discursive 'exterior' from which the discourse of subordination can be interrupted" (154). From this point of view, the perception of social subordination as oppression is not, as social history entails, the result of an act of consciousness. What individuals do is meaningfully construct oppression out of social or economic subordination and not become conscious, or not, of their oppression. Whether individuals accept or not their subordination, ascribe one or another meaning to it, or grant it a greater or lesser importance for their lives, will depend on the conceptual perspective they adopt in each case. And the same could be said of the modalities of conduct that this subordination generates, specifically, of resistance to it. Nor is conduct

a response to the existence of social subordination itself either, but a response, instead, to its specific articulation as oppression. Of course, as Laclau and Mouffe clarify, it could be admitted that wherever there is power,
there is resistance, but it must be immediately added, "only in certain
cases do these forms of resistance take on a political character and become
struggles directed towards putting an end to relations of subordination as
such" (152–53).

Just such is the case of the relation between subordination and oppression of women. Up until the seventeenth century, feminism as a movement of struggle against women's subordination could not emerge out,
since the set of discourses that constructed women as subjects fixed
purely and simply in a subordinate position. For feminism to emerge, a
discursive rupture had to occur, a displacement of the old discourse by
another, new, and different one. Therefore, even though it is historically
true that there have been many forms of resistance by women against
male domination, what is really significant for historical analysis is that
only under certain conditions and specific forms does a feminist movement, one demanding equality, emerge (153). It is indeed only from the
moment when "the democratic discourse" becomes available, one propi-
tiating the articulation of different forms of resistance to subordination,
that the conditions exist to make possible struggle against different types
of inequality, including the inequality of women. It is only when a displacement of the democratic discourse from the "field of political equality between citizens to the field of equality between sexes" occurs, that female oppression, and thus feminism, can be constituted (154). In other
words, for the object oppression of women (and its associated form of
practice, feminism) to emerge, the new democratic principles of liberty
and equality needed first to be imposed as the foundation of social imaginary (or, in the authors' terms, constituted as a fundamental nodal point
in the construction of the political). This decisive mutation in the social
imaginary of Western societies took place two hundred years ago and can
be defined in these terms: "the logic of equivalence was transformed into
the fundamental instrument of production of the social" (154–55).

This is what both authors, following Tocqueville, refer to as "democratic revolution," a term that designates "the end of a society of a hierar-
chic and inegalitarian type, ruled by a theological-political logic in which
the social order had its foundation in divine will." A society "in which the
social body was conceived of as a whole in which individuals appeared
fixed in differential positions." A social body in which politics "could not
be more than the repetition of hierarchical relations which reproduced the
same type of subordinated subject" (155). The "key-moment" of this democratic revolution was the French Revolution, since, with it, a new social
imaginary and the claim of popular sovereignty emerged; a new legiti-

macy appears and a new mode of institution of the social is established (155). This break with the Old Regime, symbolized by the Declaration of the Rights of Man, would provide the discursive conditions that made it possible to propose different forms of inequality as illegitimate and anti-natural, and thus make them equivalent as forms of oppression. "Here lay the profound subversive power of the democratic discourse, which would allow the spread of equality and liberty into increasingly wider domains and therefore act as a fermenting agent upon the different forms of struggle against subordination." Such is the case of the labor movement of the nineteenth century, whose demands were constructed, precisely, with the help of the categories of this new democratic discourse (155).

Of course, from a postsocial standpoint, discursive articulation is not only the base for the transformation of concrete social phenomena into objects. It is also the operation through which society, as a whole, is objectified, and, in particular, through which it has been objectified, in modern times, specifically as *society*—that is, as an objective, autonomous, and self-regulating structure that works as the causal foundation of social practice, identities, relations, or institutions. With the advent of postsocial history, the standard concept of society has also cracked and dissolved, at the same time as the concept itself has been reconstructed by postsocial scholarship on new bases. A reconstruction that was initiated with a historicization of the concept of society but one that has ended up in a radical rethinking of the very nature of society (or the social) as object (as well as of the notion of social causality associated with it.) In this respect, then, postsocial history begins by pointing out, as Joyce does, the following: even though the process of reification or naturalization to which every concept is subjected converts it into a common sense concept, this should not distract us from the fact that the notion of society is a historical construct and that "the idea that 'society' comprised a *system*, was one particular manifestation of this much larger history of 'society,' a manifestation taking clearer form in the eighteenth century."[24] It is indeed in this time when social reality and interpersonal relations start to be conceived as a domain that transcends and is independent of the will of individuals, at the same time as it is the unintended outcome of their actions. That is, as a domain governed by its own rules and endowed with an internal mechanism of stability and change that, by virtue of this, operates as the foundation of human life (replacing religion as the ultimate ground of order and as the ontological frame of human experience).

So far, however, we have seen nothing new. The work of theoretical reconstruction as such really starts when postsocial historians add that this understanding and conceptualization of social reality is not the result of a discovery, but of a *construction*. The notion of society did not appear because the rules that govern human society had been discerned, but because human society came to be meaningfully reconstructed through new conceptual parameters. The notion of society is not, thus, the designative label of a phenomenon that really exists, but the category through which, at a given moment, social relations began to be made sense of and converted into an object—in this case, the object "society." As Keith M. Baker argues, there is no such thing as a discovery of society, "as if it were a positivity whose true reality was simply waiting to be revealed by the eclipse of religion." Society "is not the solid reality seen by human eyes as soon as they were disenchanted with religion"—this is only the story told by the modern discourse itself. Society is not "a brute objective fact," but rather a certain meaningful construction of social reality instituted in practice. This does not imply, as Baker remarks, a denial that interdependence in human relations exists as such, but simply that "there are many possible ways in which this interdependence might be constructed." *Society* is no more than the specific conceptual construction of that interdependence forged during the Enlightenment.[25]

The historiographical repercussions of this theoretical reconstruction of the concept of society are obvious and many (although I only mention two, briefly, here). To start with, if the concept of society, coined in the modern age, is not a designative label of an objective phenomenon (that is, independent of and prior to the mediation of the concept itself), and is, instead, a historically specific way of meaningfully constructing social sphere, the latter, then, does not constitute an objective instance and should not be taken as such in historical analysis. This implies, as well, that the concept of society (in the sense of social structure) is deprived of all epistemological content and all cognitive power and that the notion of social causality also loses any utility as a tool of social analysis. Nonetheless, as social causality is dealt with in a later chapter, here I will limit myself to the other, far more concrete repercussion.

As I have indicated, the advent of postsocial history has not only involved discarding the concepts of society and social causality, but has also thwarted their reconstruction, seriously reducing, thus, the scope of their historical applicability and analytical appropriateness, an outcome already implicit in and logically deductible from the very decline the concept of society suffers. In proceeding with this theoretical reconstruction, the first statement postsocial history makes is: if society is not an objective phenomenon, as social history assumes, but a discursive construction, then it cannot have an universal existence (as social historians also tend to believe). Instead, society as objective structure can only exist during the modern period of human history and even here, only in those situations where the objectivist variant of modern discourse is in force. Hence, it is a grave mistake to extrapolate and apply the notions of society and social causality to historical periods or situations in which these notions did not exist as such, as social historians have been doing for decades.

Thus, postsocial history denies that social reality is an objective structure, but, at the same time, postsocial history recognizes that, in certain historical situations, social reality works as an objective structure, and as such causally determines the identity and practice of individuals. And therefore it could be claimed that there are relations of social causality. But this *only* occurs in those historical circumstances in which the social sphere has been articulated as "society." Only when individuals are located under the influence of the modern category of society and, in consequence, *effectively* operate and organize their practice through such a category, can such practice be considered socially determined. In other words, only when individuals explicitly define their interests, identities, or expectations out of their social conditions of existence, can it be said that society is really working as an objective structure. Which, in turn, implies that if the social sphere has been able to work, on certain occasions, over the last two centuries, as an objective structure, this has not been due to its being such but to its articulation as such. If many individuals and groups—like, for example, the class-based labor movement—have defined their identity and acted in accordance with their social position, this was not because they were really determined by it but because social position had been previously articulated as the foundation of identity. *Not even* in modern times, in which "society" and social causality have an effective existence, can the social sphere be considered the causal foundation of experience and practice. Even in this case, experience and practice are causally linked to discursive mediation, not to the social referent, or, if more helpful, to society as an object and not to society as a real phenomenon.[26]

This is why, as some authors have pointed out, when studying modern societies, historical analysis must shift "from the assumption of an objective 'society' to the study of how the category of 'the social' was formed."[27] In this case too, if the behavior of individuals is not because of their social location but because this has been articulated as a social objectivity, then to explain such behavior we have to focus our analytical attention on the process of articulation itself. It is in this process, and not in the living circumstances, where the causal origin of practice is to be found. And a similar "discursive move"[28] is required if we want to understand and explain, in general, the appearance and development of modern society, the identities that embody it, the conflicts that run through it, or certain problematics, not previously conceivable, that now come into view. In the same way, close historical analysis of the genealogy and practical deployment of the category of society is requisite in order to make intelligible all those actions aimed at acting *upon* society itself, at controlling, specifically, the conditions of social reproduction. The fact that society has been discursively objectified as an ultimately originating entity is what explains that, in the modern period, "the social" has become a mode of governance, to which forms of knowledge are so closely linked. It has become, on the one hand, an object of theory-knowledge and study and, on the other, an object of regulatory intervention, a target of policy, or a site of practice. This discursive objectivization is what explains the conception of society as susceptible to technical control and of practice in terms of social engineering and what makes, therefore, intelligible the set of actions that intends to control, plan, regulate, orient, or direct social processes. But best I avoid treading further on this path, which is not, on this occasion, the one historical research follows. Let me simply note, at this closure, that in this particular case too, the denaturalization of the concept of society seems not only to have placed the history of concept formation at the center of the stage but also to have turned such a history into the cornerstone of social theory.

4

✛

The Making of
Interests and Identities

Rethinking the nature and genesis of social objectivity and critical review of the concept of experience involve a reconstruction of two other capital concepts of historical analysis, the concepts of interest and identity. In this case, too, what postsocial historians essentially argue, as one can readily guess, is that if every experience of social reality is discursively constructed, then individuals' interests and identities cannot be objectively inscribed in their social (or material) position either. They are, instead, constituted as historical factors in the very process of articulating or meaningfully constructing such a position. But, once more, let me look at this more closely, starting with the concept of interest.

To better appreciate the terms and the depth of the rethinking of the concept of *interest* tackled by postsocial history, we should remember, if only briefly, that, in the objectivist paradigm, the interests of individuals are, in general, located in and generated by their socioeconomic position. And thus, for example, the poor, slaves, peasants, craftsmen, modern factory workers, or members of the middle class, conscious or not of the fact, would have specific interests depending on their belonging to a certain social category. Hence interests operate as a real causal connection between social structure and conscious action. This is considered so because aspirations, expectations, and purposes that individuals aim to satisfy, realize, or attain are inherent in, derive logically from, and are determined by their social features or attributes. Of course, it is accepted that this causal connection is sometimes disturbed by false consciousness, but that acknowledgment does not invalidate the theoretical assumption sketched here. Furthermore, although, with the rise of new cultural history, this objectivist assumption was reformulated, its theoretical core remained intact, as we know. For new cultural historians, individuals possess social interests, but, unlike what classical social historians upheld, these interests do not manifest themselves or historically work spontaneously, but only evince once they have been discerned, recognized, or made conscious in the course of practice. This active unveiling of social interests has to occur in order to enable them to become embodied in action. Thus, in new cultural history, conscious action continues to be anchored in the social being, although not directly but through the perceived being—which cries out, as I have indicated, begging historical analysis to add an interpretive moment to its initial explanatory endeavor.

Postsocial history shares and takes, as its starting point, this sort of theoretical move from interests to identity or perceived being, inasmuch as it also maintains that interests only operate historically if they have a conscious existence and that the notion of hidden or unconscious interests, found in social history, is crippling nonsense that needs to be discarded. Historical actors may not be conscious (and they generally are not) of the origin and process involved in the constitution of interests leading them to act in a certain way. But they certainly cannot be ignorant of the interests themselves because without awareness interests could not motivate actions. To be historical factors interests have to be facts of consciousness. However, the agreement between the two kinds of history (new cultural and postsocial) ends at this point. Postsocial history immediately questions the assumption that interests are social or objective, in the sense that they have a previous existence in the social conditions of life and are implicit in or defined by these conditions. On the contrary, the interests of individuals do not come from their social position nor, therefore, do they emerge through an act of consciousness, but are constituted as a result of the meaning social position acquires within a given social imaginary. Social properties are not, in themselves, substances of interest; they are substances of interest only if they are articulated as such. Like any other subjective entity, interests are brought to life by an operation of articulation and, therefore, individuals do not recognize or discern their interests as if these were preconstituted in the social sphere (or in any other referent), but they construct them discursively. Unlike what new cultural history sustains, language does not simply provide individuals vocabulary with which to formulate their social interests, but language is what does enable them to conceive their social interests themselves. And, therefore, these interests cannot have a historical existence or operate as causal factors outside of this operation of articulation. Thus, postsocial history, once again, does not limit itself to merely endorsing the aforementioned theoretical move toward the perceived being, but also proceeds to causally disconnect this from any social being (which, in practice, spells its dissolution).[1]

Postsocial historians believe historical scholarship is bringing to light and progressively making it more evident that the interests of individuals do not have a social foundation. No such thing as social interests actually exists and, as Margaret R. Somers points out, we should stop imputing a particular set of interests to people as members of social categories.[2] Contrary to widely accepted historical assumption, the place individuals occupy in social relations does not imply, in and of itself, certain living expectations or aims. Interests are constituted in a distinct sphere and through a process different from the one assumed by the social causality paradigm. It is the categorial matrix or prevailing social imaginary that confers, in each case, meaning on social properties or situations and makes possible for these to acquire the condition of foundation of individuals' interests.[3] If social reality has no intrinsic meanings, then the interests associated with it cannot constitute a preexisting social entity. On the contrary, as Keith M. Baker states, these interests are nothing more than "a principle of differentiation," since they are forged as the result of the relative position that individuals or groups come to occupy when being incorporated into a discursive system of differences. And therefore the interests of individuals—as well as the conflicts of interests in which these become involved—are not simply given in social position, but they depend on the meaningful relationship into which this position enters with all other social positions.[4] If interests are not given in some prediscursive ontological social structure, we are compelled to explain, in each case, why certain social positions generate certain interests, and not take for granted, as social-new cultural history does, that there is a causal or logically necessary link between the two.

Furthermore, the discursive, not social, nature of interests is what explains that similar social positions can generate different interests and that, in general, interests are precarious and unstable historical products which are always subjected to processes of redefinition or reconstruction.[5] Changes in discursive conditions not only force individuals to reformulate their traditional interests and demands and to base them on new social diagnoses (in order to gain practical efficacy), but also make it possible for *new* interests and demands, whose existence was previously impossible, to appear and be enunciated. This is what happens, for example, during the liberal revolutions, when the rise and institutionalization of the modern discourse converts political participation into a primordial interest of the lower strata of the Third Estate. Or, as Baker suggests, when the appearance of such a discourse generates, by succeeding in changing the perception of feudal relations as natural ones, an interest in abolishing feudalism, an interest that is neither contained in

nor causally deducible from feudal relations themselves, but one engendered in the process of discursive rearticulation of these very relations. In
this case too, the modern-liberal discourse is not what allows peasants to
make previously existing interests explicit, as social history would maintain, but it is the means through which interests are constituted as such. A
peasant can only become interested in abolishing feudalism once this has
been denaturalized by an external discourse, but not while continuing to
articulate it through the categories of the feudal discourse itself. And, as
Baker argues, unless we take into account new discursive conditions, we
will not be able to explain "the meanings of 'social' events" taking place
during the so-called Great Fear of the summer of 1789.[6]

As we know, by redefining the concept of interest in this way, postsocial history expels any notion of *false consciousness*, entailing, as it does, the
existence of objective social interests. If interests are not inscribed in their
social positions or material referents, then there is neither true nor false
consciousness with respect to them (nor are there normal or deviated behaviors), but simply different forms of articulating interests out of such
positions or referents. In those cases in which social actors do not seem to
behave in accordance with (or even behave in opposition to) the interests
that they allegedly possess by virtue of their social position—for example,
peasants supporting counterrevolution or workers voting conservative—
it is certainly not a question of these actors having a false consciousness
of their interests. They have articulated their interests through a categorial matrix not considered the standard one. Their behavior should not be
understood as immature expressions of the social being or as indirect
ways of realizing social interests, for example, regarding the aforementioned antiliberal peasant resistance to be merely the ideologically dis-
guised channel of the peasant revolution.

Of course, the claim that social interests do not exist should not be understood, as often occurs, in a narrowly literal sense. What this statement
means is not that interests lack a social base or that they are socially arbitrary, as it is evident that every interest is always constituted out of a referent, whether social or material. Every interest always appears as a subjective response to a given social or living situation. Nor does it mean that
interests, as revisionism maintains, are mere political or ideological constructions. What postsocial history rejects is a social essentialist conception of interests, and therefore, what it resolutely asserts is that interests
are not *objective*, in the sense that they are not something implicit in the social attributes of people that become explicit in their consciousness. What
postsocial history states is not that socioeconomic factors are irrelevant,
but that their contribution to the making of interests is always made
through the mediation of a certain discursive pattern. And that, in consequence, a given socioeconomic or physical property or feature only be-

comes a defining criterion of interests and thus begins to mold the behavior of individuals if—and only if—it has been discursively endowed with such a meaning, and not because of its mere existence. Social attributes undoubtedly constitute the necessary material support of interests, but they are not their causal foundation. Interests, as historical phenomena, are not gestated in the social sphere, but in the space of signification resulting from the interaction of such a sphere with a specific social imaginary. Interests neither exist prior to the mediation of the discourse, nor do they have exteriority with respect to this. Once social, material, or physical referents have been articulated, the resulting interests appear as their natural effects. But that should not confuse us and make us lose sight of the fact that the link between the two is natural *only* within some specific discursive framework and that this link could not have been established without the active and practical presence of such a framework. Thus, in the present historiographical phase, the debate about the concept of interest no longer consists of a confrontation between idealism and materialism, but between materialism and idealism and a history based on the concept of discursive mediation. And for the latter, discourse is the means by which interests are constituted, whereas (political) ideology is *merely* the vocabulary in which individuals talk about them.

This new concept of interest can be quite disturbing and not always easy to assimilate. In a historiographical culture deeply pervaded with reflectionism or representationalism, such a concept seems to come into conflict with the most elemental common sense. It can be admitted that in some cases the causal connection between social situation and interests is not as evident as social history has tended to believe. But when interests are of an economic or a material nature, the causal character of the connection does not seem to allow any doubt. In these cases, interests appear to be mere natural responses and, therefore, resulting behaviors not only seem to be unequivocally induced by material life, but the only possible and expected ones. Of course, there are situations in which expected responses are absent or delayed, but that would be a mere, passing anomaly. And thus, sooner or later every individual subjugated to unfavorable socioeconomic conditions ends up rebelling against them, and he/she does so in a similar manner. However, from the perspective of postsocial history, even in the cases just described, such a conclusion seems precipitate. And not only because the response does not always occur and, when it does, it is not always similar. That is, not only because contingency and heterogeneity are nonaccidental features but consubstantial ones, something, in the end, already emphasized by new cultural history. The conclusion is precipitate because in cases as elemental as these are, the emergence of interests always involves an operation of meaningful construction, however rudimentary it may be. As I have remarked, even crude economic exploitation does not become intolerable and does not generate an interest in mitigating and, much less, in eradicating it, until it is objectified through the category of exploitation itself or, in other words, until the relation of exploitation is discursively denaturalized. As Patrick Joyce observed some time ago, economic relations, however exploitative they may be (in a technical or moral sense), do not possess a single-minded meaning, but present themselves to people in countless ways, depending—I would add—on the social imaginary through which they are apprehended.[7] And, therefore, even though it is obvious that the said interest, in order to emerge, requires the prior existence of an economic relation of exploitation, it is also obvious that this relation does not generate such an interest by itself, but only insofar as it has been endowed with a specific meaning (moral, economical, political, historical, etc).

That is why saying, for example, galley slaves are interested in leaving their situation, workers in improving their wages and working conditions, or women in putting an end to their subordination,[8] is no more than empirical triviality, lacking any explanatory value, and analytically irrelevant (apart from probably being a flagrant historical anachronism). These examples simply record the existence of a relationship between social position and interests, avoiding completely the truly crucial question of why such "interests" are *activated* or not in certain historical circumstances and why they are activated in one way and not in another. For although it is an empirically obvious fact that there is a link between social position and interest, the standard response based on an act of consciousness is unsatisfactory precisely because it cannot explain why social position *historically* generates interest. That is, why galley slaves, workers, and women only manifest their interest in emancipation (or, if you prefer, why emancipation becomes thinkable, conceivable, and therefore desirable) only in certain circumstances (and not in all).

The answer from postsocial history is that such an interest only is not activated by itself or through experience, but it is activated only when individuals convert discursively their social positions into meaningful objects. Without this operation of meaningful construction, the "interest" would never have become interest in its proper sense (that is, as a conscious entity). Since any response to social environment involves and mobilizes a system of meanings, interests are not activated in a meaningless vacuum. They do not emerge simply as the result of an act of self-reflection or demystification, as if individuals faced up to their social position and ended up recognizing their essence in one way or another. On the contrary, interests are never enunciated in neutral terms and therefore the motives agents manifest are always discursively pervaded (and not just socially anchored). Thus, in order to have galley slaves, workers, and women reaching the conviction, at a given moment, that their situation is not natural and could be modified, the mere existence of that situation is not enough. Their deployment of some sort of conceptual repertoire, no matter how elemental (injustice, personal dignity, exploitation, etc.), was also necessary for them to be able to conceive their situation as unnatural, a situation, up until that moment, perceived as natural. In short, for post-social history, the fact that individuals or groups may have certain "objective" interests, in a purely abstract and ahistorical sense, lacks historical significance or analytical interest (apart from being empirically inscrutable), since the only historically existent interests are those that individuals show they have. These are the only interests that have historical effects, since they generate practices and social relations and institutions. And as far as real interests are concerned, they are always genetically linked to a discursive pattern or social imaginary, without whose mediation they would not have been able to emerge or be enunciated.

This is what happens, for example, and as I have put forward, in the case of the relationship between what Terry Eagleton calls "being a woman (a social situation) and being a feminist (a political position)." According to Eagleton, all women will not spontaneously become feminists, but *"they ought to do so,"* and a demystified understanding of their oppressed social condition would logically lead them in that direction.[9] This argument, however, not only involves a sort of epistemological teleology, but it does not even seem very plausible. If this were the case, it would imply that women, for thousands of years, were incapable of recognizing their interests and that only suddenly, at the end of the eighteenth century, did they start, in an increasingly massive fashion, to do so. Of course, a social historian would maintain that feminism emerged as a consequence of the appearance of the modern social and ideological world and that its extension, from the nineteenth century on, can be attributed to changes in the social situation of women. And that, for example, the rise of feminism in the 1960s was no more than an effect of women starting to engage in paid work on a large scale. However, in the sequence of this reasoning, there is still a need for an essential link, namely an explanation of why women experienced and meaningfully faced their new social and employment situation in these terms and not in other ones. Indeed, as put forward earlier, women's interest in equality or emancipation occurred historically when the categories and logic of equivalence of the modern discourse were put into play, and certainly not by the existence of the subordination of women. Nor did the large-scale incorporation of women into paid work, by itself, bring about a rise in feminism. Incorporation into the workplace had been articulated by discursive categories, like those of labor, that objectify productive work as the base of civil, political, and social rights, insisting these rights be granted to individuals who do such a work. In short, the changes in women's socioeconomic situation had the effect they did because they interacted with a specific discursive framework and, therefore, it was this interaction that made transformation of the legal, political, cultural, or moral status of women possible.

As I have indicated, the reticence to accept the discursive, in lieu of the objective, nature of interests diminishes when interests are not so materially immediate, but more complex in their definition and scope. That is what happens, for example, in the case of the relationship between working class and social revolution, one of the capital episodes of modern history. For a long time, historians tended to consider it obvious that the socioeconomic condition of workers (lack of property, subjection to economic exploitation, subordinate position in production relations, lower living standards, and so on) presupposes, in some way, that workers are potentially revolutionary and are objectively interested in revolutionary social change. And this view is upheld, as I have pointed out, regardless of whether said interest operates spontaneously or is symbolically activated. However, this does not seem to be the case for postsocial history. That it did seem to be so for so long was due to the fact that—apart, of course, from the practice of the labor movement itself—historical analysis of the issue employed the same social imaginary that had brought about the interest in social revolution. That is why, as soon as one moves out of that imaginary or, at least, to its limits, what previously appeared and was perceived as a natural effect or an objective process shows itself to be, instead, a rhetorical effect. Of course there is no doubt about the existence of a link between working class condition and social revolution, as the latter is an empirically demonstrable response to the former. But, this link is only material or factual, not causal. For the link to become established, the working class condition itself had to be conceptualized through categories like exploitation, class, or social revolution, or, simply, as a "social question," a problem to be resolved. Modern-socialist language did not make explicit an interest that was socially implicit, but modern-socialist language, with its mediation, did constitute interests as such. To claim that the interest in social revolution was implicit in the working class is not only risky, since it is impossible to prove, but analytically irrelevant as well. We do know that, on some occasions, groups of workers have had such an interest, but we do not know that this interest is objective. As Ernesto Laclau and Chantal Mouffe remark, although working class and socialism are not incompatible, the fundamental interests in socialism cannot be *logically* deduced from the position of the working class in the economic process.[10]

II

A similar process of theoretical rethinking involves the concept of *identity*. Like other social sciences or relatively young disciplines such as cultural studies, the field of historical studies has also been shaken up by heated debate over the question of identity. This has enabled historians to make their own contribution to that "veritable explosion"[11] of interest in this issue that has occurred in recent years. One result of this debate has been the emergence of a new notion of subject, different from both the rational subject of idealist history and the social subject of materialist history.

Before getting down to specifics, however, it is worth remarking that the starting point of the historiographical debate on identity is to be found in the critical reaction of social history to the notion of individual or rational subject. Traditional history, as will no doubt be recalled, conceived individuals as natural, autonomous, originary, unitary, and stable subjects and, therefore, as rational and fully aware agents who are the centered authors of social practice and the foundation and origin of social relations. This is why its historical research is a hermeneutical, interpretive, or comprehensive undertaking with the purpose of recovering agents' thoughts, intentions, and motives. For social history, on the contrary, identity is a social construction, not a natural attribute. Instead of a fixed entity, identity is only a historical form of closure or point of suture that changes depending on social circumstances. Individuals derive their identity from their place within social relations and, therefore, subjects are no more than historically specific expressions of the social conditions of existence, since the latter are what set the terms in which people perceive and characterize themselves. Thus, according to social history, the very notion of individual or rational subject is no more than an ideological representation of modern social conditions and, in particular, of the rise of the middle class (which is why social historians discarded any notion of human agency).

In new cultural history, with its conferring an active function to symbolic, cultural, or narrative mediation in the process of making consciousness, the concept of identity becomes more complex and dynamic. For new cultural historians, even if identity is implicit in its social referent, it is accomplished as such in the subjective sphere. It does not emerge and project itself into action spontaneously, but only when it is experientially discerned and transformed into self-consciousness. Identity, although it is inscribed in a system of structural relations, enjoys a relative autonomy. Thus, by defining it as a practical entity and by adding perceived being to social being, new cultural history stresses much more the fluid, contingent, unstable, and fragmented condition of subject, as well as its many-sided and plural character. In consequence, an image of subject has emerged which takes the form of a kind of polyhedron or even a kaleidoscopic figure, composed of different sides or facets. Furthermore, identity appears as the result of a conjunction, sometimes conflictive, of many different identity referents (class, race, gender, sex, nation, religion, etc.) that are continually rearranged and hierarchically reordered in the flow of social life and in accordance with the living strategies of the subjects themselves. A concept of identity, in sum, that is far richer in nuance, that pays more attention to the folds and modulations of everyday life, and that has a greater ambition and capacity for concrete analysis. However, as I have emphasized when dealing with the internal evolution of the social history paradigm, new cultural history never transcends the limits of this paradigm and, therefore, although it redefines the *form* of identity, it does not alter its final *nature*. New cultural historians continue to consider identity an objective social attribute. Identity is realized in the cultural sphere, but its source lies in a social context with the capacity to determine meaningfully—and not just materially—individuals' consciousness. In this point too, new cultural history is governed by the conceptual logic of the dichotomous model. Consequently, the discussion, on adopting the form of a tension between structure and agency, between individual and society, boils down to deciding which of the two instances warrants causal primacy.

However, since the theoretical dichotomous model has been denaturalized, the discussion on identity has taken on new contours, and historical scholarship has gradually shifted its gaze, starting to get around theoretical impasse and beyond seemingly unsolvable dilemma severely hindering potential advancement in the historiographical debate surrounding identity and identity-related questions. With the advent of postsocial history, reflection and discussion about identity have entered a qualitatively new phase, if only because the criticism of postsocial historians is no longer directed against the notion of rational subject only, but against the notion of social subject *also*. Of course, postsocial historians realize the subjectivist conception of identity obtains and continues to have enormous influence in the field of historical studies, even a hegemonic one in many areas. But they believe such a conception of identity has been irrevocably undermined on the theoretical level, is no longer at the leading edge of historical research, and that despite the increase in revisionist history, the battle against it belongs to an already relinquished stage of historiographical debate. Therefore, the notion of social subject is what now clamors for special attention and serious critical scrutiny.[12]

Postsocial history starts its theoretical rethinking of the concept of identity where new cultural history left it. Postsocial history takes off with the assumption that subjects or forms of social identification (the ways individuals and groups perceive themselves) are historical entities, not universal and autonomous essences. It also begins with the new cultural premise that identities are not states, but positions, that they are differential or relational entities, and that they do not make up a homogeneous whole, but a plural and fractured one. However, postsocial history then goes a step further, not just because it also submits social subject to criticism or because it has renewed the arguments against rational subject. It takes this further step because in addition to merely historicizing identity or making its physiognomy more complex, postsocial history, above all, proceeds to completely redefine the genesis and nature of identity. First, postsocial history ceases to pose the discussion on identity in dichotomous terms, stating that identity is neither a natural attribute nor a social or cultural construct (or a combination of the two). The making of identities is impossible to grasp and explain with the standard dual scheme. Second, just as the historization of subjectivity overwhelmed, in its day, the notion of natural or rational identity, so the crisis of the concept of society is subverting the notion of social subject or social identity. This is one of the fundamental sequels of recent developments in historical scholarship and historiographical debate. If social reality does not constitute an objective structure, then people's identities cannot be the expression of their social position. If meaning is about an interaction between social reality and an inherited categorial matrix then a "meaning-filled" entity like identity is also forged as the result of the interplay between social or real position and discursive social imaginary.

And this is indeed the basic theoretical premise of postsocial history. The identity of individuals—the way they conceive, classify, and characterize themselves and in accordance to which they act—is not an expression of their social position, but rather the effect of a particular way of articulating such a position and the experience of it. The way in which people identify themselves (individually or collectively) depends on the discursive patterns of identification prevailing in each historical situation. It is the discursive domain that sets out *in advance*[13] the possible modes of subjectivization, the criteria through which subjects are delimited, distributed, and formed. It is the social imaginary that, on giving social context its meaningful existence, also confers a meaning on the place that people occupy in it, thus forging their self-perception and turning them into subjects and agents within such a context. Specifically, it is just such a discursive imaginary that establishes which physical, social, economic, cultural, religious, geographical, or whichever other features define the identity of individuals, thus configuring the bearers of these features as specific subjects. Thus, according to postsocial history, the categories of subjectivization or identification not only precede identities and are not mere labels or ideological expressions of preexisting identities, but are what generate the different forms of identity when those categories are historically deployed. And thus, for example, it was the appearance and historical enthroning of categories like rational individual, class, or nation that made it possible for people to start to feel and behave as such. It was these categories that made it possible for natural qualities, location in the production relations, or place of birth to become and operate as the identity foundation of the people involved. This

process of construction of identity can, of course, be masked when identity is presented as something natural and stable. As Joan W. Scott remarks, the imposition of a categorial (and universal) subject-status (*the*
worker, *the* peasant, *the* woman, *the* black) has shrouded the operations of
difference in the organization of social life, since each category, taken as
fixed, has tended to solidify the process of subject-construction, making it
less rather than more apparent, naturalizing it instead of encouraging
analysis of it.[14] But this should not distract us from recognizing that the
origin of these forms of subject lies in such operations of difference, demanding, and certainly worthy analytical attention.

Despite the logical continuity that seems to exist between identities and
their social referents (to the extent that one tends to see the former as a
sort of natural secretion of the latter), the connection between both instances is not objective; it is not set up through an operation of representation. As I have just said, people do not define themselves, feel, or act as
subjects, in one way or another, due to the simple fact of possessing certain social or natural features, but because these features have acquired
the condition of defining traits of personality. Likewise, when individuals
perceive and identify collectively, they are not merely describing or recognizing themselves as members of a social category or group; they are
assuming the identity meaning that this membership implies. Therefore,
identity is not a mere conscious representation or reflection of its referent,
it is not a quality or feature that social referents have and that individuals,
in one way or another, become aware of and project into action. On the
contrary, identities always emerge out of a historically specific objectivization of the referent itself. For the connection between the two to be
established and for identity to be able to achieve a conscious existence, it
is not enough that referent exist. It is also necessary that referent be articulated as an *object of identity*, that is, as a criterion with which to define
people's identity. And since this is something that always comes about as
a result of applying a given categorial matrix or system of differences, individuals do not, then, recognize or discover themselves as subjects and
agents, but construct themselves meaningfully as such when they apply
such a classificatory grid.

In this case too, we should stop imputing a particular identity to people as members of a certain social category or group, since social membership is a causally inert fact. It only works as an object of identity when
it is incorporated into a materialist and representationist social imaginary.
This leads to a double conclusion of enormous transcendence to historical
analysis. On the one hand, identity is causally linked to the object, not to
the referent (its link to the referent is purely material, factual). On the
other, objects of identity do not preexist identities themselves. The two,
both objects and identities, are constituted *simultaneously* in the *same*

process of articulation of social context, because for subject and object to be able to emerge and relate to each other, an appropriate space of signification must previously exist. And thus, for example, as we will see later on, concepts like class construct not only class identity but, also, class itself as an object.

The fact that discursive patterns of identification precede the emergence of identities—and not the other way round—is what leads Patrick Joyce, for example, to question Jürgen Habermas's thesis that the public sphere or civil society is an expression of the rise of the bourgeoisie or middle class. What Habermas presents as an explanation (the bourgeoisie), argues Joyce, is really what must be explained, because the bourgeoisie, as a subject—not of course as a social group—is a consequence of the appearance and social deployment of the modern category of civil society, not its own generating cause. The appearance of the modern discourse enabled the bourgeoisie to conceive itself as a subject and to become constituted as an agent; but the bourgeoisie did not create the modern discourse. Or, in the words of Joyce himself, it was the discourse and practice of civil society and the public sphere that "enabled groups of people to view themselves as 'bourgeois' in the first place."[15] And the same could be said of other modern modalities of identity, like sexual identity. As I have already pointed out, historical research carried out in this field is revealing that it was the appearance of the category of sexuality—articulating sexual practices as criteria of individualization—that converted individuals into sexual subjects. It was, therefore, the historical process that created not only the sexual identity but also, at the same time, constructed sex (biological fact) as an object (base of identity).[16]

Thus, according to postsocial history, language does not simply name subjects, but it brings them to life, it makes them appear. It is not, as historians have usually believed up until now, that individuals express their identity through available language, but that they construct it by means of language itself. Identity is not something individuals just carry or social context simply imposes on them; identity is a position that discourse assigns individuals by articulating them through a particular system of differences. In this sense, it could be said that subjects are constituted as a result of an *interpellation* of discourse, to use an old, albeit controversial, yet still a highly expressive term.[17] Discourse, that is, addresses individuals, calling them to respond to classification in difference. If it is discourse, and not the social referent, that establishes the criteria for constituting subjectivity and if individuals become subjects on being inserted in and mobilized by the forms of identity inherent to a discursive formation, then the implication is that discourse really induces or compels individuals within its area of influence to classify themselves, individually or collectively, through the said criteria. And therefore one could say, using again that usual terminology, that the discourse really hails or recruits individuals as subjects because once some social or physical features have become objectified as marks of subjectivization, discourse really does interpellate individuals who possess those particular objectified traits as subjects and agents. Of course, discursive interpellation of individuals does not take place in a social vacuum. Discourse does not interpellate abstract, ahistorical, isolated individuals, but socially located individuals, and it mobilizes them as subjects according to their particular social properties. In this sense, postsocial history does not deny that social position pushes individuals to form groups and constitute collective subjects, but does disavow that this is an objective movement. For postsocial historians it is, instead, a movement triggered from outside by a certain social imaginary. It is true, for example, that workers were inclined in the past to form identity and political groups as workers. But what made this happen was not just that they shared a similar socioeconomic position, but that they were interpellated by the class discourse, in the same way workers furnished the identity of people decades earlier because they were interpellated by the modern-radical discourse and by its categories of people, individual, natural rights, or citizenship.[18]

It is this conception of identity that leads Keith Baker, for example, to call into question that the social divisions of late-eighteenth-century France implied, in any way, the constitution of the Third Estate as a historical subject and political agent. However much we may have tended to think these divisions were predestined to become political identities, this is not so. What really brings about this new form of political identity is a new categorial framework coming into play (which Baker calls "political culture") that objectifies certain social attributes or positions as the base of interests and identities, converting in this way its bearers into specific subjects. As indicated before, what specifically converted the Third Estate into a political subject, in confrontation with privileged orders, was the application of categories like labor-property, which established productive activity as a primordial criterion of belonging to the nation. The Third Estate does not become a political subject just because its members shared certain social conditions (being productive, compared with the unproductive privileged), but because these social conditions become objects of identity thanks to bringing the labor-nation categorial equation into play. And the same could be said of the later division of the Third Estate into different identity groups. This is why Baker argues that instead of taking it for granted that the distinction between the privileged orders and the Third Estate is objective, that it constitutes "the most basic social cleavage," or it is an effect of social division itself, one must explain how and why such a distinction suddenly became the basic criterion of identification, the crucial cleavage upon which the very definition of the social and political order now seemed to hinge, and, in consequence, the causal foundation for the practice of its members.[19]

Thus, postsocial history continues to confer on identities the triple characteristic of being contingent, unstable, and differential entities, but it does so in a somewhat different sense from that of new cultural history. For the latter, identities are contingent because, although they are implicit in the social sphere, they can become conscious or not, depending on whether they are subjectively recognized or not. For postsocial history, however, identities are contingent not only historically, but, above all, *socially*. In the sense that their existence is not pre-figured in the social referent, but it depends on the suitability or inappropriateness of the discursive conditions. Identities are contingent not because they might or might not emerge, but because they may, or may not, *be born*. As I have pointed out, it is impossible to know in advance, and regardless of discursive conditions, which referent will become an identity referent, a defining criterion of subjectivity. An object of identity is not something that is waiting to be discovered or to manifest itself, but it is something that appears and is constituted as such in the very process of articulating social reality. As Joan Scott says, "the appearance of a new identity is not inevitable or determined, not something that was always there simply waiting to be expressed" (nor is it "something that will always exist in the form it was given in a particular political movement or at a particular historical moment").[20] For this reason, precisely, we cannot confer a normative value on any identity object, nor can we establish epistemological hierarchies among the different forms of identity, as if some were natural, ontologically complete, or superior to the rest. The fact that, in a given historical juncture, a certain referent operates as an object of identity does not mean that the same thing will occur in all historical situations, and when it fails to occur, that does not mean the process of creating identity has not yet been consumed, is still in an early stage, or that it has been blocked by false consciousness, nor, simply, that the individuals involved are prey to alienation, in the sense that they have failed in their attempt to know themselves. However, if identity is causally linked to the object, and not the referent, the fact that similar social positions generate different forms of identity (or do not generate any) should not be interpreted as an anomaly, but simply as a consequence of the fact that such social positions have been articulated through different discursive patterns. This is what explains, for example, societies with similar class divisions presenting such distinct class identities, or not having any at all.

Postsocial history also admits identities are unstable, however much they may be presented as natural and fixed, in order to have, as James Vernon points out, a "sense of collective agency." This is what happens, according to Vernon, with the class identity of the nineteenth-century socialist parties or the feminine identity resulting from applying the concept of citizenship (which leads to the political exclusion of women).[21] Nonetheless, for postsocial history, the instability of identities is not just because social conditions themselves are unstable but because the discursive conditions that, in each case, stabilize identities are also unstable. Postsocial history, as previously stated, does not limit itself to historicizing identities (already done decades before by social history) nor does it limit itself to denying the natural fixity of subjects, but goes further, denying its *social* fixity. It is in this sense, and not in the conventional one, that postsocial history conceives the unstable nature of identity. And this is why it intends to leave behind not just the natural essentialism, but also the social essentialism—that is, the idea that, as Scott says, "there are fixed identities, visible to us as social or natural facts."[22] Thus, postsocial history advocates a notion of identity that stresses its nonfixity and sees it as an unstable ordering of multiple possibilities. But what postsocial historians stress is that the provisional nature of every identity is due to its constitution within an ever-changing discourse and through an operation of differential arrangement.[23]

Finally, for postsocial history identities are clearly differential entities not only because of their form, but above all, because of their nature. Postsocial history takes for granted that all identities are forged out of the contrast with and the exclusion of other identification possibilities, that is, through the production of frontier-effects. Any identity undoubtedly requires a constitutive outside that, although suppressed, is in a sense always present (and so every identity is always threatened by what it has left out). And thus, for example, in the constitution of any pair of identities (masculine-feminine, black-white, homosexual-heterosexual, or proletariat-bourgeoisie), not only does one term depend on the other (often in a hierarchical fashion), but, in addition, both imply each other. However, postsocial history also considers all identities differential because of their process of constitution, as they are the result of applying a system of differences and not just the result of the existence of a relational set of social referents.

These are, in essence, the terms in which postsocial historians are rethinking the nature of subjects of conscious action or praxis-oriented historical subjectivities. The essential aspect of this rethinking is that identity is no longer considered a property (natural or social) that language designates and transmits, but a property that is constituted *within* language itself. It could be said that, for postsocial history, the subject is no more than a *discursive position*. That does not mean, however, as I have already emphasized in relation to the concept of interest, that identities lack any social or real ground, that they are socially arbitrary, or that they are constituted independently from social conditions. If this were the case, it would only be a sort of linguistic functionalism or constructionism. Nor does this mean, as it does for revisionism, that identities are ideological or political creations, since, as is evident, every identity is not only historically located but socially anchored as well. And, of course, postsocial history does not involve giving up any notion of subject either. Instead, in Scott's words, postsocial history has succeeded in making subject an even more visible historical entity.[24] Actually, the only thing that postsocial history claims is that every identity has a *discursive dimension* implying thus that even though social referent constitutes the material base of identity, it plays no objective function in its constitution. As Scott argues elsewhere, treating the emergence of a new identity as a discursive event is not to introduce a new form of linguistic determinism, it is simply to reject a separation between "experience" and language, and to insist instead on the productive quality of discourse.[25]

It goes without saying that the new concept of identity involves a new agenda for historical research, or, as Scott puts it, a real "change of object."[26] If identities do not emerge through an act of consciousness, but thanks to an operation of meaningful construction, then to explain an identity requires more than bringing its referential link to light. From now on, it will also be necessary to clarify what discursive conditions enabled a referent to become an identity referent—and, in turn, caused other referents to be ignored or excluded. If one wishes, as Geoff Eley says, to answer the question of why or "on what bases, in different places and at different times, does identity's non-fixity become temporarily fixed in such a way as to enable individuals and groups to behave as a particular kind of agency, political or otherwise?" or if one wishes to explain "how do people become shaped into acting subjects, understanding themselves in particular ways?"[27] one will have to unravel the internal logic and the possibilities and contradictions of the underlying categorial grid in each case. What compels us, in turn, to also get a grip on the genealogy of the categorial grid itself, since this is where the origin of subjects is to be found in the end.

This new agenda seems to guide Scott herself in her work on the history of French feminism.[28] What this work shows is that what one could call feminist subject (woman understood as a subject of rights) was born as a result of the appearance of a new discursive space, the modern-liberal one. It was this that enabled women to think of their social, political, and legal position in terms of equality and difference, and thus to generate a new self-consciousness, with its respective practical logic. As Scott states, this new form of feminine identity has its origin in the interaction between what she calls republican discourse (made up by categories like equality, liberty, or natural rights) and the social situation of women. As Dena Goodman details, in this respect, "Olympe de Gougue's insistence that women had both the same political rights as men and special needs

which demanded protection" was a function "of the discursive parameters established by the declaration [of the rights of man and citizen] and
subsequent legislation."[29] To be exact, according to Scott, it was the appearance of the "universalist discourses, specifically the discourses of abstract individualism and of social duty and social rights" that enabled
women "to conceive of themselves as political agents even as those same
discourses denied women political agency" (15): the same discourse politically excludes women just as it constructs them as subjects, recognizing them as civil agents and, it is, thus, the mediation of such a discourse
that engenders feminism (20). Thus, the new feminist identity did not
emerge as a result of an act of consciousness of women's attributes or natural rights; it was, as Scott says, neither the effect of an act of recognition nor
the final stage of "a story of cumulative progress toward an ever-elusive
goal" (1). Rather, it was a consequence of a meaningful construction of the
position of women carried out through a historically specific set of tenets
and principles. It is the application of this that gives the fact of being a
woman its new identity objectivity and, therefore, that reconstructs social
and political relations between men and women and generates the new
modality of conflict. From this standpoint, the feminist identity is no more
than one of many possible articulations of the feminine identity, and not
a sort of full or supreme achievement of such an identity.

By articulating the feminist identity, the modern discourse also engenders feminism as a resistance movement. As Scott argues, the feminist
agency was constituted by that universalist discourse of individualism
(with their theories of rights and citizenship) that evokes "sexual difference" to naturalize the exclusion of women. In consequence, feminist action has to be understood "in terms of the discursive process—the epistemologies, institutions and practices—that produces political subjects, that
makes agency (in this case, the agency of feminists) possible even when it
is forbidden or denied" (16). Specifically, feminist agency—that is, feminist struggles and resistance—is grounded in the "contradiction," brought
about by the modern discourse, between the general declaration of rights
and their legal and social implementation, which implies the political exclusion of women.[30] It is such a discourse that sets up the patterns of subsequent conflict, as it provides feminism with its fundamental concepts,
demands, expectations, aims, arguments, and, even, means of struggle.
And, therefore, it is modern discourse that makes intelligible both the
feminist practice and the conflict that it embodies.

Likewise, the fact that feminist identity and the claims and practice of
feminism are causally linked to the modern-liberal social imaginary and
not to the social condition of women (that is, to the object and not to the
referent), is what explains subsequent transformations as the discourse
itself evolves throughout the nineteenth century. According to Scott, fem-

inism and feminist struggles are related to the discursive arenas in which
the very meanings of "women" and their rights were constructed (104).
Therefore, feminists formulated their claims for rights in terms of very
different epistemologies, and their arguments must be read that way—
and not as evidence of a transcendent or continuous woman's consciousness or women's experience (13). Since this causal relationship between discursive framework and feminist program remains in force over
time, the history of feminism can only be understood as "the articulation
of a set of discursive sites." Specifically, the variations and changes over
time in feminist thought can only be understood as a product of the
transformations of the liberal-republican discourse itself.[31] And thus, for
example, the revolutionary juncture of 1848 provided a different discursive context for feminism and feminist struggle. Given that, at this juncture, "the right to work and the right to vote were inextricably inter-
twined" (57), feminism built new claims for women's citizenship out of
the categories of this new discursive outlook, particularly the category of
labor, which articulates productive work as a base for political rights.
This induces the priority objective of the feminist struggle to become the
recognition of feminine work as comparable to masculine work, because,
as Jeanne Deroin reasons, women's duty to bear and raise their children
is a productive work that qualifies them for the same rights as men
(57–59). And the same relationship between feminism and discursive
arena happens during the Third Republic, even though, in this case, it is
the objectifying of politics as a sphere of representation of interests that
converts political exclusion into the primordial base of feminist identity
and action (99 and ff.).

III

The new concept of identity also underlies, to give another example,
the new notion of class identity, which has been forged as a consequence of the increasing causal uncoupling between class position and
class consciousness. In this case too, what recent historical scholarship
makes clear is that class identity and feelings are not subjective expressions of social classes, nor, specifically, of the socioeconomic changes of
the modern period (with the appearance of so-called class society). Of
course, the existence of class divisions was an indispensable requisite
for class identity to emerge, but it is a purely material requisite. However much people immersed in the modern discursive universe (including social historians themselves) tend to conceive class consciousness as a (more or less straight) natural effect of class, it did not emerge
through an act of consciousness. Instead, class consciousness emerged

as a result of the meaningful apprehension of social location and relations by means of the categories of the objectivist variant of the modern
social imaginary, specifically those of society and class.

Class is a historically inert social datum or phenomenon until such time
as it is articulated as an identity object. Therefore, as Scott points out, concepts like class are required before individuals can identify themselves as
members of such a group and can act collectively as such.[32] As Patrick
Joyce remarks, class cannot be referred to an external "social" referent as
if this were its foundation, origin, or cause. Instead, given that society is
not an objective structure, "the discourses and practices organized around
conceptions of 'society'" are no more than the means "by which different
individuals, groups and institutions come to identify and organize themselves. Amongst these groups are, of course, 'classes.'"[33] This implies at
least two things. First, class identity is a specifically modern historical
phenomenon, since it can only exist and be operative as an effective
means of social action in modern society (and that is why concepts like
class identity or class struggle should not be transferred to other historical contexts.) Second, those cases in which class identity does not emerge,
even though class divisions exist, should not be interpreted as an anomaly or a sign of false consciousness. It is simply a consequence of the fact
that the discursive conditions are inappropriate for class to have become
an identity object. In other words, in those cases individuals have articulated their social position by means of a distinct classificatory grid, one
that is different from the modern objectivist one, and they thus possess another identity.

Once this theoretical remaking of the concept of class identity has happened, the historiographical question at issue is no longer to elucidate
through which mechanism (reflection or symbolic internalization) class
becomes class consciousness, or to assess the degree of accomplishment of
the latter. From now on, the historiographical question at issue is how
class became an identity object, how "class became available as a basis for
people's cognition and their action."[34] To achieve this end requires recognition and elucidation of the categorial framework making possible this
becoming, and reconstruction of its historical genealogy. As Joyce himself
insightfully argues, if the concept of "society" is the ground upon which
the figures of class have been placed, figures that in some readings of class
have been not only social facts but collective actors on the historical stage,
then "it is necessary to go back and look at the history of this ground if the
figures that are its consequence are to be understood."[35]

This is why the genealogy of the concept of class itself has become so
central in historical analysis. It has proved to be a fundamental explanatory variable in the making of class as social object and subject. Such an
explanatory purpose is just what drives Mary Poovey to undertake her

genealogical investigation on class, because she too believes the origin of class is to be found in the historical advent of a specific "classificatory thinking."[36] Poovey starts by taking a position in the debate about what the term *class* describes—about whether it refers to an objective set of material conditions (or relations) that can be observed in every modern society, or to a mode of understanding or articulating one's place in a social hierarchy, which only became available in the nineteenth century (15). On this matter, she advocates setting aside the reflection model upon which the debate has been based in favor of a paradigm that emphasizes the historicity of the very terms in which the debate has been conducted. But Poovey also argues that the classificatory thinking that sets class as a way of arranging people long predates the appearance of so-called class society, the outcome of a conceptual shift whose origin only goes back to the mid-seventeenth century. This implies that we must move from questions about what "class" describes toward an investigation of the history of such a classificatory thinking and the assumptions frequently carried over in subsequent deployments of class analysis (15). In other words, and as Joyce argues, once class identity has stopped being an objective property, the very relevant question to be tackled and answered by historical scholarship is how a class classificatory thinking appeared and became available to people for classifying themselves as subjects and agents—specifically, how the location in social hierarchy or production relations became relevant for people's identity.

According to Poovey, the said classificatory thinking is an epistemology that was gradually consolidated in the seventeenth century and elaborated during the course of the next two centuries alongside, and in a complex relationship to, the development of the material conditions we generally associate with "class." It combined two modes of understanding the natural and social worlds. The first is a taxonomic mode that made sense of particulars of the world, grouping them into categories (or classes) according to a single feature or group of features. The second is a conceptualization of "value" in terms of features that can be quantified. When these two modes of understanding were brought together under the particular conditions of seventeenth-century England, they provided the terms for some of the characteristic concepts of modern Western societies, including the crucial notion that quantity is more important than quality and some activities are more productive (hence more valuable and significant) than others (16). Thus, the new classificatory thinking emerged as a consequence of replacing previous qualitative classificatory criteria by other quantitative ones. Specifically, it emerged as an alternative to the paradigm by which social divisions were most frequently conceptualized in this period, a paradigm that emphasized religious and political affiliations. From the mid-seventeenth century, in the wake of the radical challenge to monarchical sovereignty that had just occurred, some theorists began to invoke the language of scientific rationality and to represent social groups by criteria deemed "rational." That is, criteria that could be quantified in specific contrast to other descriptions that emphasized features considered "irrational." As Poovey notes, the rise of class and that of instrumental rationality are closely connected (18). It was this change in the prevailing classificatory thinking that allowed class as a form of identity to emerge and become operative as a character of social relations and conflicts.

One of the consequences following the adoption of the new rationalized system of representation (emphasizing the quantifiability and commodification of men and objects) was the transformation of men into instances of what Adam Smith will call *homo economicus* (29–30), that is, into rational economic agents. Thus, the new set of classificatory terms gave rise to new subject positions. One of these will be class, understood as an aggregate of individuals defined by both its opposition to an individualized disinterestedness and by the quantifiable abstraction "labor" and its relative share of the national wealth (that eventually achieves a consciousness of itself as a social group) (45). This is the classificatory logic that, through authors like Smith or Ricardo, reached Marx and allowed him to formulate his concept of class. One grounded on the assumption that the economic group whose waged and divided labor makes it an aggregate is more than a collection of individual men and just might become conscious of its disadvantages and work together for revolutionary change (48).

Thus, in carrying out such a theoretical remaking, postsocial history has substantially redefined the terms of the debate on classes and class struggle. If class identity is not a representation of social class, but instead a meaningful construction of this, then we must modify the standard terms of the discussion. To start with, the discussion no longer revolves around the question of the degree of relative autonomy of consciousness (as this would imply maintaining the assumption of the existence of an objective class). Nor does it revolve around the more general question of whether or not class determines individuals' identity and meaningful practice, since the answer is affirmative and negative at the same time. I say this because the decay of social history has led some historians to simply deny, in general, class determination and to conclude, in consequence, that class identity, when it has existed, has been a purely ideological and political construct. Many of them have even redirected discussion and inquiry toward the question of the empirical existence of social classes themselves. These historians, however, are simply carrying out an idealist inversion of objectivism while maintaining the basic terms of the debate and they, thus, remain entrapped in the same aporias. Postsocial history, on the contrary, tackles the crisis of the objectivist notion of class in a different way.

To maintain, as postsocial history does, that class is not an objective entity (but only a real one) by no means implies that it has *never* determined the identity and actions of its members. In those situations, characteristic of the modern period, in which class has been objectified as such, it has *indeed* determined them. And therefore, to understand and explain relevant historical processes of modern society like, for example, the socialist labor movement, it is indispensable to bear class in mind. It is not a question of accepting or rejecting class as a historical factor, but of rethinking, in the sense outlined above, both its nature and the nature of its link with individuals' consciousness and actions (including the consequent time and space restraint of its historical prevalence). In other words, it is a question of distinguishing between class as a social phenomenon and class as a social object.

These are the terms in which the history of labor movement has been rethought over the last few years. As I have already pointed out, recent historical research is showing that this form of identity and social practice is not an effect of the rise of capitalism or of the living and working conditions or economic location of workers. Working class identity and practice is rather an effect of the meaning these circumstances take on when they are apprehended through categories like labor, property, exploitation, society, class, or proletariat, or when they are associated with expectations of sociopolitical change through a category like rational emancipation-revolution. As Geoff Eley argues, it is increasingly difficult to maintain that the making of the working class is the logical unfolding of an economic process and its necessary effect at the levels of social organization, consciousness, and culture. And not only because the working class is heterogeneous and segmented along lines of race, gender, religion, or ethnicity, as new cultural historians have emphasized, but because working class politics (the rise of labor movements and socialist parties) is not the causal expression of an economically located class interest or a social structural position. On the contrary, class as a collective subject, that is, the insistence that class was the organizing reality of the emerging capitalist societies and of the growth of specific practices and organizations (like trade unions and socialist parties), was constituted as such in the discursive sphere, in the sense that "class emerged as a set of discursive claims about the social world seeking to reorder that world in terms of itself." And that is why, as has been stressed, "the history of a class is inseparable from the history of the category."[37] In the case of the radical labor movements, categories like natural rights or citizenship made it possible for people to become a collective subject, at the same time as they constructed democracy as a specific form of power, that is, people as the category "in whose name society and public should speak and be organized."[38]

A rethinking of this tenor is, in my opinion, what has triggered and underlies, for instance, historical researches like those of William H. Sewell and Zachary Lockman on the origins of the French and Egyptian labor movements, respectively. Sewell's work[39] basically shows that the new working class identity, appearing in France in the 1830s, was not the outcome of socioeconomic changes, the proletarianization of artisans, the appearance of factory workers, or the intensification of workplace conflicts, but was, instead, the result of working class intellectuals and organizations articulating social and political circumstances through the categories and tenets of the liberal discourse inherited from the French Revolution and reinstitutionalized by the July Revolution. Workers reconstructed their collective identity and created a new sense of belonging by becoming involved in the new discursive environment and applying such categories and tenets. At the same time, they also brought into existence a community of interests that went beyond both trade and the old corporate discursive pattern that had, until then, governed relations among workers and between workers and employers and the state.

After the Revolution of 1830, corporate language continued to be useful for internal affairs and retained its efficacy within trades. But it proved inadequate and powerless in the public or political sphere, denying workers all access to this and preventing them from communicating with the state and persuading it to accept their claims and turn them into legal regulations (*Work*, 194–95). As Sewell puts forward, in the weeks after the Revolution, the workers became clearly aware of the limitations of their idiom. The government rejected their demands (to outlaw machines, to raise wages, to establish uniform tariffs, to regulate trades, or to shorten the workday) with a mixture of shock, stupefaction, incomprehension, and stern parental reproaches, considering such demands not only unacceptable but also inconsistent, senseless, and utterly irrational. The reason for this attitude is the blatant contradiction between the corporate conception of social and labor relations, including the demands arising from them, and the liberal principles on which the new political and legal regime was based and for which the labor organizations themselves had fought. First of all, demands based on the corporate conception of social and labor relations come into conflict with the liberty of industry, labor, and contracting, that is, with the principle that relations between workers and employers are relations between free individuals or citizens. In consequence, any trade regulation supposed a violation of the liberty of industry and any collective organization of workers spelled illegal coalition, in the eyes of the state. Secondly, any demand addressed to the state had to be made individually, since the state recognized only individual citizens as subjects and interlocutors, not collective organizations, identified with the intermediate institutions of the Old Regime (*Work*, 195–96, and

"La confraternité," 651–54). Workers thus discovered that their idiom lacked moral or even cognitive force in the public sphere and that if they were to recover the efficacy lost and reestablish channels of communication with the state, they had to endow their demands and their identity with a new conceptual support. They had to re-articulate them through the social, political, moral, and theoretical categories of the liberal discourse that they themselves had helped to institutionalize. As Sewell reports, the liberal institutionalization of the right to property and the liberty of industry only allowed relations between individual citizens and prevented any association of workers—with the consequent incomprehension and repression of the state—and initially provoked a retreat of the labor movement after the Revolution. But, at the same time, that liberal incommensurability had another fundamental and unforeseen effect: it stimulated some militant workers to reformulate it from the workers' point of view (*Work*, 280 and 197, and "Artisans," 60). A new workers' identity would be born from, precisely, this process of discursive rearticulation.

In the new circumstances, the basic question facing workers' organizations was how to reestablish workers as legitimate actors and speakers in the public arena, that is, as political subjects (*Work*, 198). The answer, according to Sewell, was to be found in the creative adaptation of the liberal discourse and the rhetoric of the French Revolution (*Work*, 199, and "La confraternité," 656), in a rapid appropriation of the revolutionary language with the purpose of highlighting the moral and political standing of workers ("Artisans," 60). Specifically, the workers adopted the discourse of individual rights and democratic participation, terms in which the recent Revolution had been carried out ("How," 70), leading categories like *labor* and *liberty* to become cornerstones of the labor program. By resting, for example, on the arguments of authors like Sieyès (who excludes the nobility from the nation because it does no work useful to society), the workers went one step further and "declared that manual labor alone supported all of society," that the workers were "the most useful class of society," the producers of all wealth, and that, therefore, such gave them the condition of *sovereign people*, with the concomitant right to act on the public stage. And, in sharp contrast, the bourgeoisie was depicted as a new aristocracy separated from the nation by its privileges. That is, working-class authors applied the old concepts of aristocracy, privilege, servitude, or emancipation to the relations between the bourgeoisie and the workers, which meant "the bourgeois were dubbed 'new aristocrats,' who used their 'privilege' of property ownership to keep workers in 'servitude' as industrial 'serfs' or 'slaves.'" All of which turned the bourgeois constitutional government based on property franchise—one that excluded the workers from the political system and broke the alliance that had lead to the triumph of the Revolution—into an oppressive "feudal" tyranny and justified the workers' efforts to gain their "emancipation" (*Work*, 199, and "Artisans," 60–61). Just as the Third Estate had to wrest its rights from the privileged orders, the workers would have to take them, by revolution if necessary, from the bourgeoisie. At the same time, the Lockean theory of property was reinterpreted so as to invest political rights not in property, which this tradition regarded as a product of labor, but directly in labor itself. This converted property into an abusive privilege, one that exempted its idle owners from labor and, given the existing suffrage laws, gave them a monopoly of political power as well ("How," 71). As Sewell concludes, "revolutionary language and rhetoric not only endowed workers with the power of public speech," but "it also provided the power to re-define the moral and social world" (*Work*, 201).

However, even though the liberal discourse validated the workers as a sovereign people, as legitimate actors on the public stage, and endowed them with the power of comprehensible speech, the individualism grounding this discourse prevented them, at the same time, from formulating their collective demands ("La confraternité," 658). This difficulty would be solved by rearticulating these demands through the notion of "association," which became the key slogan of the workers' movement in the following years. According to liberal discourse, society is made up of free individuals and any attempt at collective regulation is considered an infringement on the liberty of those individuals. But, at the same time, every citizen has the right to associate freely with others, a right that is "an inseparable part of the 'liberté' proclaimed in 1789 and revived conspicuously in 1830." From this point of view, as Sewell explains, the regulations that workers' organizations proposed became not an assault on the liberty of industry, but an expression of the associated free wills of the producers, much as laws of a nation were an expression of the general will. In this way, their claims for collective regulation were made compatible with revolutionary discourse and with the principle of liberty ("Artisans," 61, and "La confraternité," 658–59). This way, in opposition to the corporation, which is organized around belonging to a trade, the association appears, which is based on the concept of individual or citizen.

As far as the issue of identity is concerned, the fundamental point is that from 1833, urban workers started to view their place in society in a different way. As a result, they could think and talk of an "association" that would encompass the societies of all trades and would fight for the rights of all workers in the face of the property-owning bourgeoisie.[40] It was in this form, association of workers of different trades, that French workers first conceived themselves as a united class, thus leading to the birth of "class consciousness," that is, the consideration that all workers form part of a group with common interests, over and above their trade (*Work*, 211, and "La confraternité," 660 and 664). This new and powerful sense of common identity among artisans working in different trades and the universalization of trade solidarity to encompass all workers is a novel phenomenon. It entails a sharp break or discontinuity with the previous situation, dominated by acute differences, generally accompanied by rivalry and hostility, between trades and in which solidarity was only conceivable within each trade.[41]

The emergence of this class consciousness coincided with a wave of strikes that occurred in 1833 and in the course of which practical collaboration between different trades intensified. According to Sewell, however, this wave of strikes and the practical experience of collaboration prove insufficient or fall short when one tries to explain the appearance of such class consciousness. These facts undoubtedly constitute an important "base" and a "favorable" factor, but they are not in themselves "a sufficient condition" ("La confraternité," 668 and 665, and *Work*, 213). For this break to occur and for class identity to replace trade identity, the workers had to begin to make sense of their situation, to define their program, and to implement their practice through the liberal discourse, specifically through the category of citizenship. As Sewell says, it was not until workers' corporations were themselves seen as free associations of *productive laboring citizens*, rather than as distinct corps devoted to the perfection of a particular art, that the wider fraternity of all workers became thinkable. In other words, class consciousness was born out of developments in the revolutionary language and rhetoric, the reformulation of corporate notions of belonging into a new idiom of association. Once this had occurred, the wave of strikes in 1833 could lead not only to practical cooperation between workers in different trades, but to a profound sense of moral fraternity and common identity on the part of "the confraternity of proletarians" (*Work*, 213, and "La confraternité," 665–66). Once the discursive conditions have led them to stop seeing themselves as members of a trade (and acting as such) and to begin seeing themselves as free productive citizens, workers can then think of themselves and arrange their practice in terms of a social group with common interests. This is how the "labor movement" was born.[42]

The main conclusion that Sewell's accounts yield is the following: class identity was not born as a representation or reflection of socioeconomic conditions—that had hardly varied—but it was born from the discursive rearticulation of these conditions through the categories of the modern-liberal discourse inherited from the French Revolution.[43] As Sewell emphasizes, the working class identity—like socialism in the 1840s—is the consequence of an appropriation, rather than an abandonment, of the revolutionary discourse. In fact, the workers who previously identified themselves as members of a trade are the *same* as those who, by endowing their situation with sense through the new categories, go on to conceive themselves as a class or unitary group. To understand and explain the emergence of the class identity and the labor movement (both in France and in England), as Sewell's work instructs, we have to focus our attention on the "conceptual transformation" of the liberal discourse from which they rise. To search for the origin of national differences would also require focus not on the heterogeneity of social conditions or capitalist accumulation so much as on the diversity of discursive traditions ("How," 72 and 70).

In Zachary Lockman's work,[44] although impregnated with many of the theoretical assumptions of new cultural history, the concept of class identity undoubtedly goes beyond the limits of the objectivist paradigm. The starting point of Lockman's argument is a criticism of the assumption that class is an entity that exists "out there" in the "real world," prior to meaning and independent of the ways in which it can be thought of and talked about in language, and that class identity is the outcome of structural economic change ("Imagining," 158). The fallacy in this assumption, argues Lockman, comes from the fact that it is grounded on a theory of knowledge that makes a dichotomy between what actually exists in the real world (in this case, a social class) and its (admittedly sometimes distorted or refracted) reflection in consciousness. Class then, defined in terms of relationship to the means of production, income level, or any other criterion, is *pregiven* in external reality and a certain class location implies a specific form of consciousness ("'Worker,'" 74, emphasis in original). In this scheme, moreover, the failure of workers to grasp the meaning of their objective structural location and their class interest and the absence of struggle to overthrow capitalism and replace it with a system that objectively fits their needs, is explained by false consciousness ("'Worker,'" 74–75). However, objects Lockman, in most cases workers' conduct differs from what is prescribed by this theoretical model. Furthermore, historical research shows that a certain consciousness or propensity to act collectively in a particular way does not derive from a determinate social situation (for example, concentration in large factories) ("'Worker,'" 75). Such is an anomaly that the concept of experience (often taken as an alternative to crude economic determinism) cannot overcome, since this continues to imply the existence of an objective social reality, supposing certain social circumstances produce in the consciousness of those on whom they impinge particular experiences, which are then handled or processed culturally to produce certain meanings ("'Worker,'" 75–76). Lockman upholds that although "worker" and "working class" are certainly identities profoundly shaped by material practices (i.e., capitalist production relations of a certain kind and scale), their coherence and social effectivity nonetheless cannot be derived either from workers' structural position or from their experience. According to him, within a specific socioeconomic matrix, identities are produced "in and through discourse," that is, "through systems of meaning expressed in language and other signifying practices, material and otherwise" ("'Worker,'" 72). Which implies likewise that neither the working class as a social actor nor workers' subjectivity—the ways in which they feel, think, and make sense of themselves and their relation to the world—can be assumed to be singular or unified or fixed in meaning, especially one derived from the Western European experience ("'Worker,'" 72).

In the particular case of Egypt, the application of the objectivist paradigm interprets working-class formation as the product of capitalist development and the exploitation to which it subjected workers. In this interpretation, development between 1882 and 1914, the fruit of foreign investment and of modern large-scale enterprises employing a growing number of wage workers, created an Egyptian working class. Later, this new class gradually acquired consciousness of itself through its experience of and resistance to exploitation, oppression, and abuse in the workplace, and responded with collective action (strikes, trade unions, political activism, etc.), thereby manifesting that they were beginning to think and act in "class" ways ("Imagining," 158, and "'Worker,'" 73). Finally, that resistance impressed on the rest of Egyptian society the existence of the working class as a social reality and a significant economic and political actor ("Imagining," 158).

However, argues Lockman, even though capitalist development did generate a category of people employed in large-scale industry, workers resisted to what they perceived as unjust or arbitrary domination, oppression, and exploitation, and their forms of struggle are similar to the European ones, one cannot establish a separation as such between experience and representation, since any experience is already representation ("'Worker,'" 76). Although "the rhetoric of class appeals to the objective 'experience' of workers, in fact such experience only exists through its conceptual organization" ("'Worker,'" 77). And consequently, the explanation of the way in which the new representation of Egyptian society emerged requires an approach very different from that which informs the standard narratives of Egyptian labor history ("Imagining, 158). Instead of starting from the premise that class *"produces"* class consciousness, we ought to challenge that dichotomy by taking very seriously the argument that both class consciousness and class are born from a certain articulation, through a coherent conceptual pattern, of the events and activities of daily life ("'Worker,'" 77, emphasis in original). What this, in turn, implies is that the resistance of workers does not result simply from their experience of domination and exploitation, nor is it always informed by some abstract, "rational" (in the capitalist-economistic sense of that term) classical "proletarian" form of subjectivity, as much of the literature seems to maintain. Instead, resistance is also a consequence of the process of articulation itself

("'Worker,'" 76). This does not mean, remarks Lockman, that the social conditions of language's existence are arbitrary or that there is no link between social being and social consciousness. What it means is that the class consciousness that emerged among workers can be understood not so much as either reflective of class position or the product of experience, but as *constructed* in and through discursive struggles about meaning.[45] In Egypt, as elsewhere, "workers" and "working class" "as forms of identity, perceived social categories or forms of subjectivity and historical actors," can be seen as products or *"effects"* not only of certain material practices (for example, wage employment in large enterprises). They are also products "of a particular discourse that, by providing categories of worker and class identity, gives people a language with which to make sense (or rather, to make one of several possible kinds of sense) of their experience and to interpret the world and their own place and possibilities within it" ("'Worker,'" 77, and "Imagining," 158–59, emphasis in original).

Before the arrival of class language in Egypt, the social referent of identity and action and the criterion of social classification was the trade, not position in the relations of production. The Arabic-speaking urban male population was classified in terms of affiliation to a specific craft or trade, rather than as members of a class that incorporated all wage workers across occupational lines (so that both masters, owners of the means of production, and journeymen belonged to the same category) ("'Worker,'" 78). In the representation of society, there was no notion of working class and the dominant discourse conceptualized most (if not quite all) individuals as part of some occupational group ("Imagining," 157–58). Thus, during the entire nineteenth century, craftsmen, even when employed for a wage, are not conceived of as "workers" by virtue of their structural position, nor is there any hint that "working class" is as yet a socially meaningful category ("'Worker,'" 81). Even at the beginning of the twentieth century, when many Egyptians were already employed in large industrial or transport enterprises and staged conflicts with their employers, they do not seem to have perceived themselves, or to have been perceived by other Egyptians, as belonging to or constituting a "working class," that is, as possessing a collective social identity and agency. In fact, despite the social, economic, and political changes that the Egyptian society experienced, this "occupational identity" still remained powerful until well into the twentieth century ("'Worker,'" 80).

However, at the end of the first decade of that century and, of course, around the time of World War I, some (though by no means all) Egyptians had come to regard workers as a distinct social category, to perceive the working class as a component of Egyptian society, and to see class conflict as an indigenous movement ("Imagining," 158). What was this change due to? And why did the new form of identity emerge? If socioeconomic transformations were not the cause, what was? ("Imagining," 177). According to Lockman, the new form of identity emerged as a result of articulating socioeconomic conditions through a category—namely, class—that *is of an external origin* (created in nineteenth-century Europe, spreading subsequently around the world, and reaching Egypt in the early twentieth century). Such a category did not spring from the social practice or experience of the Egyptian workers, but is external and prior to these and, therefore, it was this category that endowed social reality with its meaning and constructed experience and practice themselves. Thus, while socioeconomic changes and the appearance of a working class were a necessary material condition, they were not a sufficient one, because without interaction between Egyptian social conditions and the class discourse of European origin, class identity would not have emerged. It was just as craft workers, self-employed artisans, and small masters, as well as workers employed in large modern enterprises, began to gain access to the European model of working-class identity and agency, that they posited class as a (or even *the*) central feature of the social order and "workerness" as a means of organizing individual experience ("Imagining," 186, emphasis in original).

As Lockman explains, the introduction of the class discourse into Egypt took place through two channels, at a time when various political forces tried to organize groups of people around some pole of identity in order to realize a particular sociopolitical project, by promoting certain representations of self, society, and the world ("Imagining," 159). The first channel to introduce European categories was the Egyptian "Westernized intellectual elite" (the *effendiyya*) and, in particular, the nationalists. The shift took place when some segments of the *effendiyya*, especially the nationalist intelligentsia, adopted a new way of "imagining" the lower classes, with the consequent redefinition of Egyptian peasants and workers as distinct components of the nation ("Imagining," 178). Thus the nationalists, by adopting, adapting, and deploying the new "model" or discourse, posited class as a significant feature of the social order, defined "workerness" as a specific form of subjectivity, and incorporated them into a representation of their society which had hitherto been largely innocent of class ("Imagining," 161). Specifically, one path along which this model may have reached Egyptian workers was through the efforts of Nationalist Party activists to organize, from the second half of the first decade of the century onward, certain groups of Egyptian workers, creating institutions and introducing practices in which a certain conception of working class identity inhered ("Imagining," 179). For this reason, from at least 1906 onward, we can observe the lower classes in Egypt being imagined by segments of the *effendiyya* in this new way, and it was in part through this process that a working class was discursively constructed

("Imagining," 179). Through this process, says Lockman, some Egyptians came to "see" their society as composed of classes and to denote others or themselves as a kind of person called a "worker," who, along with others of "his kind," collectively constituted a "working class" possessing certain distinctive attributes ("Imagining," 177). As a consequence, political struggle came to be inscribed into different discursive parameters, and the workers' conflicts, although they had existed for a long time, began to acquire new social meanings, to be constructed as distinct objects within a new conception of Egyptian society, and to be articulated within a narrative of labor activism modeled on that of Western Europe. The second channel for the introduction of the class discourse refers to Greek and Italian workers who migrated to Egypt. Foreign workers who had been involved in trade unionism, had participated in strikes, and had even been members of socialist, anarchist, and anarcho-syndicalist movements or groups in their countries of origin, and who brought these ideas and experiences with them to Egypt ("Imagining," 186).

The essential conclusion that can be drawn from Lockman's account is that working class identity did not emerge as a consequence of capitalist development in Egypt. It emerged because the class discourse, on reaching Egypt, triggered a real reconceptualization of Egyptian society and of workers' identity, endowing their experience and practices (i.e., the organization of labor, space, and time in the workplace, exploitation, and oppression, modes of living, working, thinking, and resisting) with "working class" meaning ("Imagining," 186–87). This is not to say, Lockman insists, that the structural, economic, and political factors were irrelevant, that class identity was merely an imposition of the intelligentsia, or that Egyptian workers passively adopted a fixed model and came to perceive self and society in the same way as a contemporary English, Italian, or German worker did. On the contrary, this was a creative process, in which the workers themselves played a key role and in which Egyptians not only assimilated a certain set of practices; they also combined it with elements drawn from other systems of meaning ("Imagining," 187). But, the fact that the workers played an active role in crafting their own identity and making sense of their own world does not mean that we can explain the adoption of working class identity as simply the product of a certain "experience" of exploitation and oppression in the workplace. Instead, as suggested earlier, one must examine the discursive field that provided the workers with the ways of comprehending (or, to be more precise, structuring) their circumstances, their experiences, and themselves, including those ways that posited class (in whatever particular sense) as a meaningful category ("Imagining," 185–86). As it was within and through this discursive field that "workerness" came to be a subject position for certain people and that working conditions (low wages, miserable working conditions, abusive foremen, etc.) were constructed not only as oppressive and exploitative in a specifically structured way, but also as potentially "resistible," even changeable, by means of certain kinds of activities (strikes, trade unions, etc.). Because, as Lockman stresses, it was not "resistance" itself that was learned in the process—Egyptians have always found ways to resist or evade oppressive authority—but rather certain *forms* of resistance specific to the new discursive field ("Imagining," 186).

5

A New Concept
of Social Action

I

Denaturalization of the concept of society as objective structure and ensuing theoretical rethinking of the notions of experience, interest, and identity have sunk the concept of *social causality* into a deep crisis. As I have repeated, the main theoretical driving force behind recent developments in historical studies has been the growing critical doubt cast on the assumption that the consciousness of individuals is a reflection or representation of their social conditions of existence and that, therefore, the explanation of their actions is to be found in such conditions. As Geoff Eley states, once the commitment to grasping society as a unitary, underlying whole has passed into crisis, the concepts of society and social causality can no longer be maintained—as there is no structural coherence deriving from the economy, from a social system, or from some other overarching principle of order. This crisis spells the following: even though particular phenomena (an event, a policy, an institution, an ideology, a text) have particular social contexts, in the sense of conditions, practices, sites that conjoin in producing an essential part of their meaning, there is no underlying structure of which such phenomena can be expression or effect.[1]

Upon observing what seems an obvious relation between a certain social situation and a particular form of behavior, one tends to regard the latter as a causal effect of the former. However, argues postsocial history, this is due more to the prevalence of certain theoretical assumptions or habits of thinking than to the actual existence of a causal connection. Indeed, less indulgent and external scrutiny of the explanatory scheme of social history has exposed theoretical naïveté and shattered the seemingly commonsensical character of social causality, making clear the failure of social history to fully explain through which specific mechanism social context translates into conscious action. Paraphrasing Stuart Hall, social history does not contain any developed account of the actual mechanisms through which material factors reproduce their knowledge (or of the mechanisms under which the transparency of the social could be obscured by false consciousness).[2] In short, it is now crystal clear that social history never elaborated or made explicit the micro-fundamentals of its social theory. Basing their work on the concept of reflection, social historians took the existence of a mechanism of causal connection for granted and converted mere assumption into unquestionable premise. Or, to be more exact, social history assumed that since there is a material link between the two spheres, the relationship between them must be a causal one. However, once one reaches a postsocial theoretical horizon, what had hitherto been indubitable premises became questions that obliged clarification. For, what is it exactly to reflect the social or to act as social context determines? In what sense and on what basis can it be claimed that a form of consciousness or behavior is caused by, or inherent in, a certain social position? The existence of a material and empirically verifiable link or of an evident spatial and time correlation between a social situation and a certain course of action falls far too short to justify inferring a causal relationship between the two, in the sense that the social presupposes, if only potentially, action. There is not even enough to sustain the inference in those cases, carefully discussed already, wherein agents claim or believe they are acting in accordance with their social position. Therefore, although a link or correlation may clarify purely material practices, neither can explain meaningful ones.

The first symptom of theoretical weakening of the social causality paradigm in historical studies was the emergence of new cultural history. As we have seen, in an effort to mitigate the increasing difficulty encountered when trying to account for meaningful practices with social location and attributes of subjects exclusively, new cultural historians introduced the notion of symbolic mediation, making action, thus, an effect of the cultural internalization of social conditions. However, as the concept of reflection gradually lost explanatory authority, was emptied of content, efforts to enlarge the territory of subjective creativity and individual autonomy were no longer considered sufficient. Instead, to wholly rethink and redefine the very nature of social practice became, for many, sine qua non. Theoretical diminishment of the objectivist framework (together with simultaneous resistance to any recourse to the idealist model) facilitated the possibility of formulating alternative explanation. From this propitious atmosphere, a new conception of social action took shape and gave rise to an image of society governed by a causal logic different from any previously assumed in historical scholarship. Succinctly put, the decay of objectivism has led postsocial historians to offer a new answer to the basic question of why people act as they do. Obviously, any answer offered by postsocial history lies outside the parameters of traditional history—people freely and rationally decide—and of social history—social circumstances compel them—and, specifically, postsocial history formulates the premise that meaningful actions are neither acts of rational choice nor effects, be they immediate or symbolic, of the social context. On the contrary, meaningful actions are the outcome of the specific articulation that individuals make of this context and of their place in it. The relations of cause and effect between social context and action are not inscribed in, or fixed by, the former, but are constituted as such in the sphere of discursive mediation. And, therefore, if people act as they do, it is not because they occupy a certain social position, but, at the most, because that position has been endowed with a certain meaning within a given social imaginary.

Thus, as far as the concept of *social action* is concerned, what postsocial history claims is that if individuals are not preconstituted rational subjects and society is not an objective structure—and if, in consequence, neither of the two can be the source of subjectivity—then it is obvious that neither of them has the power to causally determine the meaningful actions of historical actors. Specifically, if objectivity is not an attribute that reality bears, but one that it acquires when articulated, and if, in consequence, the meanings and standards of rationality are not cultural or ideological representations of such a reality, then the actions that individuals undertake based on, or guided by, them should not be taken as effects of social determination. On the contrary, if these meanings and patterns of rationality are forged by an operation of discursive mediation, then not only context does not start to determine actions until it has been objectified, but also the nature of its determination (as well as its results) depends on the specific way in which context itself has been objectified. Thus, actions do not have their causal origin in social context, but in the discursive mediation itself and, therefore, their explanation must be sought, in the last analysis, in the body of categories through which individuals have endowed their social environment with meaning and entered into meaningful interaction with it—as well as through which they have shaped themselves as subjects. It is in bringing into play such a categorial body that a certain *regime of practical rationality* is established, thus defining which behaviors are logical or natural and what course or program of action is the suitable one in each case. If discursive patterns underlie the conscious perceptions that individuals have of their environment, as well as of themselves and their existence, then individuals as agents always behave

in accordance with the terms of such discursive patterns. To be more precise, if people construct their own experience, interests, and identity by locating themselves within a social imaginary, then the latter necessarily enables their actions and guides their conduct. This imaginary allows agents
to make a diagnosis of their place in the world and thus to acquire the set
of beliefs, intentions, feelings, passions, aspirations, hopes, frustrations,
or expectations that motivate, underlie, accompany, justify, or confer
sense on their actions, be these the most daily and ordinary actions or the
most complex and intellectually elaborated ones.

Thus, postsocial history starts from the assumption of social history
that individuals are not natural entities, but subjects are historical constructions, and that the latter, and not the former, are the only ones that
undertake meaningful actions. It also assumes that the standards of rationality that underlie practice are historical products and that the historical process that converts individuals into subjects is what also shapes and
empowers them as *agents* or subjects of action. From this point of view,
agency is not a capacity that individuals possess immanently, but a capacity they acquire when they are constituted as subjects. As I have emphasized, subjects cannot be free agents who make rational choices because the subjectivity that guides their behavior is a derived entity.
Indeed, the very notion of rational subject or self (as well as the notion of
human agency, inherent to it) is no more than a historically specific (modern) form of identity. This certainly invalidates both notions as foundations for a theory of action. But, postsocial history does not limit itself to
questioning the structural character of social reality and the notion of natural subjectivity. It also turns sharply from the social history horizon and
places human action within a new causal and intelligibility framework. If,
as I have just said, subjectivity is a meaningful construction, then actions
only become intelligible and can be explained if one takes into account
and unravels their discursive matrix. Thus, postsocial history continues to
take it for granted that actions are a response to the pressure of social context, but they are *discursively mediated* responses, in the sense that actions
are causally linked to the operation of discursive mediation that underlies
them, and not to their social contexts of reference. From which it follows
not only that discursivity is an ontological condition of human action and
social life, but that, in consequence, historical scholarship must adopt a
new agenda. As I have already noted and highlight later, in any effort to
explain the practice of historical actors, reenacting their reasons or un-
covering their social conditions no longer suffice, but careful consideration of the context of meanings in which such a practice is rooted is also
required.

For postsocial history, it is not only that social practice is always inscribed in a particular discursive regime, but that the latter also operates

as a real causal foundation. As Joan W. Scott states, social practice is "a discursive effect."[3] Individuals assess and reproduce their living conditions or draw up their projects for the future always within a world—which includes themselves—that has been meaningfully constructed. What social practice does is to deploy, mobilize, and actualize the meanings and the regime of practical rationality of a certain discourse. Agents are constantly working in a universe of signification and deploying its content, possibilities, and conditions in a practical fashion, embodying it in beliefs, relations, institutions, social norms, or value systems. As Keith Baker writes, agents are constantly "playing at its [language] margins, exploiting its possibilities and extending the play of its potential meanings, as they pursue their purposes and projects." Moreover, continues Baker, although this play of discursive possibility may not be infinite, it is always open to individual and collective actors. However, as he qualifies further, by the same token "it is not necessarily controllable by such actors."[4] In the postsocial view of human action, individuals do not use discourse as a means of action. Rather it is the discourse itself that, on actively mediating, establishes the *conditions of possibility* of action. Which is just why the latter is not merely an *event*, but an *episode* too, insofar as it is inserted in a grid of signification that not only triggers it, but also provides it with its intelligibility.

This theoretical premise should be understood in its exact sense. In this case too, to avoid misinterpretations or hasty judgments, a brief explanatory note should be added. Postsocial history does not deny that social conditions are a conditioning and constraining factor on practice, as if it were merely an idealist reaction against materialism. What it does deny is that this conditioning or constraining is objective or structural, in the sense that a given social situation involves, in any way, in and of itself, a certain response or specific course of action. To put it in Foucauldian terms, postsocial history does not question the existence of either discursive and nondiscursive practices, but it does maintain that the latter are always articulated by the former and that, consequently, nondiscursive practices have no autonomous capacity of causation. That social reality imposes limits on action—that all practices are socially situated and constrained by unknown factors and that social context constantly presses individuals and compels them to act—constitutes an empirically obvious fact. It is also evident that social context defines the field of possibilities of action (and therefore precludes or excludes certain actions), which is the referential framework of decisions and choices, and that it provides agents with their material, cultural, or organizational resources. Postsocial history argues, however, that it is not social context which provides agents with either the categories or meanings on which they base their actions and that, therefore, although such a context is undoubtedly the material matrix of practice, it is not its causal matrix. Even though social conditions constrain, determine, empower, limit, influence, or simply affect actions, they only do so on the material or physical level, not on the meaningful level. In fact, postsocial history considers social context incapable of explaining anything because it is not ontologically independent of the discursive practices that construct it. Thus, social reality can generate certain material responses or reactions in individuals, but not meaningful responses or reactions or, therefore, affect the meaningful dimension of social practice. For postsocial history, even though individuals and their social context are in permanent interaction in the course of practice, the analytically relevant point is that it is not an interaction with primary or original instances. Instead, it is always an interaction between meaningful entities, between individuals and a social context that have previously been articulated or constructed as subjects and object respectively.

Thus, if one had to answer Eley's question of what place is left, specifically, for social determination once the notion of society as a totalizing category is dissolved, it must be said, first, that postsocial history at no time discards social causality; second, that postsocial history does, though, restrict social causality to the area of the material and does subordinate it to discursive mediation. The former means that if, as Eley himself writes, "the social" is "constituted *through* discourse," then "social explanation" can only explain material practices, but not the meaningful ones, that is, the ones that imply, mobilize, or deploy some kind of system of meanings. The latter means that "the social" has lost all independent causal efficacy outside the discursive mediation itself, in the sense that any pressure or determination of the social context on practice is always, and necessarily, exercised *through* a certain discursive matrix.[5]

The epistemological dissatisfaction that has led postsocial authors to make this distinction between social causality and discursive mediation is the same one that underlies other distinctions with which it has some points in common. Here, I am thinking, for example, about the distinction that William H. Sewell establishes between mechanistic and semiotic forms of explanation of social life. The former based on a material relation of cause and effect and the latter on the "codes" or "paradigms" that enable human action or practices.[6] Sewell maintains that mechanistic causality is essential for explaining social processes, because elements like demographic, economic, geographic, or institutional conditions are determining factors of practice. But, at the same time, he insists these factors must be simultaneously analyzed with the semiotic ones, as they are both closely entwined and interact with each other. On this occasion, however, Sewell covers very little of the path traveled by postsocial history. Since he reduces "semiotic logic" to a set of formal or cultural devices (gestural, iconic, ritual, and so on) and, in consequence, he does not take into account the existence of historically specific patterns of meaning, Sewell continues to conceive of the link between social conditions and consciousness essentially in terms of the old dichotomous theoretical model. That is, in terms of interaction between social reality and cultural resources (for example, between "changes in rural class structure" and "agrarian ritual").

Nevertheless, from the perspective of postsocial history there are practices (or essential aspects of them) associated with these social changes that would remain unexplained without giving consideration to certain networks of signification. To take Sewell's own example and argumentation: a connection between demographic changes and fluctuations in prices and wages and poverty obviously exists but it is not an exclusively mechanistic connection nor do the consequences listed encompass the whole historical phenomenon in question. Remaining on a merely material plane denies that phenomenon all historical relevance. Other circumstances have to be taken into consideration, those surrounding demographic changes for example. The latter do not exercise their pressure in a vacuum, but through agents who embody patterns of meaning, and resulting practices are, thus, dependent on the specific manner in which the changes themselves or their effects are made meaningful. The demographic situation, or its relation with food resources, can explain (at least in principle) the fall in wages, the rise in prices, or the increase in poverty, but not the responses that these phenomena give rise to. We already know, as Sewell himself has studied elsewhere, that such phenomena can be conceptualized in very different ways and the responses vary historically (resigned acceptance of natural and inexorable facts at one extreme or social rebellion at the other) depending on the prevailing discursive regime in each case. Moreover, and something worth remembering, demographic changes themselves are not merely natural or biological phenomena, but they also involve a set of meaningful practices.

And the same could be argued, in general, with regard to the defense of social causality or determination undertaken by Sewell himself in a later work.[7] Over the last few years, he says, an effective *thinning* of the social in historical scholarship has taken place, coinciding with an increasingly semiotic approach to both documents and reality in historical research. Historical sources read or examined not as means of gaining information about reality but as specific ways of perceiving and arranging it. For example, Joan Scott, in her paper on a statistical inquiry into work in Paris in 1847 and 1848, treats statistical categories as discursive instead of just considering the numbers they produce as objective data about social life (215).[8] But, for Sewell, who does see the linguistic turn as a positive development in historical studies, a robust sense of the social (217) needs to be sustained because, he upholds, social context imposes objective limits on human action. On this occasion too, he illustrates his stance with two examples. The first is the influence of the world currency market on political decision makers, industrial workers, or strategies for unionization (220). In the case of shop floor politics in Korea, for instance, exchange rates of the yuan against the dollar act as a structural constraint on the nature of union demands on management (221). The second example is that of a premodern, predominantly rural population in which a mutation of the plague bacillus extends the average life span by several years. This, he argues, has several effects: children can only expect to inherit their parents' assets, a precondition for marriage and characteristic requisite for starting a new family, at a much later age and such deferral spells significant changes in the society's form of life. It could, for example, lead to later marriages or more lifetime celibacy, to a burgeoning of bandit gangs, monasteries, and nunneries, to changes in the value or composition of dowries or bride prices, or to an increase in the number of people who migrate to cities where excess labor might find employment in manufacturing. It seems obvious, adds Sewell, that we cannot hope to explain which of these possible changes might actually result from the lengthening of the life span without also trying to understand the cultural or discursive milieu in which it took place. But it would be equally absurd, in his opinion, to claim that such a discursive reconstruction alone provides an adequate account of the change, and extremely foolish to disdain the use of objectivist demographic theory and methods to determine the effects of rising life expectations on the age structure of the population. In short, such banal and undeniable facts—we age and die or we cannot be in two places at the same time—have far-reaching effects on the shapes and possibilities of human social life and discourse, effects that cannot be fully accounted for by discursive analysis (221–22). All this leads Sewell to conclude that historical analysts should treat contextual events as objective or structural constraints, at least strategically, and that therefore strategic methodological resort to objectivism is virtually impossible to avoid (221).

Even at the cost of being too repetitive or tedious, let me stress once again what is really at stake concerning the social in historical studies today and try as well to dispel some misunderstandings that seem to run through Sewell's argument. Once the postsocial theoretical horizon has been reached, it is not a question of dispensing or not with social context when explaining people's practice. The key issue lies with the question of conferring a different explanatory role on social context. Specifically speaking, social reality continues to be regarded as the material ground of practice but is no longer considered its objective ground. Postsocial history does not deny that social factors constrain practice; this is something that it takes for granted. What it does deny is that such a constraining is objective, in the indicated sense that a real event or situation is able, even if potentially, to compel people to behave or react in a certain way. For postsocial authors, social context necessarily takes part in making practice. But, just how, the specific way people respond to contextual pressure is always dependent on the meaning that context acquires when articulated through a given set of assumptions about how society works and might work, and therefore on what is appropriate or normal behavior in each juncture. The standard notion of social causality, even a thoroughly reformulated version, cannot properly grasp this kind of bond between social context and action.

To focus on previous examples, there can be no doubt that the world currency market is an external, uncontrollable factor that influences and constrains collective bargaining, but it does so in one or another way depending on how it is understood and explained. Just how workers conceive of currency exchange fluctuations—unavoidable or natural facts or an imposition of imperialism—is crucial to explaining their attitude, specifically to accepting or not a cut in their wages. What is just happening nowadays, and as Sewell himself points out so well, is a highly efficacious articulation of economy as an inexorable and natural process, one deeply affecting, of course, union or workers' practice. If the prevailing articulation of economy were another one, the practical outcome would undoubtedly be very different. Thus, in this case too, the question is not whether the international currency market influences or not workers' practice, because it is obvious that it does indeed. The question is whether the workers' response is in any sense implicit in the present state of the currency market or does their response stem, instead, from the way workers make sense of that market and from the way they incorporate such sense-making into their practice. And the same happens with demographic fluctuations, as I have just argued. The empirical fact that demographic changes can affect marriage practices or forms of life is not under discussion. Such a factor exists and must be taken into account. The crucial point is how demographic changes take part in shaping practices and forms of life and, specifically, if there is indeed a cause-effect relationship between the two as depicted by Sewell. Marriage as a merely empirical fact can be determined by demographic circumstances, but as a meaningful or historically placed practice, it is dependent on how such circumstances are conceptually experienced. What can explain, in other words, how similar demographic settings give rise to quite different marriage practices historically?

I have the impression that Sewell's approach to the social is hindered by a problem of incommensurability between theoretical outlooks. Specifically, by the difficulties the postsocial distinction between the real and the objective and between language as vocabulary and language as a pattern of meanings can pose when approached through the categories of the dichotomous paradigm. This problem prevents a proper understanding of the terms in which postsocial authors have rethought both the social and social constraint on practice. A dichotomous paradigm precludes any consideration of a third component of historical process different from both the real-objective and the cultural-subjective. This is a very common problem among social-new cultural historians who, in general, fail to grasp the said distinction and find it extremely difficult, if not impossible, to conceive of any real world that is not objective or of any social constraint that is not structural.[9]

It seems clear that, with its resolute move from social causality to discursive mediation, postsocial history has placed the debate on human action within new theoretical coordinates. Since postsocial historians are dissatisfied "with both structuralist and voluntarist models of social action"[10] (as well as with any combination of the two), reflection and discussion on social action are no longer posited in terms of a dilemma or tension between free will and social determination, between structure and action, or simply between individual and society. As I have said, this dilemma or tension would make sense if at least one of the two instances involved constituted a primary component or pregiven condition of action, but not once the existence of both rational subjectivity and social objectivity has been rejected. Consequently, in the present historiographical phase, it is no longer a question of advocating either human agency or social coercion, but of placing human action in a new space of causality and intelligibility. The crucial question to be answered is not what is the exact degree of autonomy of action or of liberty of agents with respect to social environment, but what discursive conditions have made it possible that a given social environment has generated a particular modality of practice. Otherwise any historical inquiry on the question would be a rather sterile endeavor, its only fruits a merely descriptive account of the space-time correlation between the two instances, without any kind of explanatory relevance and not even able to explain the genesis of the correlation itself.

II

The crisis of the concept of social causality and the new theory of social action underlie, for instance, the critical review that Margaret R. Somers and William H. Sewell have made of the history of the British labor and the sans-culotte movement respectively. In both cases, the questioning of social explanation is followed by a new account founded explicitly on the assumption that interests, identities, and practices are forged out of the mediation of a categorial framework that comes from outside their social referent. In the case of Somers, she starts from a double critical rethinking.

She begins by emphasizing that the history of the British labor movement has been embedded in an objectivist meta-narrative that conceives society as a natural self-regulating entity. As a consequence, the labor movement appears as the effect on the conscious realm of the changes experienced by British society, specifically its transition from a traditional society to a modern capitalist one, via industrialization. According to this meta-narrative, there is a causal link between the societal and economic changes of the industrial revolution (class in itself) and the emergence of a revolutionary class consciousness (class for itself). The societal transformation, whether it is called industrialization, modernization, or proletarianization, "ushers in the 'birth of class society.'"[11] Specifically, economic changes (commercialization, increasing division of labor, and technological development) gradually break the bonds of relatively static pre-industrial economies and give way to the appearance of "class relations," as well as the liberal state, the framework and support of the laissez-faire economy. Through this process, continues Somers, "traditional" relations were transformed into class relations and community artisan cultures organized by moral economies were supplanted by the force of new class alignments—from, in her graphic words, the "bread nexus to the wage nexus" (596–97).

Once the premise claiming a causal link between social transformation and class-consciousness has been established, it operates as a real meta-narrative for historical inquiry, defining its patterns, objectives, and questions to be posed and answered, as historians themselves take meta-narrative categories to be labels of reality. As Somers indicates, as long as the question of working-class action is bound a priori to the industrial societal transformation and the birth of class society, the research task will be limited to elaborating different versions of a merely presumed, but undemonstrated, causal relationship between societal transformation and working-class consciousness (598). Once the condition of objective foundation of the labor movement, along with its "response" in the form of collective action, is conferred on socioeconomic changes and proletarianization, the only thing remaining for explanation would be the "historical variations" of this fundamental scheme. However, according to Somers, such a premise is not only an unquestioned one but also mistaken since working-class identity and practice are not responses to or expressions of social changes and the appearance of a class society, but the result of a completely different process. In this case too, as she states in her criticism of Ira Katznelson, something requiring empirical demonstration, namely the causal primacy of proletarianization, must not be assumed to be a theoretical foundation.[12]

Before reaching this point in her argument, however, Somers raises another critical objection and an equally outstanding one for historiographical discussion. The aforementioned meta-narrative and its theory of class formation define, normatively, what should be the natural behavior of the working class, and, therefore, it conceptualizes those behaviors that do not fit as a problem of *deviance* or *anomalousness* (596). This is the inevitable corollary when applying the objectivist assumption that a certain social position entails a certain conduct. Thus, since such a meta-narrative sets a general model of the relation between industrialization and proletarianization and the birth of class society and the expected behavioral response of the working class, the problem, obsessing and informing all studies of working-class formation, is "why the failure (or incoherence, peculiarity, or deviance) of the 'real' working class" (594). The weight and articulating power of the objectivist meta-narrative have managed to bring about the historiographical conviction that this failure lies with the working class itself, precluding any pondering whatsoever over the meta-narrative instead. This is why, as Somers says, social labor history has always tended to place the *epistemology of absence* (596) in the foreground. Consequently, studies of labor movement have concentrated not so much on analyzing the effective constitution of the identity of individuals or groups being studied, but on the "exceptions" to the prediction. They have not focused on explaining what is or has been empirically present, but rather on the failure of people to behave correctly in accordance with a theoretical normative model. Thus, Somers concludes, studies of working-class formation have a most peculiar property: "rather than seeking to explain the *presence* of radically varying dispositions and practices, they have concentrated disproportionately on explaining the *absence* of an expected outcome, namely the emergence of a revolutionary class-consciousness among the Western working class."[13] These studies seem inexorably driven to conceptualize the history of labor movement basically in terms of deviance and not, for example, in terms of *variation*.

Thus, the first implication—both theoretical and epistemological—that follows from Somers's argument is that concepts—including those of social history itself—are not mere designative labels of real phenomena; they are, instead, the fruit of a meta-narrative articulation of them. But there is a second, equally significant, implication, namely that any attempt to renew labor history must start by deconstructing such concepts, naturalized by the long-term social and analytical influence of a meta-narrative based on the notions of society and social determination. As Somers herself states, if we wish to revise class formation theory, we must recognize, reconsider, and challenge that meta-narrative (593). That is, suspending judgment on the causal equation between social change and working-class identity is the only way of unblocking historical conundrum in this field.

What historical explanation of the making of labor movement follows from this criticism of social explanation and the call for a denaturalization of the modern meta-narrative? If labor movement is not an expression or effect of social modernization, then what is it? The conclusion that can be drawn from Somers's account is that labor movement was not constituted in the social sphere, but it emerged through a historical process different from the one taken for granted by social-new cultural history. The British labor movement in the first half of the nineteenth century was the fruit not of socioeconomic transformations, but of the meaningful apprehension of them. It was the outcome of articulating social and political relations through a certain discursive pattern (or, in Somers's terminology, a "narrative") and of deploying, in the terrain of practice, their basic constitutive categories. In this case too, just such mediation turned the social situation into action. The discursive pattern in question is the liberal-radical discourse, whose essential categorial principle (or "narrative theme") was that "working people had inviolable *rights* to particular *political* and *legal* relationships" (612). It is this category of rights that articulates experience, interests, and identity and that generates the ways of action and political practice of the members of the labor movement. According to Somers's account, such a narrative included rights of citizenship, a certain notion of people, and a particular conception of the law, including a notion of the legal relationship between the people and the law. At the same time, its conception of rights defined independence and autonomy as inexorably linked to the property rights of working people. Rights that were "only in part the fruits of individual labor; they primarily rested on membership of the political community" (612). As Somers herself stresses, this "language of rights" was "the explanatory prism through which class issues and other aspects of social distress were *mediated and made sense of*" (613, emphasis mine). It was this linguistic pattern that made possible the emergence of labor movement as such, as it was through it that events were assessed, explained, and given meaning, thus providing a guide for action and the methods for the remedies of wrongs and distress (612).

According to Somers, such a pattern of meanings (one that had been shaped over the previous centuries) includes specific guidelines of action and protest and it is the means by which "working families" articulate their identities at the beginning of the nineteenth century. The content of the underlying linguistic pattern is what explains, in Somers's words, that "in the midst of the worst economic distress of their lives, English industrial families based their protests not on economic demands or those of a 'moral economy.'" Instead, they based them "on a broadly conceived claim to legal rights to participation, substantive social justice (Poor Laws), local government control, cohesive family and community relations, 'modern' methods of labor regulation (trade unions) and the right to independence—be it from capitalists, the state, or from other workers." Specifically, their reliance on plot lines "driven by a conception of justice and *rights of membership* to explain their distress and guide their action," elucidates their directing their protests against law, legal authorities, legal ideals of universality and equity, local politics, and legal institutions (612).

Sewell's work on the sans-culotte movement clearly leads toward a similar critical rethinking of social explanation.[14] Sewell also calls into question the existence of a truly causal connection between the socioeconomic position of the sans-culottes and their conscious practice and he doubts, as well, that the latter should be regarded as an effect of the former. His account starts with critique of the materialist interpretation of this historical phenomenon, especially Albert Soboul's classical formulation. Let me briefly freshen memories on this point. Heeding Sewell's own depiction, the social explanation Soboul offers is based on the assumption that identity groupings—or collective historical subjects—are expressions of socioeconomic groupings. Specifically, the consciousness, program, and political practice of the sans-culotte movement would have risen directly from the social conditions of a distinct socioeconomic category or social group identifiable as "the sans-culotterie." A group that is not, of course, a class (it included both employers and employees), but whose diverse members shared a common interest as consumers. Bread prices and not wages were the great economic issue of the day and it was hunger that united everyone against the great merchant, the nobleman, or the speculating bourgeoisie. Furthermore, according to Soboul, this unity of consciousness was due to the influence of the master artisans over their workforce. Although masters and journeymen have different relationships with the means of production and there are conflicts between them, the small scale of production and the consequent intimacy between masters and journeymen resulted in an essential unanimity of outlook on the social world. Concerning specifically the sans-culottes' view of the food supply, Soboul also conceives this as arising naturally from the sans-culottes' economic condition (250).

Sewell upholds that the movement's consciousness and practice were not expressions of the material conditions of existence of its members. Because, even though the economic condition of the Parisian *menu peuple* was an important source of political discourse about subsistence in 1793, the determination of economic factors was not, as Soboul claims, either so direct or so immediate. Furthermore and according to Sewell once more, the sans-culotterie itself, understood as a unified social and economic category, did not exist as such and, therefore, its social circumstances and experiences could hardly be the source of sans-culottes' ideas (252–53). Which leads him to conclude that if "the rhetoric of economic terror" was not "an unsurprising consequence of sans-culotte social being," then its existence needs "considerable explanatory exegesis" (250). An exegesis that has to take into consideration other factors or ingredients of the process involved in the constitution of this rhetoric out of the socioeconomic situation.

Once he has established these general principles, Sewell applies them to the analysis of one of the essential components of the sans-culotte program, the question of subsistence (the prices and supply of food), the sans-culottes demanding, basically, control and condemnation of hoarders and the establishment of a maximum. Sewell's central point here is that the "sans-culotte rhetoric of subsistence" was not causally determined by the living conditions of the members of the movement or by the scarcity and high prices of food in particular. Instead, the program of demands put forth by the sans-culottes was constituted in a different sphere from the social one. Such a program is the result of the meaningful apprehension and arrangement of the social situation in general, and of the state of subsistence in particular, through certain categories or principles. These are what, by conferring their meaning on social events, define the objectives to be attained and, by being projected in practice, determine the character, orientation, and the forms of the movement's political action. In other words, mostly from Sewell himself, the social standing or the formal political affiliations of the sans-culottes did not define the sans-culotte rhetoric of subsistence; it was defined, instead, "by its discursive characteristics." Subsistence rhetoric, he goes on, may be characterized as a self-consistent discourse whose autonomous dynamics and political effects are not reducible to the social interests or projects of any particular social category. In fact, Sewell emphasizes, immediately thereafter, such a discourse was not only articulated by the sans-culottes but was used by other political options as well, constituting "a publicly available rhetorical system that served as a meeting ground for political actors from widely varying social backgrounds and with distinct institutional commitments who were engaged in quite different overall projects" (253).

Sewell then goes on to specify which principles generated the sans-culotte program of action. First of all, states Sewell, the sans-culotte program was not only an assertion of the interests of the urban poor; it was also full of moral exhortations and metaphysical pronouncements and, in particular, of hostility against the Church. Specifically, by secularizing the drama of religious salvation and replacing it with the drama of mankind's salvation on Earth (253), the politics of food found its place within the cosmic drama of good and evil (254). The second discursive principle was a consideration of nature as the sacred source of truth and of physical and spiritual sustenance. For republicans, life was the supreme gift of nature and assuring the continuation of life through nature's bounty was the most fundamental political duty. The third principle was the definition of the right of subsistence as "a sacred and imprescriptible right of man" (254). Principles like these, operating as organizing patterns of the experience and interests and objectifying certain social facts as problems to be solved, generated the sans-culotte movement and converted its members into historical subjects. Scarcity, for example, was conceptualized not as a consequence of poor harvests but of speculation (because nature produces enough to feed the population), and the proposed solution was the repression of the hoarders. As Sewell puts forward, by operating on the assumption that abundance is natural and that shortage can only be a result of manipulation, the sans-culottes came to consider scarcity an "artificial" fruit of hoarding and believed hoarders sought the destruction of the Republic (256), requiring, thus, severe laws be passed against them (257). This articulation of the social and economic situation was also the means by which the aforementioned principles were projected into action. And thus, for example, the natural right to subsistence was translated into a demand for fixing the price of goods of prime necessity and for subordinating the right of property to such a natural right. Thus, the sans-culottes saw the Republic as possessing the right to regulate prices (254), and considered growers and merchants necessarily subordinate to the public welfare, which is why they were equated to civil servants—public servants with the duty to supply food (255). Finally, the fact that this articulation was made through a new categorial grid is what explains why food shortages and high prices did not simply produce, as in previous periods, subsistence riots but actions of political protest. According to Sewell, it is precisely the existence of this network of mutual implication, linking the rhetoric of subsistence with the larger discursive framework of terror (against hoarders because they are counterrevolutionaries) that raises serious doubts about Soboul's explanation of the social origins of sans-culotte ideology. Because it was not just a question of a material claim for food supply, but this claim was inserted in a wider program of struggle against counterrevolution and of demand for rights. In this case, too, interests are not mere social or material attributes that become manifest in the political sphere, but they are meaningful constructions themselves.[15] This does not mean, as we already know, that the socioeconomic situation and, in particular, hunger, were not essential factors in the shaping of the sans-culottes' program and practice. Nor does it mean, as Sewell makes clear, "that either the substance of the rhetoric or its role in the politics of the revolution were without social determinants" (253). Hunger, of course, not only existed, it was also the material ground of the rhetoric of subsistence. Hunger was a real issue and a chronic problem in the time of the Revolution; poor harvests were frequent and people spent half their wages on food, so any rise in prices spelled dreaded hunger. Therefore, there were good reasons for people to worry about hunger and, in fact, not only was hunger one of the reasons for the urban uprisings of 1789, but memory of privations remained alive in the years following. Nobody can doubt, as Sewell asserts, "a real economic basis" (261) to the sans-culottes' rhetoric of subsistence.

What is under discussion, however, is not the existence of hunger or its obvious connection with the sans-culottes' program and practice. What is under discussion is the nature of this connection, that is, the answer to the question of why hunger generated this specific kind of reaction, attitude, demands, and political action. And this cannot be explained by the mere existence of hunger; it is necessary to take into consideration the mediation of categories like those listed above (struggle between good and evil, nature as a source of life, and the natural right to subsistence).[16] In fact, the main shortcoming of the social explanation lies in its taking for granted that hunger, by itself, generates a certain kind of response in individuals, without realizing that such a response will depend on the varying objective existences (i.e., meanings) that hunger acquires depending on the prevailing social imaginary in each case. Furthermore, the very existence of a response depends on hunger having been objectified in a certain way: for example, not as a natural or providential phenomenon, but as a *social* problem to be resolved. The sans-culottes did not react as they did because they were hungry but because, by perceiving and experiencing their hunger through the modern imaginary, hungry became a violation of a natural right, as well as a social evil, one that political measure could and should address. Such political resolution was, in turn, thinkable and perceived as suitable for putting into practice only because the aforementioned discursive principles already existed. Consequently, anyone who wishes to understand and explain sans-culottes practice in this terrain cannot just record the existence of hunger and its condition as being central to the sans-culottes' concerns and program. One must also explain why and how hunger was objectified in this specific way and gave, thus, rise to a certain social and political practice.

To reinforce his argument, Sewell resorts to comparing Paris in 1793 with Paris in 1848. According to him, this comparison should make clear the insufficiency of the arguments of both Soboul and George Rudé. In 1848, food prices were moderate but people had also just emerged from a period of terrible hunger, the relation between wages and prices was similar, and factory industry had hardly advanced, small workshops and manual work still remained predominate. However, in the Parisian revolution of 1848, "hardly a word was said about the problem of subsistence." On the contrary, labor, not subsistence, was the burning issue. Instead of demonstrating for a maximum and for punishments against hoarding, Parisian workers demonstrated for a reformed "organization of labor" and were forcing their employers to grant more favorable wage schedules (*tarifs*) (262). Thus, "although economic conditions in Paris in the mid-nineteenth century were surprisingly similar to those in the

1790s, the political demands of the Parisian poor were utterly different" (262). What can this clarify and what can help explain such pronounced contrast? According to Sewell, what it tells us is that economic conditions do not give rise to politically salient interests in the direct and obvious fashion Soboul and Rudé assume, but such interests are "profoundly shaped by the surrounding political culture."[17] In 1848, the ordinary people of Paris defined their interests as workers because the category of labor had been socially established in the past two decades and had made the political identity "worker" particularly potent. Therefore, the contrast is due to the articulation of similar social and economic conditions through very different discursive principles. Which, in turn, makes interests, forms of identity, program, and political practice different too. That is why Sewell concludes that "to understand why similarly situated Parisians in 1793 defined their interests as consumers, we must know more than that bread made up a large proportion of their expenditures; we must be able to explain how the political culture of their time made the price and availability of bread the crucial question, rather than focusing their attention on the financially equivalent question of obtaining sufficient wages to pay for bread" (262). In other words, we must know through what discursive categories (natural right to subsistence or labor) meaning has been conferred on the social situation and the corresponding program of action designed to deal with it (demand of a maximum or reorganization of labor).

III

The new theory of social action outlined here underlies the conception of *political action* furthered by postsocial history. For a long time, historians had conceived of politics either as a causally autonomous subjective sphere (traditional history and revisionism) or as a representation of social interests and identities (social history). Postsocial history, however, by making a distinction between political *discourse* and political *vocabulary* (that is, between the underlying categorial matrix and the forms of consciousness or ideologies that result from applying it to political life), confers a new causal origin on political action. Since it is the mediation of political discourse that provides individuals with the diagnosis of their situation, constitutes them as political subjects, and defines their interests in this terrain, it is such a mediation that prefigures a certain course of action and makes certain conflicts and power relations natural.[18] As Margaret Somers asserts, political action is not an exteriorization of social interests, but the result of deploying a "conceptual network," like the "Anglo-American citizenship theory," which constitutes a "structural relational matrix of theoretical principles and conceptual assumptions" according to which individuals organize, configure, and make sense of their political practice.[19]

This is, for instance, the theoretical stance adopted by Keith Baker in his analysis of the French Revolution. Baker also takes the distinction between categorial framework (what he calls "political culture") and subjectivity as his starting point, thus maintaining that the former is neither a reflection of social context nor is it a subjective device created and handled by agents. Instead, "political culture" is a prior instance that takes an active part in the shaping of political identities and the conflicts that divide them and which molds, guides, and makes sense of political practice. In the specific case of the French Revolution, Baker argues, political language is not an instrument in the hands of revolutionary actors. On the contrary, these revolutionary actors "were constantly swept away by the power of a language that each proved unable to control."[20] Consequently, the causes of the Revolution are not to be found in either the socioeconomic context or in the ideological sphere, but in the mediation of a political culture that forges the actors themselves and authorizes their actions. In his own words, this political culture "comprises the definitions of the relative subject-positions from which individuals and groups may (or may not) legitimately make claims one upon another and, therefore, of the identity and boundaries of the community to which they belong. It constitutes the meanings of the terms in which these claims are framed, the nature of the contexts to which they pertain, and the authority of the principles according to which they are made binding. It shapes the constitution and powers of the agencies and procedures by which contestations are resolved, competing claims authoritatively adjudicated and binding decisions enforced" (4–5). According to Baker, social history, by conceiving Revolution as the result of the "rise of the bourgeoisie to power as an expression of an objective historical necessity," is incapable of perceiving the key phenomenon, namely the appearance of a new form of political discourse that institutes new modes of political action. It is incapable of grasping the constitutive intervention of the language that underlies the revolutionary process (18).

That is why Baker criticizes the theses of authors like François Furet and Lynn Hunt that what happens during the Revolution is that subjectivity becomes *temporarily* independent of its social base and the conflict of social interests is replaced by a symbolic struggle around the conceptual definition of legitimacy. As Furet argues, according to Baker, the collapse of royal authority in 1789 caused the relationship between power and social interests to be disrupted. As a consequence, social interests were suspended in favor of an outbidding of the idea over real history and the social order was reconstituted at the level of ideology. It is not, however, Baker objects, that, in a juncture of crisis and very rapid change, the symbolic sphere becomes provisionally independent of its social base and language and by virtue of this acquires such a performative capacity. It is, rather, that language *always* has this capacity and it is *always* an active generator both of interests and of the political behavior implicit in them. The "linguisticality" is not an exceptional parenthesis or a peculiar feature of the French Revolution, but a *permanent* historical condition (7–8). Both Furet and Hunt, operating with a dichotomous theoretical model, are unable to distinguish between political discourse and vocabulary and, therefore, any causal detachment of political action with respect to social context leads them inexorably to restoring intentional explanation. However, as Baker argues, political action is not a symbolic practice but a discursive one. Which is precisely why, in order to understand and explain the French Revolution, it is necessary to identify the field of political discourse and to reconstitute the political culture or the set of linguistic patterns and relationships that made it possible (24).

The political culture that generated the Revolution was, argues Baker, forged over the eighteenth century by substituting the absolutist mold with a new discursive framework that, by having the concept of *public opinion* as its cornerstone, triggered a shift in the source of legitimacy of political authority from the crown to civil society. This new political culture was the result of a disaggregation of the attributes traditionally bound together in the concept of monarchical authority—reason, justice, and will—and of its reconceptualization in a language of "social science" and natural and rational order that made the French Revolution "thinkable" and, therefore, possible. It was this language that supported the program of administrative uniformity, civil rights, fiscal equality, and representation of social interests through participation in political management. It provided, as well, the foundations for reconstituting the new social order on principles like property, public utility, rights of man, national sovereignty, and representation or responsible government (24–26 and 199).

It is the decline, precisely, of the instrumentalist notion of political language and of the representationist conception of politics that has forced historians to redefine the genesis and nature of both political conflicts and political power. Let me take a brief look at this. Previously, political struggles had been conceived in terms of ideological confrontation or, as some authors put it, of a struggle to appropriate or adjudicate meanings to political concepts and, thus, impose one criterion of legitimacy or another. This conception is based on the assumption that political identities are pregiven in another sphere and concur to political arena for the purpose of attaining interests (be they natural or social) that are also pregiven. However, if, as postsocial history maintains, such identities, as well as their interests, are constituted in the space of signification created by the mediation of political discourse, then the relationships they enter into and the conflicts between them cannot have an external causal foundation either. Instead, they must be forged through the same process of discursive mediation. It is this process that creates the conditions of emergence of certain conflicts, that establishes the terms, objectives, and the scope of the confrontation, that makes mutual demands intelligible, and that provides agents with the rhetorical resources they use. Thus, it is not a case of different political options trying to impose their definitions of categories like democracy, liberty, or equality, to mention an ordinary example. It is the existence of such categories that allows the corresponding conflicts to emerge around them. As I have already noted, the major political conflicts of modern society are not triggered by political exclusion, deprivation of rights, or social inequalities, but by the fact that these circumstances have been made meaningful (and, in consequence, regarded as unjust or unnatural) through categories like democracy, liberty, or equality.

This implies that political struggles are always causally immersed within a *shared discourse* and that it is what defines the object, the terms, and the scope of the disputes to which all the political options involved adhere. As sociologists Jeffrey Alexander and Phillip Smith state, referring to the so-called discourse of American Civil Society, a shared discourse constitutes "a semantic commensurability" or underlying common code that imposes an "underlying consensus" on all political options.[21] This seems to be the case, for instance, in the relationship between socialism and liberalism, as both share the same basic assumptions of the modern discourse to which they belong (what would also explain that socialist revolutions have not been able to transcend liberal society). Historians such as Patrick Joyce, James Vernon, and Keith Baker have paid careful attention to the presence, historical role, and explanatory relevance of shared discourse. Joyce has expressly pointed out different situations in which diverse, even opposing, political options share and operate within the same discursive pattern or social imaginary. According to him, this is what occurs in France after the revolution of 1848, when "the social," like the expression of "progress" and the "modern," became the common substrate of political and social struggles.[22] Likewise, social relations in Victorian England "can in large part be understood in terms of the concordances and discordances operating within shared discourses about the social, whether we think of these in terms of collective subjects like humanity, myths of origin such as those clustering around the value of independence, or the 'roles' of gender."[23] James Vernon, in his study of nineteenth-century British politics,[24] also maintains that the constitutionalist discourse represents a "master narrative" or "shared" language within which are constituted in this period not only the competing political groups

and their constituencies of support, but also the conflicts between them
(295–96). Beyond the particular interpretations of the constitution, there is
a conceptual framework, common to Tories, Whigs, and radicals, which
imposes a limited range of interpretative possibilities, which enables the
different political options to make themselves mutually intelligible, and
which defines the patterns of their confrontation.[25] The "genius of the constitutional master-narrative," writes Vernon, was not only "that it enabled
political groups to make this great mass of diverse and often conflicting
identities coherent, and thus empowered its subjects with a sense of
agency," but also that all the competing groups based their own interpretation of the nation's past and its future destiny on the same "shared
tropes" (328).

The appearance of postsocial history has also, then, brought with it a
new concept of political power. In the past, historians had conceived of
and analyzed political power in terms of social control and ideological imposition. These historians rely on a double assumption. First, that political power is an effect or function of social divisions. Second, that the
prime means through which political domination is settled, kept up, and
legitimated is ideology, understood as a false consciousness imposed on
the dominated to prevent them from recognizing their objective interests
and from achieving full identity self-awareness. At the same time, the existence of an objective social structure was the condition for the appearance of a true consciousness. The dominated have the possibility, in the
course of practice and by means of ideological criticism, of ripping the
ideological veil between their consciousness and reality, replacing false
consciousness with a true one, and of, thus, winning the dispute over the
control of objectivity. However, in the light of postsocial's theory of society, this conception of political power has been shown to be excessively
reductionist and formal, as well as analytically unsatisfactory. Postsocial
history upholds that while political power always has a social base, the
former is not a causal effect of the latter. Political power is the result of applying a certain regime of political rationality, or, expressed in Foucauldian terms, a certain mode of governmentality. This is fundamentally
so because, as I have stressed, the organizing categories of political power
are not ideological creations of the dominant identity, but come from a
discursive substrate that not only precedes and transcends such an identity, but it is also what enables it to become constituted as such.[26] Which
entails, as well, that the political relationship between the dominant and
the dominated is not previously inscribed in the sphere of socioeconomic
relations, but depends on the specific way both are subjectified, as well as
on the historical function implied in this subjectivization. From this point
of view, power is not just simply something that the dominant apply to or
impose upon the dominated, but a *meaningful relationship* in which the

two are involved. Political power is not just a vertical link, it is also, if I may use the metaphor, a dense horizontal weft. Nor should the state only be conceived, in a literal sense, as an apparatus of domination (which it is), but also as the institutionalization of a certain modality of meaningful articulation of political power. Baker has defined this new concept of political power very clearly. He carefully argues the following: if "a community exists only to the extent that there is some common discourse by which its members can constitute themselves as different groups within the social order and make claims upon one another that are regarded as intelligible and binding" and if, moreover, the "interaction involved in the framing of such claims is constrained within that discourse, which it in turn sustains, extends and on occasions transforms," then political authority is indeed "a matter of linguistic authority." First, "in the sense that political functions are defined and allocated within the framework of a given political discourse," and second "in the sense that their exercise takes the form of upholding authoritative definitions of the terms within that discourse."[27]

None of this should be understood to be saying political domination does not exist or that it has no connection whatsoever with socioeconomic stratification. What postsocial history does (once again in Foucauldian terms) is to distinguish between a state of domination on the one hand and power relations on the other. That is, between the mere material fact of political domination of some social groups by others and the meaningful arrangement this domination adopts, depending on the social imaginary through which it has been erected and according to which it is exercised. This is not a merely formal distinction between two components of political power. It implies that all political domination is always articulated by certain power relations, in the sense that domination is not generated by social divisions, but by the specific way in which these are made meaningful through a particular political discourse. The connection between social supremacy and political domination exists, but the connection is not natural or causal but rhetorical, and therefore power is not just a social relation, but also a discursively constructed relation. That is why, postsocial historians stress that in order to explain why political domination adopts a given form and follows certain logic, it is not anywhere near sufficient to simply identify the social groups in conflict. It is also necessary to reconstruct the system of meanings within which they have been constituted as political subjects and act as such. Otherwise, for example, the enduring perception of political relations between the middle class and the working class in terms of revolution *versus* antirevolution would be unintelligible. What explains such a political relation it is not the social inequality between the two classes, but the fact that the modern discourse objectified the working class as a revolutionary subject. As well as the fact that the bourgeoisie, whose members share with those of the working class the same discursive community, gave credit to such an objectivization.

The fact that political power is exercised not through but within discourse has a double implication. On the one hand, what guarantees the efficacy of political domination is not ideological manipulation (founded on a supremacy of social resources), but the existence of a basic discursive consensus between the dominant and the dominated to which this domination is logically, conceptually, and rhetorically anchored. On the other hand, it is this discursive consensus that also confers efficacy on the *resistance* to domination. Domination and resistance are not two incommensurable forces fighting to impose their respective forms of legitimacy. They are two differential components of the same system of meaning and therefore they presuppose each other. The same categories, principles, or social imaginary that establish the conditions that make domination possible are what organize and authorize resistance to it. In the standard view, resistance is the result of the fact that dominated groups either create a counterideology (social history) or they appropriate the dominant ideology and reuse it as a weapon against the dominant (new cultural history). As Marc W. Steinberg says, for example, in a classical new cultural formulation based on Bakhtinian dialogism, resistance is a "process of counter-hegemony."[28] For postsocial history, however, what happens is not that the dominated appropriate the dominant ideology, but that the same discourse that institutionalizes domination authorizes, makes thinkable, and sets the patterns of the political contestation to this domination. The categories that settle and authorize domination are the same ones that make resistance thinkable. And, therefore, what dominated groups do is not to express their social interests by means of the dominant ideology, but to articulate them through the same discourse and develop the possibilities and contradictions of it. As we have seen, for example, the categories of the liberal discourse (like property or labor) that laid the foundations of political exclusion are the same ones that made conceivable and gave rise to the resistance to such exclusion. As Joan Scott argues, the issue is less one of opposition between domination and resistance, control and agency, than one of a complex process that constructs possibilities for and puts limits on specific actions undertaken by individuals and groups.[29] From this point of view, a revolution would not be— as social history claims—an ideological unmasking of domination, but a collapse of the discursive community and of its power relations. A revolution is, as Baker states, no more than a discursive break, the appearance of a new form of discursive rationality constituting new modes of political and social action. That is, "a transformation of the discursive practice of the community, a moment in which social relations are reconstituted and the discourse defining the political relations between individuals and groups is radically recast" (as happened in France in 1789).[30]

At this point I consider it crucial to insist on the necessity of avoiding a common historiographical error, namely, mistaken equation of the post-social approach with revisionism, specifically in the field of political history. Many scholars often fail to distinguish between, on the one hand, revisionist endeavor to make the political realm or ideologies autonomous (from social context) and, on the other, postsocial assertion that the terms of political practice are always set by a shared background of categories or principles. This is, for instance, a distinction that Richard Price ignores, leading him to conflate revisionist and discursive approaches to popular politics in nineteenth-century Britain.[31] However, since they still work within the dichotomous model, revisionist historians, like Eugenio Biagini for example, disconnect any causality whatsoever between political action and social location of actors. The same occurs, as I have noted, in Gareth Stedman Jones's rethinking of Chartism. In following the so-called Cambridge School or contextualism, Jones limits himself to stating that the ideology and practice of Chartist movement lack any causal relationship with the socioeconomic situation or living conditions of its members. Postsocial historians, on the contrary, as we have just seen, desist from thinking politics in standard dual terms and seek explanation of political practice in the mediation of the political rationality prevailing in each juncture. Thus, for them, it is not a question of making political identities more or less independent of their social referents, but of recovering the very constructive process by which the political itself and the involved identities are produced. This point is clear, for example, in James Vernon's critical review of the book by Catherine Hall, Keith McClelland, and Jane Rendall.[32] As Vernon argues, referring to the Rendall approach to the exclusion of women from the political arena, it is not a question of broadening our conception of the political to incorporate women's participation, but of analyzing how the political was constituted in order to prevent such a participation. For liberalism is not simply an ideology but a way of structuring political identities and struggles, including those of the movement for women's suffrage. And the same could be said, according to Vernon, about Hall's approach to class and race. In this case too, liberalism managed to produce the colonial order of things or the liberal political subject and its racialized others. Vernon certainly criticizes, therefore, "the latent materialism of the book," but not with the purpose of replacing it with idealism and restoring the autonomy of political actors, but of highlighting, instead, the constitutive role of linguistic settings that are beyond the control of these agents.

IV

So far I have mainly referred to society as an object of perception, but I have said very little about society as a real entity. I should not, however, conclude without drawing attention to the fact that both aspects are inextricably linked and presuppose each other, as the new concept of social action involves a profound rethinking of the nature of society as a phenomenon. To start with, if the meaningful actions of individuals have their origin in discursive mediation—and not in social determination—then society would not be an autonomous sphere endowed with an internal mechanism of self-reproduction, but rather the result of the practical projection of a certain discursive pattern. If meta-narrative categories and their social imaginary arrange people's meaningful practice, then they also arrange the social relations these people enter into and produce the social context that will be, later, the object of meaningful grasping. Thus, discourse does not only make, in the terms outlined, a meaningful construction of society. It also makes an *effective* construction of society, as discourse is continually becoming embodied in social relations, institutions, and norms. This is what leads postsocial authors to conceive of society not as a rational (traditional history) or as an objective (social history) entity nor as a symbolic (new cultural history) one, but to conceive of society as a *semiotic* entity.

The work of Richard Biernacki gives us an example of discursive construction of social relations and of the semiotic character of these relations. Here the focus is on the relations of production.[33] Biernacki's inquiry shows that the relationships individuals enter into in production and the specific way in which production is organized do not obey a kind of logic inherent in the economic sphere or in production itself, but depend on the conceptual background prevailing in each case. This background operates as an independent historical variable that does not merely mediate in the interpretation of reality but takes an active part in shaping this reality and imposes its logic on it. According to Biernacki, a comparative study of the wool textile industry in Germany and Britain during the nineteenth century demonstrates that even though economic circumstances surrounding the development of this branch of the industry are similar in both countries, the relations between employers and employees and the organization of production vary, depending on differences in conceptual patterns, specifically on the concept of labor as a commodity each country holds. German employers and workers understood employment as timed appropriation of workers' labor power and disposition over the workers' labor activity, whereas British owners and workers saw employment as the appropriation of workers' materialized labor via its products. In the case of Germany, when employers and workers enacted the conveyance of labor as an abstract substance, they founded the transaction on the sale of the disposition over the workers' labor activity and on the appropriation of labor power. In contrast, in the British case, employers and workers enacted the principle that the capitalist employment relations rested on the appropriation of abstract labor as it was carried in tangible products. The essential point is that this difference in the definition of the concept of labor structured the most fundamental aspects of industrial relations, including methods of remuneration, definition of wages, calculation of output and costs, disciplinary techniques, rights to employment, formulation of grievances, the design of factory buildings, and even the apperception of time and space. And thus, for example, whereas the British weavers were required to deliver products at a regular pace to their employers, but not necessarily their personal labor time, German weavers contracted for disposal over their personal labor time itself and had to show up in person. In the same way, the piece rate scales in each country reflect this difference between the transfer of "embodied labor" (Britain) and the transfer of the disposition over the labor activity (Germany). In the former case, payment is based on the inches of cloth produced, whereas in the latter case it is based on the number of shots executed. And that is why German workers complained about the intensification of work in terms of thousands of shots executed, not in terms of inches of cloth delivered (as in Britain).[34]

With the advent of postsocial history and its concept of social action, not only has the notion of social structure as an instance that bears intrinsic meanings entered into decline, but postsocial history has also triggered the crisis swirling around the notion of society as an autonomous entity located outside human action, generated and reproduced independently of any such action. In the materialist paradigm, society is conceived as possessing an internal mechanism of working and transformation, and therefore human action, since it is socially determined, appears as merely implementing or realizing such a mechanism. Social history admits, of course, that socioeconomic relations are constituted of meaningful actions, and not just of material ones. But on considering both as immediate expressions of social structure, it makes no ontological distinction between the two. New cultural history, on asserting the symbolic nature of meaningful actions, grants these a power to re-create social structure that was previously absent.[35] Nevertheless, given the symbolic (and, therefore, representational) nature of meaningful actions, new cultural historians continue to be constrained within structural limits and, in the last analysis, they end up reproducing the logic of the social structure itself.

However, if the historical agents' subjectivity is not a representation, of whatever kind, of socioeconomic conditions but the result of the meaningful articulation of them, then society does not generate or reproduce itself through action. Instead, society *is produced and reproduced by action itself.* In other words, if social practice and the resulting social relations are the outcome of a discursive mediation, then social conditions are not reproduced by themselves, but through discursive mediation itself. Which means that new social situations are not objectively implicit in the former ones but are engendered in the process of interaction of the former with a certain discursive pattern. It is in this way, for example, that a process of social change like the transition from feudalism to capitalism should be explained. This transition is not the effect of a structural contradiction that manifests itself and is resolved on the plane of political action, but this political action is born, instead, of the rearticulation of social conditions through a new pattern of meanings or social imaginary. Such a transition, then, did not come about because new socioeconomic conditions emerge, but as a consequence of the meanings with which these conditions were endowed through the categories of modern discourse. Beyond this articulation, there is no structural causal factor (hidden or underlying), but only an accumulation of social and material facts that are objects of meaningful construction. Postsocial history avows the following: no social phenomenon—be it production or human rationality—is outside of discursive mediation or can operate as the final, unconditioned causal foundation of social relations and exchanges, and social relations including their transformation over time originate in constant interaction between meta-narrative matrices and the other domains of society. Postsocial history thus replaces the former organic picture of society with a new, dynamically complex depiction.

Conclusion

A New Agenda
for Historical Studies

If my analysis concerning the recent developments and current theoretical state of historical studies is actually accurate, then it would not seem too audacious to conclude that historical science is presently experiencing a new change of paradigm and not a merely thematic or methodological shift. And, if indeed such significant transformation has occurred, historians would want to consider adopting a different agenda for historical research and would be encouraged, as well, to reexamine prior historical interpretations, just as social historians did decades ago. Furthermore, if my survey of the path traveled by historical scholarship in the last few years is near the mark, postsocial history not only exists but also entails explicit discontinuity, a sharp break from previous kinds of history, and specifically so with respect to the immediately preceding kind—new cultural history—from which to a large extent postsocial history has emerged. Even though much background does lay in rethinking and making more flexible the connection between social reality and consciousness, fundamental matter for new cultural historians, postsocial history is not a mere continuation of the tendency to confer greater relative autonomy upon cultural sphere and human intentionality. Instead, postsocial history involves steady shedding of the dichotomous theoretical model and its constitutive terms. Finally, if postsocial history has done more than just rethink the form of the relationship between social position and consciousness and has, as I claim, substantially redefined the very nature of such a relationship, then this makes postsocial history basically incompatible with new cultural history.

Unlike the appraisal many scholars sustain, "linguistic turn" is not a continuation of "cultural turn."[1] Discursive history is not an extension or

radicalization of new cultural history, as such a radicalization relentlessly
leads to restoration, whether partial or total, of human agency and inherently implies eschewal, far from even slight endorsement, of linguistic
mediation. Let me draw attention to what is, in my opinion, a highly illustrative sample of the theoretical logic actually driving new cultural historians (as well as of the iron tyranny of the dichotomous model) expressed in a recent piece by Sarah Maza. She begins by claiming cultural
realm is not just mere epiphenomenon nor reflection of social conditions,
but that the cultural sphere plays an active role in shaping social processes
by providing historical actors with the symbolic devices through which
they understand reality. Then, Maza goes on to equate cultural autonomy
and human agency, given her assumption that any weakening of the social in historical explanation involves a strengthening of agents' freedom.
She finally ends up conferring autonomy on ideas, converts the social into
a subjectively imagined entity, and advocates fully restoring human
agency. According to her, "restoring agency to actors in the past includes
granting *them* the freedom to imagine and define the social world in
which they lived."[2] In front of this, conciliation between the two kinds of
history, making them compatible (or at least complementary), as some
purport, defies the feasible. Assertions like that of Marc Steinberg that
new cultural history and postsocial history "can be wedded," as well as
his subsequent argumentation, seem to be founded on rather inaccurate
understanding of the terms, depth, and implications of present-day theoretical shift in historical studies.[3] According to Steinberg, the autonomy
new cultural historians (like E. P. Thompson) conferred on "culture, politics, and language" foreshadowed the new outlook on "the determinative
force of discourse." There is, he argues, a homology to be observed when
comparing the gap between social being and social consciousness and the
gap between signifier and signified. In both cases, according to him, discourse mediates people's engagement with the social world, providing
them with the foundations for human agency and the diachrony of social
change.[4] Here, Steinberg seems to fall prey to a patent mistake, as he not
only confuses cultural mediation with discursive mediation but also
mixes up the notions of language on which each is found. For new cultural history, language continues to be a cultural entity and a means of expression, even if symbolic, of objective meanings. And therefore, the effect
of its mediation can do no more than confer greater freedom of action to
individuals vis-à-vis the structural coercion of social context. For postsocial history, in contrast, language is a specific historical entity whose mediation generates both objectivity and subjectivity and arranges the relationship into which the two enter.

For similar reasons, postsocial history should not be confused, as sometimes happens, with the explicit move toward a return to subjectivism

that so-called revisionism advances. As some historians emphasize, the new theory of society is not an *inversion* of the dichotomous objectivist model of social history, but one that entails a new theoretical scheme. As Joan Scott succinctly remarks, since the new type of history abandons any opposition between objective determination and its subjective effects, it cannot be considered the reverse of social history.[5] To put it in the words of John E. Toews: the ongoing theoretical shift in historical studies is indeed a question of abandoning both the "psychological and sociological theories that provided models for relating experience to meaning in terms of representation, cause or expression." That is, as he elucidates further, a question of adopting other theories that "recognize language in all its density and opacity as the place where meaning is constituted," namely, as a set of impersonal and anonymous procedures and rules which determines "what can be said and how it can be said" and which constructs, "in a very practical and active sense," the "world of objects and subjects, the world of 'experience.'"[6]

As a result of this recent theoretical shift, historians have been compelled to increasingly embrace a new agenda for historical research. I have previously referred, time and again, to this issue but it is worth stressing one final time. For traditional history, given its subjectivist outlook, the goal of historical inquiry is to reenact and comprehend the motives and intentions of agents and their intellectual universe and system of ideas, beliefs, and values in general, all of which are considered rational human creations. For social history, given its objectivist outlook, the conscious practice of agents is no more than an expression of social context, and therefore the aim of historical inquiry is to reenact such a context. It is obvious, however, that with the advent of postsocial history and its questioning of both intentional and structural explanation (as well as the new cultural combination of the two), historical inquiry must change its goals. Postsocial history brings into view convincing argumentation that people always experience their social world or enter into meaningful relation with it through the active mediation of a discursive social imaginary and the latter endows social reality with meaning, confers historical existence on interests and identities, and triggers, guides, and gives sense to meaningful actions. If this depiction is an essentially correct one and if, above all, as postsocial history upholds, discourse does, by projecting itself in practice, actively contribute to the making of social events, processes, relations, and institutions, then the prime objective of historical research must be to identify, specify, and unravel the categorial system of meanings that operate in each case. This means, specifically, historical studies need to analyze the exact terms of discursive mediation between individuals and their social and material conditions of existence and to assess the performative effects of that mediation on the making of practices and social relations. This is what would enable us to explain the forms of consciousness and the modalities of action, to make historical processes and changes intelligible, and to explain the genesis and evolution of societies.

Patrick Joyce provides an astute and pithy commentary on needed historical focus: if the social world is at bottom a discursive construct, then it is only by looking at the principles of its construction that any headway will be made—and this applies to both the history of the social and the theory of the social.[7] Which, in turn, implies, as I have already indicated, that any explanation of social actions and events requires a thorough analysis of the process of historical formation of concepts themselves. Only this kind of analysis, argues Joan Scott, enables us to satisfactorily respond to essential questions like the following ones: "How have categories of representation and analysis—such as class, race, gender, relations of production, biology, identity, subjectivity, agency, experience, even culture—achieved their foundational status? What have been the effects of their articulations? What does it mean for historians to study the past in terms of these categories and for individuals to think of themselves in these terms?"[8]

The arrival of this new analytical imperative is what explains why, in recent times, language has become more and more the point of entry or starting position when embarking upon historical inquiry today. As Richard Biernacki shrewdly notes, historians are inclined to concentrate increasingly on the implicit schemes organizing practice, instead of on representations *of*, or *for*, practice.[9] Without crucial, requisite attention to language and its performative role in making both meanings and social relations, the imposition of oversimplified models on the study of society would persist and continue to perpetuate conventional understandings and close the door shut against the promising possibilities of new explanatory probes.[10]

Notes

INTRODUCTION

1. This theoretical shift is not of course an isolated phenomenon, or exclusive to history; it affects other social sciences at the same time.

2. Some authors have expressed themselves in these terms. See, for instance, Lawrence Stone, "History and Post-Modernism," *Past and Present* 135 (1991): 217.

3. Patrick Joyce, "The End of Social History?" *Social History* 20, no. 1 (1995): 74.

4. The impact on social sciences of the denaturalization of modern categories has been attentively and perceptively dealt with by authors like Margaret R. Somers. She is the one who insists on the necessity of a "historical sociology of concept formation" and who would give this a crucial role in the theoretical and epistemological renewal of social sciences. See especially, "What's Political or Cultural about Political Culture and the Public Sphere? Toward an Historical Sociology of Concept Formation," *Sociological Theory* 13, no. 2 (1995): 113–44; "Narrating and Naturalizing Civil Society and Citizenship Theory: The Place of Political Culture and the Public Sphere," *Sociological Theory* 13, no. 3 (1995): 229–74; and "The Privatization of Citizenship: How to Unthink a Knowledge Culture," in *Beyond the Cultural Turn: New Directions in the Study of Society and Culture*, ed. Victoria E. Bonnell and Lynn Hunt (Berkeley and Los Angeles: University of California Press, 1999), 121–61.

In the task of studying the historical emergence and transformation of concepts, so-called conceptual history has become, of course, an essential tool. Both in its idealist-oriented version of Anglophone contextualism (authors like J. G. A. Pocock or Quentin Skinner) and in its social-oriented version in German scholarship, for example, Reinhart Koselleck and the *Begriffsgeschichte*. This is a salient episode in historical scholarship that I cannot consider here.

5. In his own words, "the last two decades have seen a dizzying intellectual history. We have moved from a time when social history and social analysis seemed

to be capturing the central ground of the profession and the force of social determinations seemed axiomatic to a new conjuncture in which 'the social' has come
to seem ever less definite and social determinations have surrendered their previous sovereignty. The road from 'relative autonomy' and 'structural causality' (the
hard-won gains of the 1970s) to the 'discursive character of all practices' (the post-
structuralist axiom of the 1980s) has been rapid and disconcerting, and the per-
suasiveness of the antireductionist logic has been extraordinarily hard to with-
stand (rather like an up escalator with no way down)." (Geoff Eley, "Is All the
World a Text? From Social History to the History of Society Two Decades Later,"
in *The Historic Turn in the Human Sciences*, ed. Terrence J. McDonald [Ann Arbor:
University of Michigan Press, 1996], 213–14).

6. Of course, other names could be used. For reasons that will become clear
later on, it could, for example, be called *Discursive History*. In any case, if this historiographical shift becomes consolidated, future debate will undoubtedly give us
the definitive name.

CHAPTER 1

1. In this case too, I refer to the abundant literature available, of which I can
only mention a small sample here. For an overview of the internal evolution of so-
cial history, see, for example, Lynn Hunt, "Introduction: History, Culture and
Text," in *The New Cultural History*, ed. Lynn Hunt (Berkeley and Los Angeles: Uni-
versity of California Press, 1989); Peter Burke, "Overture: The New History, Its
Past and Its Future," in *New Perspectives on Historical Writing*, ed. Peter Burke
(Cambridge, U.K.: Polity Press, 1991), 1–23, and *Varieties of Cultural History* (Ithaca,
N.Y.: Cornell University Press, 1997); and Georg G. Iggers, *Historiography in the
Twentieth Century. From Scientific Objectivity to the Postmodern Challenge* (Hanover,
N.H.: Wesleyan University Press, 1997), part III. See also the brilliant account by
Ronald Grigor Suny, "Back and Beyond: Reversing the Cultural Turn?" *American
Historical Review* 107, no. 5 (2002): 1476–89.

2. Joyce Appleby, Lynn Hunt, and Margaret Jacob, *Telling the Truth about History*
(New York: W. W. Norton and Company, 1994), 218 and 220. The emphasis is
mine. Lawrence Stone had already expressed himself in similar terms in his well-
known article of 1979. According to Stone, this historiographical reorientation has
its roots in the "disillusionment with the economic determinist model of historical
explanation and this three-tiered hierarchical arrangement to which it gave rise."
And he also added, later on: "many historians now believe that the culture of the
group, and even the will of the individual, are potentially at least as important
causal agents of change as the impersonal forces of material output and demographic growth." (Lawrence Stone, "The Revival of Narrative: Reflections on a
New Old History," *Past and Present* 85 [1979], 8–9.)

3. Lynn Hunt, "History Beyond Social Theory," in *The States of "Theory": History, Art and Critical Discourse*, ed. David Carroll (New York: Columbia University
Press, 1990), 102.

4. Raphael Samuel, "Reading the Signs," *History Workshop Journal* 32 (1991): 90
and 92.

5. The expression is from Peter N. Stearns, "Toward a Wider Vision: Trends in Social History," in *The Past Before Us: Contemporary Historical Writing in the United States*, ed. Michael Kamen (Ithaca, N.Y.: Cornell University Press, 1980), 224.

6. This is, for example, the expression used by Karin J. MacHardy, "Crisis in History, or: Hermes Unbounded," *Storia della Storiografia* 17 (1990): 6. The term *crumbling* was made popular by François Dosse's work *L'histoire en miettes. Des "Annales" à la "nouvelle histoire"* (Paris: La Découverte, 1987), devoted to the analysis of the aforementioned thematic shift toward cultural realm and the weakening of the classical social history paradigm it implies.

7. The attitude of some social historians, of course, was to dig in against the advance of so-called culturalism, which provoked an early division between "hard-nosed social historians still busy analysing impersonal structures" and "historians of *mentalité*, now chasing ideals, values, mind-sets and patterns of intimate personal behaviour—the more intimate the better." (Stone, "The Revival of Narrative," 21.) A good sample of the former could be the structuralist criticism of Thompsonian "culturalism" (see, for example, respective debate in *History Workshop Journal* 6, 7, and 8 (1978 and 1979).

8. Hunt, "History Beyond Social Theory," 97.

9. These terms are taken from Pierre Bourdieu, a sociologist worth mentioning here, because his work is an explicit point of reference for many new cultural historians. (See Pierre Bourdieu, *The Logic of Practice* [Cambridge, U.K.: Polity Press, 1990], part one.) In the terminology of the sociologist Anthony Giddens (another unavoidable reference in this chapter), it would be a case of escaping from both the "imperialism of the subject" and the "imperialism of the social object." (*The Constitution of Society: Outline of the Theory of Structuration* [Cambridge, U.K.: Polity Press, 1984], 2.)

10. As Roger Chartier writes, "all relations, including those that I call economic or social relations, are organized according to differing forms of logic that put into play and into operation the schemata of perception and appreciation of a variety of social subjects and consequently, the representations that comprise what one can call a 'culture.'" (*Cultural History: Between Practices and Representations* [Cambridge, U.K.: Polity Press, 1988], 47.)

11. In this respect, let us remember, once again, the well-known and reiterated passage from *The Making of the English Working Class*:

> The making of the working class is a fact of political and cultural, as much as of economic, history. It was not the spontaneous generation of the factory system. Nor should we think of an external force—the 'industrial revolution'—working upon some nondescript undifferentiated raw material of humanity, and turning it out at the other end as a 'fresh race of beings.' The changing productive relations and working conditions of the Industrial Revolution were imposed, not upon raw material, but upon the free-born Englishman—and the free-born Englishman as Paine had left him or as the Methodists had moulded him. . . . The working class made itself as much as it was made. (Harmondsworth: Penguin, 1991), 213.

12. See, for example, Edward P. Thompson's argument in "Alcune osservazioni su classe e 'falsa coscienza,'" *Quaderni Storici* 36 (1977): 907.

13. A sample of this "populist turn," as James Epstein has labeled it, is, for example, the work of Patrick Joyce, *Visions of the People: Industrial England and the Question of Class, 1848–1914* (Cambridge: Cambridge University Press, 1991). See James Epstein, "The Populist Turn," *Journal of British Studies* 32 (1993): 177–89.

14. Roger Chartier, *On the Edge of the Cliff: History, Language and Practices* (Baltimore: Johns Hopkins University Press, 1997), 4–5.

15. Roger Chartier, "Différences entre les sexes et domination symbolique," *Annales ESC* 4 (1993): 1007.

16. And this, according to Levi, explains the importance of biography, as this is "an ideal place for verifying the interstitial—but important—nature of the liberty available to agents and for observing the concrete operations of normative systems, which are never totally free of contradictions." ("Les usages de la biographie," *Annales ESC* 6 [1989], 1333–34.)

17. Patrick Joyce, "The End of Social History?" *Social History* 20, no. 1 (1995): 75.

18. The notion of "complementarity" was used, for example, by Eric J. Hobsbawm in his response to Lawrence Stone's article. ("The Revival of Narrative: Some Comments," *Past and Present* 86 [1980]: 3–8.)

19. Peter Schöttler, "Mentalities, Ideologies, Discourses: On the 'Third Level' as a Theme in Social-Historical Research," in *The History of Everyday Life: Reconstructing Historical Experiences and Ways of Life*, ed. Alf Lüdtke (Princeton, N.J.: Princeton University Press, 1989), 72–115.

20. Roger Chartier, "The World as Representation," in *Histories: French Constructions of the Past*, ed. Jacques Revel and Lynn Hunt (New York: The New Press, 1995), 551–52. ["Le monde comme représentation," *Annales ESC* 6 (1989): 1513.] Emphasis mine. On this point, Chartier follows Emile Durkheim and Marcel Mauss.

21. Lynn Hunt, *Politics, Culture, and Class in the French Revolution* (Berkeley and Los Angeles: University of California Press, 1984), 13.

22. Hans Medick, "'Missionaries in the Rowboat'? Ethnological Ways of Knowing as a Challenge to Social History," in *The History of Everyday Life*, ed. Alf Lüdtke, 43.

23. Judith Walkowitz, *City of Dreadful Delight. Narratives of Sexual Danger in Late Victorian London* (London: Virago Press, 1994), esp. 85–86 and ff., and Michael Sonenscher, "The Sans-Culottes of the Year II: Rethinking the Language of Labour in Revolutionary France," *Social History* 9 (1984): 301–28, and *Work and Wages: Natural Law, Politics and the Eighteenth Century French Trades* (Cambridge: Cambridge University Press, 1989), esp. 354–55 and 356–58.

24. Carroll Smith-Rosenberg, *Disorderly Conduct: Visions of Gender in Victorian America* (New York: Oxford University Press, 1985), 45. Elsewhere she writes: "While linguistic differences structure society, social differences structure language." ("The Body Politic," in *Coming to Terms: Feminism, Theory, Politics*, ed. Elizabeth Weed [New York: Routledge, 1989], 101.)

25. See, for instance, Raymond Williams, *Marxism and Literature* (Oxford: Oxford University Press, 1977), esp. chapter 2. This mixed conception of language supports, for example, Gabrielle M. Spiegel's well-known historiographical proposal. Applying her concept of the "social logic of the text" implies, as she writes, that "text both mirror *and* generate social realities, are constituted *and* constitute the social and discursive formations which they may sustain, resist, contest, or seek to transform, depending on the case at hand." ("History, Historicism, and the

Social Logic of the Text in the Middle Ages," *Speculum* 65, no. 1 [1990]: 77, and "History and Post-Modernism, IV," *Past and Present* 135 [1992]: 203 and 206.) Spiegel has put her theoretical conception into practice in *Romancing the Past: The Rise of Vernacular Prose Historiography in Thirteenth Century France* (Berkeley and Los Angeles: University of California Press, 1993.)

26. In my opinion, this is the case of historians like Gareth Stedman Jones (see his "The Determinist Fix: Some Obstacles to the Further Development of the Linguistic Approach to History in the 1990s," *History Workshop Journal* 42 (1996): 19–35). I have discussed and attempted to characterize the Jones's stance in Miguel A. Cabrera, "Linguistic Approach or Return to Subjectivism? In Search of an Alternative to Social History," *Social History* 24, no. 1 (1999): 76–78.

27. See Bernard Lepetit, dir., *Les formes de l'experience. Une autre histoire sociale* (Paris: Albin Michel, 1995), especially the two contributions of Lepetit himself.

28. Natalie Z. Davies, "The Shapes of Social History," *Storia della Storiografia* 17 (1990): 30.

29. Giovanni Levi, "On Microhistory," in *New Perspectives on Historical Writing*, ed. Peter Burke (Cambridge, U.K.: Polity Press, 1991), 94–95. The literature on microhistory is already enormous; for a general introduction, I would suggest the following works: Edoardo Grendi, "Micro-analisi e storia sociale," *Quaderni Storici* 35 (1977): 506–20; Edward Muir and G. Ruggiero, *Microhistory and the Lost Peoples of Europe* (Baltimore: Johns Hopkins University Press, 1991); Carlo Ginzburg, "Microhistory: Two or Three Things That I Know about It," *Critical Inquiry* 20, no. 1 (1993): 10–35; and Jacques Revel, "Micro-analyse et construction du social," in *Jeux d'échelles: La microanalyse à l' expérience*, dir. Jacques Revel (Paris: Gallimard/Le Seuil, 1996), 15–36.

30. Alf Lüdtke, "Sui concetti di vita quotidiana, articolazione dei bisogni e 'coscienza proletaria,'" *Quaderni Storici* 36 (1977): 916–17.

31. Geoff Eley, "Labor History, Social History, *Alltagsgeschichte*: Experience, Culture and the Politics of the Everyday—A New Direction for German Social History?" *Journal of Modern History* 61 (1989): 317. The literature on this topic is also enormous. For a general introduction, see, for example, David F. Crew, "*Alltagsgeschichte*: A New Social History 'From Below'?" *Central European History* 22, nos. 3–4 (1989): 394–407; Carola Lipp, "Writing History as Political Culture: Social History Versus 'Alltagsgeschichte'—A German Debate," *Storia della Storiografia* 17 (1990): 67–100; Alf Lüdtke, ed. *The History of Everyday Life*; or Mathieu Lepetit, "Un regard sur l'historiographie allemande: les mondes de l'*Alltagsgeschichte*," *Revue d'Histoire Moderne et Contemporaine* 42, no. 2 (1998): 466–86.

32. This seems to be what some historians propose. See, for example, Bryan D. Palmer, "Critical Theory, Historical Materialism and the Ostensible End of Marxism: The Poverty of Theory Revisited," *International Review of Social History* 38 (1993): 133–62, and *Descent into Discourse: The Rectification of Language and the Writing of Social History* (Philadelphia: Temple University Press, 1990); or Neville Kirk, "In Defense of Class: A critique of Recent Revisionist Writing upon the Nineteenth-Century English Working Class," *International Review of Social History* 28 (1987): 2–42; and "History, Language, Ideas and Post-Modernism: A Materialist View," *Social History* 19, no. 2 (1994): 221–40.

33. Jon Lawrence and Miles Taylor, "The Poverty of Protest: Gareth Stedman Jones and the Politics of Language—A Reply," *Social History* 18, no. 1 (1993): 5.

CHAPTER 2

1. Margaret R. Somers, "What's Political or Cultural about Political Culture and the Public Sphere? Toward an Historical Sociology of Concept Formation," *Sociological Theory* 13, no. 2 (1995): 131–32.

2. Obviously, this concept of discourse has nothing to do with (nor should it be confused with) the conventionally used concept to designate the language in use, that is, expressions, texts, speech acts, communicational or conversational events, or disciplinary or professional vocabularies. Likewise, although it is distantly related to it, the postsocial concept of discourse should not be confused with the notion that is characteristic of the so-called historical analysis of discourse, developed in the 1970s, especially in France, by some social historians, since in this case the concept of discourse is essentially synonymous with ideology.

3. Joan W. Scott, "Deconstructing Equality versus Difference: or, the Uses of Post-Structuralist Theory for Feminism," *Feminist Studies* 14, no. 1 (1988): 35 and 34.

4. James Vernon, "Who's Afraid of the 'Linguistic Turn'? The Politics of Social History and its Discontents," *Social History* 19, no. 1 (1994): 91.

5. And thus, for example, as Somers herself points out, categories such as "husband breadwinner," "union solidarity," or "women must be independent above all" will selectively appropriate the happenings of the social world, arrange them in some order, and normatively evaluate these arrangements. ("Narrativity, Narrative Identity and Social Action: Rethinking English Working-Class Formation," *Social Science History* 16, no. 4 [1992]: 601 and 602.)

6. Charles Taylor, "Modern Social Imaginaries," *Public Culture* 14, no. 1 (2002): 91–124. In what follows, page numbers are indicated in parentheses. The term *social imaginary* is used in a similar sense, for example, by the following authors: Ernesto Laclau and Chantal Mouffe, *Hegemony and Socialist Strategy: Towards a Radical Democratic Politics* (London: Verso, 1985); Patrick Joyce, *Democratic Subjects: The Self and the Social in Nineteenth-Century England* (Cambridge: Cambridge University Press, 1994), 4; or Mary Poovey, "The Liberal Civil Subject and the Social in Eighteenth-Century British Moral Philosophy," in *The Social in Question*, ed. Patrick Joyce (London: Routledge, 2002), 44–61. As Poovey well notes, Taylor has clearly drawn upon Cornelius Castoriadis, *The Imaginary Institution of Society* (Cambridge, Mass.: MIT Press, 1987).

7. Patrick Joyce, "Introduction," in *The Social in Question: New Bearings in History and the Social Sciences*, ed. Patrick Joyce (London: Routledge, 2002), 5. Here Joyce explicitly draws upon Mary Poovey and Taylor himself.

8. Trevor Purvis and Alan Hunt, "Discourse, Ideology, Discourse, Ideology, Discourse Ideology. . . ." *British Journal of Sociology* 44, no. 3 (1993): 485.

9. Margaret R. Somers, "Narrating and Naturalizing Civil Society and Citizenship Theory: The Place of Political Culture and the Public Sphere," *Sociological Theory* 13, no. 3 (1995): 237 and 234.

10. The expressions are from Somers, "What's Political or Cultural about Political Culture and the Public Sphere?" 135 and 136.

11. The literature on the concept of discourse as system of meanings is abundant. For an excellent overview, see David Howarth, *Discourse* (Buckingham: Open University Press, 2000). You can also see Sara Mills, *Discourse* (London:

Routledge, 1997); Jacob Torfing, *New Theories of Discourse: Laclau, Mouffe and Zizek* (Oxford: Blackwell, 1999), esp. 85–100; David Howarth and Yannis Stavrakakis, "Introducing Discourse Theory and Political Analysis," in *Discourse Theory and Political Analysis: Identities, Hegemonies and Social Change*, ed. David Howarth, Aletta J. Norval, and Yannis Stavrakakis (Manchester, U.K.: Manchester University Press, 2000), 1–23; David Howarth, "An Archeology of Political Discourse? Evaluating Michel Foucault's Explanation and Critique of Ideology," *Political Studies* 50, no. 1 (2002): 117–35; and James Martin, "The Political Logic of Discourse: A Neo-Gramscian View," *History of European Ideas* 28, no. 1 (2002): 21–31. Mariana Valverde offers an interesting view on discourse studies in "Some Remarks on the Rise and Fall of Discourse Analysis," *Histoire Sociale/Social History* 33, no. 65 (2000): 59–77. On the genealogy of the concept of discourse itself, see the suggestive account by R. Keith Sawyer, "A Discourse on Discourse: An Archeological History of an Intellectual Concept," *Cultural Studies* 16, no. 3 (2002): 433–56.

12. David Harlan, "Intellectual History and the Return of Literature," *American Historical Review* 94, no. 3 (1989): 591–92. My emphasis. Harlan refers to J. G. A. Pocock, *Virtue, Commerce and History: Essays on Political Thought and History, Chiefly in the Eighteenth Century* (New York: Cambridge University Press, 1985). In fact, contextualism is one of the most advanced points to which the old hermeneutic and comprehensive history is able to reach without abandoning the concept of rational subjects. Thus it has become one of the main trenches from which many historians are nowadays opposing the new concept of language that has spread over the last two decades. For a general characterization of contextualism, see, for example, Preston King, "Historical Contextualism: The New Historicism?" *History of European Ideas* 21, no. 2 (1995): 209–33.

13. Joan W. Scott, "Reply to Criticism," *International Labor and Working-Class History* 32 (1987): 40; and "On Language, Gender and Working-Class History," *International Labor and Working-Class History* 31 (1987): 1. That is precisely why, as Mariana Valverde remarks, Joan W. Scott's main criticism of Gareth Stedman Jones and his idealist conception of society is that Jones does not understand the concept of language, as he thinks it refers to "words" as opposed to things. ("Poststructuralist Gender Historians: Are We Those Names?" *Labour/Le Travail* 25 [1990], 231.)

14. Stuart Hall has expressed it with far greater propriety and precision: "Meaning is not a transparent reflection of the world in language but arises through the differences between the terms and categories, the systems of reference, which classify out the world and allow it to be in this way appropriated into social thought, common sense." ("Signification, Representation, Ideology: Althusser and the Post-Structuralist Debates," *Critical Studies in Mass Communication* 2, no. 2 [1985]: 108.)

15. The expression is taken from Somers, "What's Political or Cultural about Political Culture and the Public Sphere?" 136. Emphasis mine.

16. Keith Michael Baker, *Inventing the French Revolution: Essays on French Political Culture in the Eighteenth Century* (New York: Cambridge University Press, 1990), 6.

17. John E. Toews, "Intellectual History after the Linguistic Turn: The Autonomy of Meaning and the Irreducibility of Experience," *American Historical Review* 92, no. 4 (1987): 882.

18. Ernesto Laclau and Chantal Mouffe, "Post-Marxism without Apologies," *New Left Review* 166 (1987): 86.

19. For the different senses of the concept of culture in social sciences, see, for example, William H. Sewell Jr., "The Concept(s) of Culture," in *Beyond the Cultural Turn. New Directions in the Study of Society and Culture*, ed. Victoria E. Bonnell and Lynn Hunt (Berkeley and Los Angeles: University of California Press, 1999), 35–61.

20. Anson Rabinbach, "Rationalism and Utopia as Language of Nature: A Note," *International Labor and Working-Class History* 31 (1987): 31.

21. As Mariana Valverde argues, the fundamental effect of introducing the concept of discourse has been to circumvent the words/things dichotomy through understanding social relations as systems of meaning. ("Poststructuralism Gender Historians," 231.)

22. Joyce, *Democratic Subjects*, 12–13 and 14. Anne E. Kane puts it in other words: "*analytically* social action is the 'last stop' in the interpretive process of meaning construction. Because meaning is embodied in the specific arrangement of symbols in cultural models, and cultural models are the first point of reference when people interpret experience, these structures should be the initial theoretical and analytic focus in studying meaning construction. In no case should the internal structure of culture be omitted from the analysis of meaning construction." ("Theorizing Meaning Construction in Social Movements: Symbolic Structures and Interpretation during the Irish Land War, 1879–1882," *Sociological Theory* 15, no. 3 [1997]: 251.)

23. As Ernesto Laclau and Chantal Mouffe say, the fact that objects are meaningful constructions has *nothing to do* with the fact that there is a world external to thought or with the realism-idealism opposition (*Hegemony and Socialist Strategy*, 108).

24. Ian Hacking, "The Making and Moulding of Child Abuse," *Critical Inquiry* 17 (1991): 253. In what follows, page numbers are indicated in parentheses. Of course, Hacking hardly analyzes the historical process of constituting child abuse as an object, and therefore the door is left open for an explanation based either on socioeconomic changes in American society or on the notion of moral progress of human thought. But here I am merely giving an example of object, not of postsocial analysis.

25. Patrick Joyce, "History and Post-Modernism I," *Past and Present* 133 (1991): 208. See Geoff Eley, "Is All the World a Text? From Social History to the History of Society Two Decades Later," in *The Historic Turn in the Human Sciences*, ed. Terrence J. McDonald (Ann Arbor: University of Michigan Press, 1996), 213.

26. William H. Sewell Jr., "How Classes are Made: Critical Reflections on E. P. Thompson's Theory of Working-Class Formation," in *E. P. Thompson: Critical Perspectives*, ed. Harvey J. Kaye and Keith McClelland (London: Polity Press, 1990), 69.

27. William H. Sewell Jr. "Artisans, Factory Workers and the Formation of the French Working Class, 1789–1848," in *Working Class Formation: Nineteenth Century Patterns in Western Europe and the United States*, ed. Ira Katznelson and Aristide Zolberg (Princeton, N.J.: Princeton University Press, 1986), 59.

28. Baker, *Inventing the French Revolution*, 3–4 and 10–11.

29. This weakness has been pointed out, for example, by a critical author like Laura Lee Downs, who censures Joan W. Scott for the fact that, although she studies how discourses work, she does not, however, explain how they change in time.

(Laura Lee Downs, "If Woman Is Just an Empty Category, Then Why Am I Afraid to Walk Alone at Night? Identity Politics Meets the Post-Modern Subject," *Comparative Studies in Society and History* 35, no. 3 [1993]: 422.)

30. This lack is evident, for example, in the work of authors like Keith M. Baker and, specifically, in his studies on the emergence of concepts like those of public opinion or representation, studies that are often limited to a mere descriptive report of the conceptual mutations that have happened. (*Inventing the French Revolution*, chapters 8 and 10.)

31. Marshall Sahlins, *Islands of History* (Chicago: University of Chicago Press, 1985), 144–46 and 148. Of course, as we will see right away, the affinities between Sahlins and postsocial history stop at this point, as he then goes on to rescue the concept of rational subject, since he considers individuals capable of handling inherited categories at will and that, therefore, intentional or rational action is the driving force behind its transformation. However, this position seems to contain contradiction, because, if subjectivity is constituted as such within an inherited categorial framework, it could hardly transcend this to handle it at will.

32. A similar argument can be found in Anne E. Kane, "Theorizing Meaning Construction in Social Movements," 250–51. According to Kane, the meaning system is transformed as people apply it in new contexts and thus recast the previous conceptual set. On this matter, I have also drawn upon John G. Gunnell, "Time and Interpretation: Understanding Concepts and Conceptual Change," *History of Political Thought* 29, no. 4 (1998): 641–58.

33. See, for instance, Giacomo Marramao, *Potere e secolarizzazione* (Roma: Editori Riuniti, 1983) and *Cielo e terra. Genealogía della secolarizzazione* (Roma: Laterza, 1994).

34. See Mary Poovey, "The Liberal Civil Subject and the Social in Eighteenth-Century British Moral Philosophy," in *The Social in Question*, ed. Patrick Joyce (London: Routledge, 2002), 44–61; David A. Bell, *The Cult of the Nation: Inventing Nationalism, 1680–1800* (Cambridge, Mass.: Harvard University Press, 2001), chapters 1 and 2; and "Lingua Populi, Lingua Dei: Language, Religion, and the Origins of French Revolutionary Nationalism," *American Historical Review* 100, no. 6 (1995): 1403–37.

35. William H. Sewell Jr., *Work and Revolution in France: The Language of Labour from the Old Regime to 1848* (New York: Cambridge University Press, 1980), 277. In what follows, page numbers are indicated in parentheses.

36. Laclau and Mouffe, *Hegemony and Socialist Strategy*, 110 and 146 (note 20).

37. Somers, "Narrating and Naturalizing Civil Society and Citizenship Theory," 234 and 236.

38. Christine Stansell, "A Response to Joan Scott," *International Labor and Working-Class History* 31 (1987): 28.

CHAPTER 3

1. David Mayfield, "Language and Social History," *Social History* 16, no. 3 (1991): 357.

2. Joan W. Scott, "A Reply to Criticism," *International Labor and Working-Class History* 32 (1987): 40–41.

3. Here, I am paraphrasing Ernesto Laclau and Chantal Mouffe, "Post-Marxism without Apologies," *New Left Review* 166 (1987): 85.

4. Scott, "A Reply to Criticism," 41.

5. Margaret R. Somers, "Narrating and Naturalizing Civil Society and Citizenship Theory: The Place of Political Culture and the Public Sphere," *Sociological Theory* 13, no. 3 (1995): 237.

6. Although I cannot deal with the question here, let me say that the history of sexuality has been one of the fields postsocial history has most developed and within which historiographical renewal of the theory of society has been outstanding.

7. Elaine Abelson, David Abraham, and Marjorie Murphy, "Interview with Joan Scott," *Radical History Review* 45 (1989): 47.

8. Mary Poovey, *Making a Social Body: British Cultural Formation, 1830–1864* (Chicago: University of Chicago Press, 1995), 5 and 7–9.

9. Mary Poovey, *A History of the Modern Fact: Problems of Knowledge in the Sciences of Wealth and Society* (Chicago: University of Chicago Press, 1998). For a general overview of Poovey's conceptual outlook and conclusions, see "Introduction" and chapter 1.

10. On the concept of articulation, see, for example, Trevor Purvis and Alan Hunt, "Discourse, Ideology, Discourse, Ideology, Discourse, Ideology. . ." *British Journal of Sociology* 44, no. 3 (1993): 492.

11. Geoff Eley, "Is All the World a Text?—From Social History to the History of Society Two Decades Later," in *The Historic Turn in the Human Sciences*, ed. Terrence J. McDonald (Ann Arbor: University of Michigan Press, 1996), 222. According to Eley, "the nineteenth-century discourse of citizenship, no less than the related conceptions of class-collective identity, were immensely complex and powerful formations of this type, which finely ordered the social and political world and structured the possibilities of what could and could not be thought."

12. The expressions in quotation marks are taken from Ernesto Laclau, "Politics and the Limits of Modernity," in *Universal Abandon? The Politics of Post-Modernism*, ed. Andrew Ross (Edinburgh: Edinburgh University Press, 1989), 67, and Mariana Valverde, "Poststructuralist Gender Historians: Are We Those Names?" *Labour/Le Travail* 25 (1990): 229, respectively.

13. Joan W. Scott, "The Evidence of Experience," *Critical Inquiry* 17 (1991): 773–97. Quote from 775–76. In what follows, page numbers are indicated in parentheses. Scott's essay has been widely cited and discussed over the last few years. See, for example, John H. Zammito,"Reading 'Experience': The Debate in Intellectual History among Scott, Toews, and LaCapra," in *Reclaiming Identity: Realist Theory and the Predicament of Postmodernism*, ed. Paula M. L. Moya and Michael R. Hames-García (Berkeley and Los Angeles: University of California Press, 2000), esp. 296–303; Shari Stone-Mediatore, "Chandra Mohanty and the Revaluing of 'Experience,'" *Hypatia* 13, no. 2 (1998): esp. 116–22; and Bruce McConachie, "Doing Things with Image Schemas: The Cognitive Turn in Theatre Studies and the Problem of Experience for Historian," *Theatre Journal* 53, no. 4 (2001): esp. 569–75. For two illuminating overviews on the critical rethinking of the concept of experience and its implications for social studies, see Michael Pickering, *History, Experience, and Cultural Studies* (New York: St. Martin's Press, 1997), and Craig Ireland,

"The Appeal to Experience and its Consequences: Variations on a Persistent Thompsonian Theme," *Cultural Critique* 52 (2002): 86–107.

14. Scott, "A Reply to Criticism," 40. The reference is to Christine Stansell, "A Response to Joan Scott," *International Labor and Working-Class History* 31 (1987): 24–29.

15. Joan W. Scott, "The Tip of the Volcano," *Comparative Studies in Society and History* 35, no. 3 (1993): 439 and 442. This article is a reply to Laura Lee Downs, "If 'Woman' Is Just and Empty Category, Then Why Am I Afraid to Walk Alone at Night? Identity, Politics Meets the Postmodern Subject," Ibid., 414–37. See also Laura Lee Downs, "Reply to Joan Scott," Ibid., 444–51.

16. Scott, "A Reply to Criticism," 39. She refers to Bryan D. Palmer, "Response to Joan Scott," *International Labor and Working-Class History* 31 (1987): 14–23.

17. Scott, "A Reply to Criticism," 40.

18. Scott, "A Reply to Criticism," 41. My emphasis.

19. Joan W. Scott, *Gender and the Politics of History* (New York: Columbia University Press, 1988), 3–4.

20. Patrick Joyce, *Democratic Subjects: The Self and the Social in Nineteenth-Century England* (Cambridge: Cambridge University Press, 1994), 12.

21. Patrick Joyce, ed., *Class* (Oxford: Oxford University Press, 1995), 128.

22. Zachary Lockman, "Workers and 'Working Class' in pre-1914 Egypt: A Rereading," in *Workers and Working Classes in the Middle East: Struggles, Histories, Historiographies*, ed. Zachary Lockman (Albany, N.Y.: State University of New York Press, 1994), 102–103.

23. Ernesto Laclau and Chantal Mouffe, *Hegemony and Socialist Strategy. Towards a Radical Democratic Politics* (London: Verso, 1985). In what follows, page numbers are indicated in parentheses.

24. Joyce, *Democratic Subjects*, 1–2 and 5. Of course, the genealogy of the category of society is an affair that goes beyond the objectives of this essay. In any event, there is accessible and increasingly abundant literature on this subject that one can consult.

25. Keith M. Baker, "Enlightenment and the Institution of Society: Notes for a Conceptual History," in *Main Trends in Cultural History*, ed. Willem Melching and Wyger Velema (Amsterdam: Rodopi, 1994), 114. Some of the expressions used in the previous paragraph also come from this work (111–13 and 119).

26. And the same could be said, of course, about the other basic organizing category of modern social life, that of individual or rational subject. If this category has operated as a guide for practice, it has not done so as an objective phenomenon (that does not exist), but as an object, that is, as one of the historically specific ways of articulating individuals and bodies and, consequently, to confer identity on them (and, of course, of articulating society itself as well, in this case, not as an objective structure, but as a spontaneous aggregate of rational subjects).

27. Nicholas B. Dirks, Geoff Eley, and Sherry B. Ortner, eds., *Culture/Power/History: A Reader in Contemporary Social Theory* (Princeton, N.J.: Princeton University Press, 1994), 29. Eley puts it in similar terms in "Is All the World a Text?" 217.

28. The expression is from Eley, "Is All the World a Text?" 217.

CHAPTER 4

1. Although postsocial historians always refer to interests as historical, explicit phenomena (because it is as such that they condition social practice), they have abandoned every notion of essential interest. This notion was analytically pertinent while historical discussion and inquiry revolved around the greater or lesser fit between consciousness and social structure, but ceases to be pertinent once the existence of the latter is in doubt.

2. Margaret R. Somers, "Narrativity, Narrative Identity and Social Action: Rethinking English Working-Class Formation," *Social Science History* 16, no. 4 (1992): 606.

3. And this is why, as Mariana Valverde argues, to make sense of social action it is indispensable to identify the categories through the mediation of which said interests have emerged. ("The Rhetoric of Reform: Tropes and the Moral Subject," *International Journal of the Sociology of Law* 16 [1990]: 65.)

4. Keith Michael Baker, *Inventing the French Revolution* (Cambridge: Cambridge University Press, 1990), 5. In the words of Baker, "individuals in any reasonably complex society can invariably be seen as occupying any number of relative positions vis-à-vis other individuals, and, therefore as possessing any number of potentially differentiating 'interests.'"

5. As Baker writes, "the nature of 'interest' (or difference) that matters in any particular situation—and in consequence, the identities of the relevant social groups and the nature of their claims—are continually being defined (and redefined)." (*Inventing the French Revolution*, 5–6.)

6. Baker, *Inventing the French Revolution*, 5.

7. Patrick Joyce, *Visions of the People: Industrial England and the Question of Class, 1848–1914* (Cambridge: Cambridge University Press, 1991), 16.

8. These examples are taken from Terry Eagleton, *Ideology: An Introduction* (London: Verso, 1991), 206–11.

9. Eagleton, *Ideology*, 211.

10. Ernesto Laclau and Chantal Mouffe, *Hegemony and Socialist Strategy. Towards a Radical Democratic Politics* (London: Verso, 1985), 84.

11. The expression is Stuart Hall's, one of the leading voices in the ongoing debate on identity. ("Introduction: Who Needs 'Identity'?" in *Questions of Cultural Identity*, ed. Stuart Hall and Paul du Gay [London: Sage, 1996], 1.)

12. That is why, from the perspective of historical studies, it seems so striking, disconcerting, and theoretically disappointing that a substantial part of the discussion on identity not only remains anchored in this primitive phase of struggle against subjectivism (and even against biological essentialism), but above all that it presents arguments that have been around for a long time in the social sciences as if they were something new. This is what can be observed, for example, in the long list of works devoted to attacking the essentialist conception of women, self, race, sex, or nation by merely historizing them, that is, with the postulate that they are all social constructions or cultural creations. However, even if the notion of natural identity has not disappeared from social sciences—and there is no sign that it will do so in the near future—once the notion of social identity has been

questioned, we cannot continue to oppose the former simply with the standard arguments of social causalism. This not only deviates and distances us from the core of the debate, but it also prevents us from making any kind of innovative contribution to this.

13. At this point, I have not been able to resist the temptation to paraphrase Judith Butler's words (*Gender Trouble: Feminism and Subversion of Identity* [London: Routledge, 1990], 1). My emphasis.

14. Joan W. Scott, "The Evidence of Experience," *Critical Inquiry* 17 (1991): 791–92.

15. Patrick Joyce, ed., *Class* (Oxford: Oxford University Press, 1995), 183.

16. The literature on the history of sexuality written from this standpoint is too abundant to fully cite here. As a general introduction, I recommend Arnold I. Davidson, "Sex and the Emergence of Sexuality," *Critical Inquiry* 144 (1987–1988): 14–48. See, also, for merely sampling, the following works by David M. Halperin: "Is There a History of Sexuality?" *History and Theory* 28, no. 3 (1989): 258–74; "Forgetting Foucault: Acts, Identities, and the History of Sexuality," *Representations* 63 (1998): 93–120; "How to Do the History of Male Homosexuality," *GLQ* 6, no. 1 (2000): 87–124; and *How to Do the History of Homosexuality* (Chicago: Chicago University Press, 2002).

17. The concept of interpellation, that comes from Jacques Lacan, was used by Louis Althusser, although in this case in relation to the notion of ideology. Here, I have paid special consideration to the re-elaboration of this concept drawn up by authors like Stuart Hall, "Signification, Representation, Ideology: Althusser and the Post-Structuralist Debates," *Critical Studies in Mass Communication* 2, no. 2 (1985): 102–3, and "Introduction: Who Needs 'Identity?'" 5–7.

18. It is precisely for this reason that the old discussion about the social base of the labor movement (whether they were artisans or industrial workers) has become obsolete and has had to be reconsidered. Because the explanation for the appearance of the labor movement as a form of identity and practice does not lies so much in socioeconomic changes as in the interaction of these changes with a discursive regime that converts into identity objects entities or facts like property, work, exploitation, class position, or the exclusion of the political system.

19. Baker, *Inventing the French Revolution*, 6.

20. Scott, "The Evidence of Experience," 792.

21. James Vernon, "Who's Afraid of the 'Linguistic Turn'? The Politics of Social History and its Discontents," *Social History* 19, no. 1 (1994): 90.

22. Scott, "The Evidence of Experience," 791.

23. Some expressions have been taken from Geoff Eley, "Is All the World a Text? From Social History to the History of Society Two Decades Later," in *The Historic Turn in the Human Sciences*, ed. Terrence McDonald (Ann Arbor: University of Michigan Press, 1996), 220.

24. Joan W. Scott, "The Tip of the Volcano," *Comparative Studies in Society and History* 35, no. 3 (1993): 439.

25. Scott, "The Evidence of Experience," 792–93.

26. Scott, "The Evidence of Experience," 792.

27. Eley, "Is All the World a Text?," 220.

28. Joan W. Scott, *Only Paradoxes to Offer: French Feminists and the Rights of Man* (Cambridge, Mass.: Harvard University Press, 1996). Page numbers are indicated in parentheses.

29. Dena Goodman, "More than Paradoxes to Offer: Feminist History as Critical Practice," *History and Theory* 36, no. 3 (1997): 394–95. This article is a review of Scott's book.

30. It is not, of course, a contradiction, as social history maintains, between the discourse and an objective social exterior (the situation of women), but a contradiction engendered by the discourse itself and that therefore can only acquire an existence and become thinkable within this discourse. It is the social institutionalization of the categories of modern-liberal discourse and the simultaneous constitution of the feminist identity that made possible the emergence of a conflict between declaration of rights and feminine exclusion, a conflict that could not exist previously. The political subordination and exclusion of women is only a motive of conflict and of identity affirmation once the aforementioned discourse is applied. One could say therefore that it is a conceptual, rather than an objective, contradiction, because, as Scott herself says, "the repetitions and conflicts of feminism" are "symptoms of contradictions in the political [*sic*] that produced feminism and that it appealed to and challenged at the same time. These were the discourses of individualism, individual rights and social obligation of democratic citizenship in France" (*Only Paradoxes to Offer*, 3).

31. Goodman, "More than Paradoxes to Offer," 396. Although, obviously, the relationship between feminism and discursive transformation is not a one-sided but a dialectic one, since feminist practice is, in turn, one of the driving forces of such a transformation.

32. Joan W. Scott, "A Reply to Criticism," *International Labor and Working Class History* 32 (1987): 41.

33. Joyce, ed., *Class*, 6 and 183.

34. Joyce, ed., *Class*, 128.

35. Joyce, ed., *Class*, 7.

36. Mary Poovey, "The Social Constitution of 'Class': Toward a History of Classificatory Thinking," in *Rethinking Class: Literary Studies and Social Formations*, ed. Wai Chee Dimock and Michael T. Gilmore (New York: Columbia University Press, 1994), 15–56. In what follows, page numbers are indicated in parentheses.

37. Eley. "Is All the World a Text?," 218.

38. The expressions are from Joyce, ed., *Class*, 14–15.

39. William H. Sewell Jr., *Work and Revolution in France: The Language of Labour from the Old Regime to 1848* (New York: Cambridge University Press, 1980); "La confraternité des prolétaires: conscience de class sous la Monarchie de Juillet," *Annales ESC* 4 (1981): 650–71; "Artisans, Factory Workers and the Formation of the French Working Class, 1789–1848," in *Working Class Formation: Nineteenth Century Patterns in Western Europe and the United States*, ed. Ira Katznelson and Aristide Zolberg (Princeton, N.J.: Princeton University Press, 1986), 45–70; and "How Classes Are Made: Critical Reflections on E. P. Thompson's Theory of Working Class Formation," in *E. P. Thompson: Critical Perspectives*, ed. Harvey J. Kaye and Keith McLelland (London: Polity Press, 1990), 50–77. Sewell also unfolds his arguments in "*Corporations Républicaines*: The Revolutionary Idiom of Parisian

Workers in 1848," *Comparative Studies in Society and History* 21 (1979): 195–203, and "Property, Labor, and the Emergence of Socialism in France, 1789–1848," in *Consciousness and Class Experience in Nineteenth-Century Europe*, ed. John M. Merriman (New York: Holmes and Meier Publishers, 1979), 45–63. Page numbers are indicated in parentheses.

40. The notion of association not only designates the union of all workers, it also includes the solidarity among them and a collectivist reorganization of production with a view to triumphing over individualism and the anarchy of the liberal economic system ("La confraternité," 658–60, and "Artisans," 62). I will not, however, deal with these latter meanings here.

41. Here, of course, class identity or consciousness should be understood as simply the sense of *belonging* to a social group that includes the workers from all trades. As Sewell says, this is a "descriptive designation" (*Work*, 283), since this is not an identity based on the concept of class, as occurs in later stages of the labor movement, but on the concept of individual. Sewell himself expressly establishes this distinction by stating that class-consciousness and struggle in the 1830s and 1840s was still quite different from that embodied in the class-conscious proletarian parties of the late nineteenth and twentieth centuries. This difference lies in the meaning of the term "class" itself. At this time, class is only a descriptive social category, and only after the spread of Marxism, he says, class came to refer mainly to social categories in a relationship of superordination or subordination and began to take on connotations of moral solidarity. "Class loyalty" would have been reprehensible to workers in 1848, as it would have implied a loyalty to some selfish interest against the common interest. By 1900, "class loyalty" had come to imply a selfless devotion to the cause of all workers (*Work*, 282). Consequently, here one can talk of class only as the sum or aggregate of more or less homogeneous individuals in the socioeconomic and cultural aspects, but not as a specific social entity and, much less, as a historical subject. In fact, strictly speaking, one should talk simply of *workers' identity*.

42. In this case too, one must clearly distinguish between this movement *of* workers, with a liberal base, and the later workers' movement based on class.

43. This is, of course, a conclusion Sewell would presumably not agree with either totally or literally. As Sewell continues to operate, up to a point, with the dichotomous theoretical model, and for him, the categories that articulate working class identity and practice remain, to a great extent, ideological entities. And that is why, apart from leaving the door open to an idealist interpretation of his work, he ends up by suggesting, first of all, that if class consciousness is not an expression of social conditions, then it is a political construction (i.e., subjective). And, second, that the aforementioned categories are imposed by the state and by the dominant classes and, therefore, what happens is that workers are forced to submit ideologically to them ("La confraternité," 668). However, the political language as the subjective embodiment of a discourse's category is one thing, and the discourse itself is another. By not making this distinction, Sewell overlooks two crucial details. First, the making of both the dominant class as a subject and the new form of state is also the result of a process of discursive mediation and that, therefore, these are not mere social entities. Second, the power relations between the labor movement and the dominant class are inscribed in a certain discursive

regime, which is what has articulated them both as subjects and agents, and therefore they both share a common social imaginary and are guided by common criteria of naturalness. Thus, what workers do is not just simply submit to the ideological definitions imposed by the state and the bourgeoisie, but they renaturalize their identity and practice in accordance with the new discursive rationality.

44. Zachary Lockman, "'Worker' and 'Working Class' in pre-1914 Egypt: A Rereading," in *Workers and Working Classes in the Middle East: Struggles, Histories, Historiographies*, ed. Zachary Lockman (Albany, N.Y.: State University of New York Press, 1994), 71–109, and "Imagining the Working Class: Culture, Nationalism and Class Formation in Egypt, 1899–1914," *Poetics Today* 15, no. 2 (1994): 157–190. Page numbers are indicated in parentheses.

45. His exact words, theoretically more ambiguous, are: "in and through political and ideological struggles—which are always discursive struggles, struggles about meaning" ('Worker,' 77).

CHAPTER 5

1. Geoff Eley, "Is All the World a Text?—From Social History to the History of Society Two Decades Later," in *The Historic Turn in the Human Sciences*, ed. Terrence McDonald (Ann Arbor: University of Michigan Press, 1996), 213.

2. Stuart Hall, "The Toad in the Garden: Thatcherism among the Theorists," in *Marxism and the Interpretation of Culture*, ed. Cary Nelson and Lawrence Grossberg (Urbana: University of Illinois Press, 1988), 44.

3. Joan W. Scott, Review of *Heroes of Their Own Lives. The Politics and History of Family Violence*, by Linda Gordon, *Signs* 16 (1990): 851.

4. Keith M. Baker, *Inventing the French Revolution: Essays on French Political Culture in the Eighteenth Century* (New York: Cambridge University Press, 1990), 6.

5. Geoff Eley, "Is All the World a Text?" 214.

6. William H. Sewell Jr., "Language and Practice in Cultural History: Backing Away from the Edge of the Cliff," *French Historical Studies* 21, no. 2 (1998): 250–52.

7. William H. Sewell Jr., "Whatever Happened to the 'Social' in Social History?" in *Schools of Thought. Twenty-Five Years of Interpretive Social Science*, ed. Joan W. Scott and Debra Keates (Princeton, N.J.: Princeton University Press, 2001), 209–26. In what follows, page numbers are indicated in parentheses. This seems to me one of the most significant contributions to the present-day theoretical debate in the field of historical and social studies. Because even though Sewell continues to advocate social causality, he openly recognizes the existence of and seriously tackles the challenge of the emerging postsocial theoretical paradigm. And in doing so, he clearly helps to move such a debate beyond the limits of the standard dichotomous horizon.

8. He refers to Joan W. Scott, "A Statistical Representation of Work: *La Statistique de l'industrie à Paris, 1847–1848*," in Joan W. Scott, *Gender and the Politics of History* (New York: Columbia University Press, 1988), 113–38.

9. This inability to properly understand the distinction between real fact and objective fact is patent, and striking, for example, in an otherwise sophisticated

new cultural historian like Roger Chartier, on whom Sewell sometimes relies here (218). This is clearly the case throughout the Chartier's book *On the Edge of the Cliff: History, Language, and Practices* (Baltimore: Johns Hopkins University Press, 1997).

10. The expression is from Mariana Valverde, "The Rhetoric of Reform: Tropes and the Moral Subject," *International Journal of the Sociology of Law* 18 (1990): 61.

11. Margaret R. Somers, "Narrativity, Narrative Identity and Social Action: Rethinking English Working Class Formation," *Social Science History* 16, no. 4 (1992): 595–96. In what follows, page numbers are indicated in parentheses. Of course, as Somers herself affirms elsewhere, at the heart of this objectivist scheme is "Marx's 'class in itself-for itself' problematic—an ideal typical formulation that predicts the development of a working-class revolutionary consciousness out of capitalism's 'objective' class structure." ("Class Formation and Capitalism: A Second Look at a Classic," *European Journal of Sociology* 37, no. 1 [1996]: 180, and "Workers of the World, Compare!" *Contemporary Sociology* 18 [1989]: 325.)

12. "Workers of the World, Compare!" 328. It refers to Ira Katznelson, "Introduction: Working-Class Formation: Constructing Cases and Comparisons," in *Working-Class Formation: Nineteenth-Century Patterns in Western Europe and the United States*, ed. Ira Katznelson and Aristide R. Zolberg (Princeton, N.J.: Princeton University Press, 1986), 3–41.

13. This is what explains, likewise, adds Somers, that the scholarly outcome of this "failure" of the Western working class "to behave correctly" is so striking: "Rather than a rich literature explaining variations among working-class histories, countless explanations can be found for why any given working-class 'deviated' from the prediction." ("Class Formation and Capitalism," 180, and "Workers of the World, Compare!" 325.)

14. William H. Sewell Jr., "The Sans-Culotte Rhetoric of Subsistence," in *The French Revolution and the Creation of Modern Political Culture*, vol. 4: *The Terror*, ed. Keith M. Baker (Oxford: Pergamon, 1994), 249–69. In what follows, page numbers are indicated in parentheses. In the Sewell's account, of course, the elements of postsocial history are interwoven with those of new cultural history. However, I will take into account only the former, as my purpose here is not to reproduce the author's arguments in their entirety, but to highlight the contribution of this work to the shaping of the new theory of society.

15. That this causal equation between scarcity and the program on subsistence does not exist is, precisely, what leads Sewell to consider "untenable" (262) the Soboul and George Rudé's thesis that the small scale of urban industry and the high proportion of income spent on bread "assured that popular classes of Paris would define their interests as consumers rather than as producers and that they would be obsessed with the supply and price of food rather than with wages and working conditions" (261–62).

16. That is why Sewell states that "although it is undoubtedly true that hunger and the fear of hunger gave rise to a widespread concern about the supply and price of food in revolutionary Paris, only a very indirect route can lead us from hunger to the elaborate and compulsively repeated rhetorical figure of a counter-revolutionary plot to starve the people and destroy the republic. The suggested cause [hunger], while certainly relevant, seems utterly insufficient to explain the

extravagant effect. Explaining the emergence of a specific sans-culottes rhetoric of subsistence in the revolutionary discourse of 1793 requires a far more complicated story than Soboul attempted to tell" (261).

17. Nor does Sewell expressly define the concept of "political culture." However, this concept does not seem to refer simply to a set of political *ideas*, but a specific historical instance. In any case, we should remember, on this point, that the fact that modern discourse frequently adopts a political form—and not, for example, a religious one—should not lead us to confuse the political *language* as a pattern of meaning with its subjective projection in the form of political *vocabulary*.

18. Political practice, of course, also depends on the specific historical way in which politics itself is articulated as a social sphere and field of activity. Thus, for example, the fact that modern discourse objectified politics as *public sphere* was what conferred the condition of primordial means of social intervention and creation, regulation and transformation of social relations on political action.

19. Margaret R. Somers, "What's Political or Cultural about Political Culture and the Public Sphere? Toward an Historical Sociology of Concept Formation," *Sociological Theory* 13, no. 2 (1995): 134.

20. Baker, *Inventing the French Revolution*, 7. Page numbers are indicated in parentheses.

21. Jeffrey C. Alexander and Phillip Smith, "The discourse of American Civil Society: A New Proposal for Cultural Studies," *Theory and Society* 22, no. 2 (1993): 165. According to the authors, although within this discourse there are differing cultures and traditions, they are all based on a single more basic framework (constituted by elements like fear of power and conspiracy and positive values like individual autonomy and contractual relations, honesty, trust, cooperation, or egalitarianism). Therefore, it could be said that the discourse of civil society constitutes "a general grammar from which historically specific traditions draw to create particular configurations of meanings, ideology and belief" (165–66). This leads Alexander and Smith to propose giving up both instrumentalist and structuralist conceptions of political conflicts, because they are not simply ideological or value disputes, but the effects of a certain conceptual logic. At least, they say, in the American context, "conflicting parties within the civil society have drawn upon the same symbolic (sic) code to formulate their particular understandings and to advance their competing claims." And therefore, to understand American politics, one must understand the codes of civil society that act as its basis (197–98).

22. Patrick Joyce, ed., *Class* (Oxford: Oxford University Press, 1995), 185. At this point Joyce implicitly turns to the work of Jacques Donzelot.

23. Patrick Joyce, *Democratic Subjects: The Self and the Social in Nineteenth-Century England* (Cambridge: Cambridge University Press, 1994), 148. The concept of shared discourse is indeed the cornerstone of Joyce's analysis and argument in this work. As he argues elsewhere, "much of nineteenth-century social relations in Britain was played out in terms of 'civility': these terms, those of 'civilization' and 'civil society,' enacted power relations (in the family or schoolroom, say) and created the collective identities upon which liberal democracy rested, identities that involved exclusion and conflict, as well as unities of various sorts (terms like 'humanity,' 'people,' 'the public,' and the realm of 'public opinion')" (*Class*, 185).

24. James Vernon, *Politics and the People: A Study in English Political Culture, c. 1815–1867* (Cambridge: Cambridge University Press, 1993), especially chapter 8. Page numbers are indicated in parentheses. See also his "Notes towards an Introduction," in *Re-reading the Constitution: New Narratives in the Political History of England's Long Nineteenth Century*, ed. James Vernon (Cambridge: Cambridge University Press, 1996), 12–13. For an illuminating overview on this new approach to politics, see Andrew Chadwick, "Studying Political Ideas: A Public Political Discourse Approach," *Political Studies* 48, no. 2 (2000): 283–301.

25. That is why, as Patrick Joyce says, "Toryism was every bit as adept as radicalism and the Whigs at appropriating the constitutional cause" (*Democratic Subjects*, 193).

26. I have already given the example of the relation between middle class and liberalism. I have also stressed, on the one hand, that the bourgeoisie as a political identity is not an expression of the bourgeois class and, on the other, that liberalism is not the ideology of the bourgeoisie, but the discursive pattern that converts it into the dominant political identity and enables it to exercise its domination. As Patrick Joyce writes, "liberalism cannot be viewed as the expression of class interest. Rather, it is a mode of governmentality, which cannot be given a class origin" (*Class*, 184). Of course, new cultural history had already stressed the contingent character of the connection between the middle class and its political identity. However, since this history never dispenses with the dichotomous model and social causality, what it does is simply give a relative autonomy to political identity with respect to middle class. An insightful example of such a new cultural conception can be found in Dror Wahrman, *Imagining the Middle Class: The Political Representation of Class in Britain, c. 1780–1840* (Cambridge: Cambridge University Press, 1995).

27. Baker, *Inventing the French Revolution*, 5 and 17–18.

28. Marc W. Steinberg, "'The Labor of the Country Is the Wealth of the Country': Class Identity, Consciousness and the Role of Discourse in the Making of the English Working Class," *International Labor and Working-Class History* 49 (1996): 7. His arguments are repeated in "'A Way of Struggle.' Reformations and Affirmation of E. P. Thompson's Class Analysis in the Light of Postmodern Theories of Language," *British Journal of Sociology* 48, no. 3 (1997): 471–92. To Steinberg, the resistance of labor movement should be explained in these terms. As he writes of the silk weavers, they "were confronted with the onslaught of capitalist degradation after half a century of relative protection. To counter the hegemony of political economy through which large manufacturers and government officials sought to restructure their world, the weavers appropriated pieces of bourgeois language and retooled it as a weapon of the weak. In this process, they were true Bakhtinian practitioners; they saw the words in use were half theirs" ("'A Way of Struggle,'" 472).

29. Joan W. Scott, Review of *Heroes of Their Own Lives*, 852. As Scott says, referring to the work of Gordon, "it was, after all, the existence of welfare societies that not only made family violence a problem to be dealt with but also gave family members a place to turn, a sense of responsibility, a reason for acting and a way of thinking about resistance" (851).

30. Baker, *Inventing the French Revolution*, 18.

31. Richard Price, "Languages of Revisionism: Historians and Popular Politics in Nineteenth-Century Britain," *Journal of Social History* 30, no. 1 (1996): 229–51.

The paper is a review essay of several books, namely works by Eugenio F. Biagini, Alastair J. Reid, Miles Taylor, James Vernon, and Patrick Joyce.

32. James Vernon, "What Is a Cultural History of Politics?" *History Workshop Journal* 52 (2001): 264–65.

33. Richard Biernacki, *The Fabrication of Labor. Germany and Britain, 1640–1914* (Berkeley and Los Angeles: University of California Press, 1995), part one. The author has summarized his research in "Work and Culture in the Reception of Class ideologies," in *Reworking Class*, ed. John R. Hall (Ithaca, N.Y.: Cornell University Press, 1997), 169–92. Biernacki puts forward and argues his theoretical framework in "Method and Metaphor after the New Cultural History," in *Beyond the Cultural Turn: New Directions in the Study of Society and Culture*, ed. Victoria E. Bonnell and Lynn Hunt (Berkeley and Los Angeles: University of California Press, 1999), 62–92. See also his "Language and the Shift from Signs to Practices in Cultural Inquiry, *History and Theory* 39, no. 3 (2000): 289–310. A basically similar argument— in this case, on the relation between corporatist discourse and heavy industry in Wilhelmine Germany—can be found in Dennis Sweeney, "Corporatist Discourse and Heavy Industry in Wilhelmine Germany: Factory Culture and Employer Politics in the Saar," *Comparative Studies in Society and History* 43, no. 4 (2001): 701–34.

34. Because, in effect, the definition of exploitation, and, consequently, the demands and protest practice of workers and unions, also depend on the concept of labor. In the case of Britain, on thinking that capitalists extract a profit manipulating the relations of exchange through which they secured and disposed of products, the workers' materialized labor, workers considered the marketplace the locus of exploitation and, therefore, demanded fair returns in the realm of exchange. In Germany, in contrast, on conceiving exploitation as an extraction of surplus and by locating it, in consequence, in production and not in the marketplace, what workers demand is a modification of property relations. Biernacki devotes part three of his book to the relationship between the concept of labor and the demands and practice of labor movement. Furthermore, he deals with such a relationship with full details in "Labor As an Imagined Commodity," *Politics and Society* 29, no. 2 (2001): 173–206.

35. A classical formulation of the new cultural view can be found in William H. Sewell Jr., "Toward a Post-materialist Rhetoric for Labor History," in *Rethinking Labor History: Essays on Discourse and Class Analysis*, ed. Lenard R. Berlanstein (Urbana: University of Illinois Press, 1993), 15–38. Essentially, what Sewell argues is that economy is not a purely material sphere, but it is also made up of symbolic practices and elements. Or, as he says, "like activities that go on in other spheres— say government, learning, religion, or warfare—production and exchange entail a complex mixture of what we would usually call the ideal and the material" (20).

CONCLUSION

1. This mistake is patent, for example, in William H. Sewell Jr., "Whatever Happened to the 'Social' in Social History?," in *Schools of Thought: Twenty-Five Years of Interpretive Social Science*, eds. Joan W. Scott and Debra Keates (Princeton, N.J.:

Princeton University Press, 2001), 212–13. For Seweel, "linguistic turn" is a step
further in the cultural and anthropological shift experienced by historical studies
from the mid-1970. The continuity thesis is also unfolded in Victoria E. Bonnell
and Lynn Hunt, eds., *Beyond the Cultural Turn: New Directions in the Study of Society and Culture* (Berkeley and Los Angeles: University of California Press, 1999),
8–9. Frustrated with the limitations of social history and historical sociology, Bonnell and Hunt tell us, historians and sociologists began to turn in a cultural direction. Later, this "linguistic turn" went on being fueled by the emergence of structuralism and poststructuralism. Underlying such a thesis is, of course, an equation
between "culture" and "language" (9). This is however a mistake that other authors do not commit. For Ronald Grigor Suny, for example, the cultural turn is neither the same as the linguistic turn nor coterminous with poststructuralism or
postmodernism, even though they have overlapped temporally and intellectually
and shared a number of concerns. ("Back and Beyond: Reversing the Cultural
Turn?" *American Historical Review* 107, no. 5 [2002]: 1482.)

2. Sarah Maza, "The Social Imaginary of the French Revolution: The Third Estate, the National Guard, and the Absent Bourgeoisie," in *The Age of Cultural Revolutions: Britain and France, 1750–1820*, ed. Colin Jones and Dror Wahrman (Berkeley and Los Angeles: University of California Press, 2002), 106–23. The sentence in
quotation marks is on page 123.

3. Marc W. Steinberg, "'The Labor of the Country Is the Wealth of the Country': Class Identity, Consciousness and the Role of Discourse in the Making of the
English Working Class," *International Labor and Working-Class History* 49 (1996): 5.

4. Marc W. Steinberg, "Culturally Speaking: Finding a Commons between Post
Structuralism and the Thompsonian Perspective," *Social History* 21, no. 2 (1996): 202.

5. Joan W. Scott, *Gender and the Politics of History* (New York: Columbia University Press, 1988), 5.

6. John W. Toews, "Intellectual History after the Linguistic Turn: The Autonomy of Meaning and the Irreducibility of Experience," *American Historical Review*
92, no. 4 (1987): 898 and 890.

7. Patrick Joyce, "The End of Social History?" *Social History* 20, no. 1 (1995): 91.

8. Joan W. Scott, "The Evidence of Experience," *Critical Inquiry* 17 (1991): 796.

9. Richard Biernacki, "Method and Metaphor after the New Cultural History,"
in *Beyond the Cultural Turn: New Directions in the Study of Society and Culture*, ed.
Victoria E. Bonnell and Lynn Hunt (Berkeley and Los Angeles: University of California Press, 1999), 75.

10. Here I am paraphrasing Joan W. Scott, "Deconstructing Equality-versus-
Difference: or the Uses of Poststructuralist Theory for Feminism," *Feminist Studies*
14, no. 1 (1988): 34–35.

Bibliography

Abelson, Elaine, David Abraham, and Marjorie Murphy. "Interview with Joan Scott." *Radical History Review* 45 (1989): 41–59.

Alexander, Jeffrey C., and Philip Smith. "The Discourse of American Civil Society: A New Proposal for Cultural Studies." *Theory and Society* 22, no. 2 (1993): 151–207.

Baker, Keith Michael. "Enlightenment and Revolution in France: Old Problems, Renewed Approaches." *Journal of Modern History* 53 (1981): 281–303.

——. "Politique et opinion publique sous l'Ancien Régime." *Annales ESC* 42, no. 1 (1987): 41–71.

——. "Revolution." Pp. 41–62 in *The French Revolution and the Creation of Modern Political Culture, Vol. 2: The Political Culture of the French Revolution*, edited by Colin Lucas. Oxford: Pergamon, 1988.

——. "Closing the French Revolution: Saint-Simon and Comte." Pp. 323–39 in *The French Revolution and the Creation of Modern Political Culture, Vol. 3: The Transformation of Political Culture, 1789–1848*, edited by François Furet and Mona Ozouf. Oxford: Pergamon, 1989.

——. *Inventing the French Revolution: Essays on French Political Culture in the Eighteenth Century*. New York: Cambridge University Press, 1990.

——. "Defining the Public Sphere in Eighteenth-Century France: Variations on a Theme by Habermas." Pp. 181–211 in *Habermas and the Public Sphere*, edited by Craig Calhoun. Cambridge, Mass: MIT Press, 1993.

——. "A Foucauldian French Revolution?" Pp. 187–205 in *Foucault and the Writing of History*, edited by Jan Goldstein. Cambridge, Mass.: Blackwell, 1994.

——. "Enlightenment and the Institution of Society: Notes for a Conceptual History." Pp. 95–120 in *Main Trends in Cultural History*, edited by Willem Melching and Wyger Velema. Amsterdam: Rodopi, 1994. Also pp. 84–104 in *Civil Society: History and Possibilities*, edited by Sudipta Kaviraj and Sunil Khilnani. Cambridge: Cambridge University Press, 2001.

——. "The Idea of a Declaration of Rights." Pp. 154–96 in *The French Idea of Freedom: Origins of the Declaration of the Rights of Man and of the Citizen*, edited by Dale Van Kley. Stanford, Calif.: Stanford University Press, 1994. Also pp. 91–140 in *The French Revolution. Recent Debates and New Controversies*, edited by Gary Kates. London: Routledge, 1998.

——. "Transformations of Classical Republicanism in Eighteenth-Century France." *Journal of Modern History* 73, no. 1 (2001): 32–53.

Biernacki, Richard. *The Fabrication of Labor. Germany and Britain, 1640–1914*. Berkeley and Los Angeles: University of California Press, 1995.

——. "Work and Culture in the Reception of Class Ideologies." Pp. 169–92 in *Reworking Class*, edited by John R. Hall. Ithaca, N.Y.: Cornell University Press, 1997.

——. "Method and Metaphor after the New Cultural History." Pp. 62–92 in Bonnell, Victoria E., and Lynn Hunt, eds., 1999.

——. "Language and the Shift from Signs to Practices in Cultural Inquiry." *History and Theory* 39, no. 3 (2000): 289–310.

——. "Labor As an Imagined Commodity." *Politics and Society* 29, no. 2 (2001): 173–206.

Bonnell, Victoria E., and Lynn Hunt, eds. *Beyond the Cultural Turn: New Directions in the Study of Society and Culture*. Berkeley and Los Angeles: University of California Press, 1999.

Brantlinger, Patrick. "A Response to *Beyond the Cultural Turn*." *American Historical Review* 107, no. 5 (2002): 1500–11.

Cabrera, Miguel A. "Linguistic Approach or Return to Subjectivism? In Search of an Alternative to Social History." *Social History* 24, no. 1 (1999): 74–89.

——. "On Language, Culture, and Social Action." *History and Theory* 40, no. 4 (2001): 82–100.

Canning, Kathleen. "Feminist History after the Linguistic Turn: Historicizing Discourse and Experience." *Signs* 19, no. 2 (1994): 368–404.

Censer, Jack R. "Revitalizing the Intellectual History of the French Revolution." *Journal of the History of Ideas* 50, no. 4 (1989): 652–66.

——. "Social Twists and Linguistic Turns. Revolutionary Historiography a Decade after the Bicentennial." *French Historical Studies* 22, no. 1 (1999): 139–67.

Chadwick, Andrew. "Aristocracy or the People? Radical Constitutionalism and the Progressive Alliance in Edwardian Britain." *Journal of Political Ideologies* 4, no. 3 (1999): 365–90.

——. *Augmenting Democracy. Political Movements and Constitutional Reform during the Rise of Labour, 1900–1924*. Aldershot: Ashgate, 1999.

——. "Studying Political Ideas: A Public Political Discourse Approach." *Political Studies* 48, no. 2 (2000): 283–301.

Childers, Thomas. "Political Sociology and the 'Linguistic Turn'." *Central European History* 22, nos. 3-4 (1989): 381–93.

Cook, Kathryn and Renea Henry. "The Edge. Interview with Joan Wallach Scott." *Differences* 9, no. 3 (1997): 132–55.

Corfield, Penelope J., ed. *Language, History and Class*. Oxford: Blackwell, 1991.

Curry, Patrick. "Towards a Post-Marxist Social History: Thompson, Clark and Beyond." Pp. 158–200 in *Rethinking Social History: English Society 1570–1920 and its Interpretation*, edited by Adrian Wilson. Manchester: Manchester University Press, 1993.

Eley, Geoff. "De l'histoire sociale au 'tournant linguistique' dans l'historiographie anglo-américaine des années 1980." *Genèses* 7 (1992): 163–93.
———. "What Is Cultural History?" *New German Critique* 65 (1995): 19–36.
———. "Is All the World a Text? From Social History to the History of Society Two Decades Later." Pp. 193–243 in Terrence J. McDonald, ed., 1996.
———. "Problems with Culture: German History after the Linguistic Turn." *Central European History* 31, no. 3 (1998): 197–228.
Eley, Geoff, and Keith Nield. "Starting Over: The Present, the Post-Modern and the Moment of Social History." *Social History* 20, no. 3 (1995): 355–64.
Eley, Geoff, and Ronald Grigor Suny. "Introduction: From the Moment of Social History to the Work of Cultural Representation." Pp. 3–37 in *Becoming National: A Reader*, edited by Geoff Eley and Ronald Grigor Suny. New York: Oxford University Press, 1996.
Finney, Patrick. "Still 'Marking Time'? Text, Discourse and Truth in International History." *Review of International Studies* 27, no. 3 (2001): 291–308.
Formisano, Ronald P. "The Concept of Political Culture." *Journal of Interdisciplinary History* 31, no. 3 (2001): 393–426.
Frader, Laura L. "Dissent over Discourse: Labor History, Gender, and the Linguistic Turn." *History and Theory* 34, no. 3 (1995): 213–30.
Geary, Dick. "Labour History, the 'Linguistic Turn' and Postmodernism." *Contemporary European History* 9, no. 3 (2000): 445–62.
Goodman, Dena. "More than Paradoxes to Offer: Feminist History as Critical Practice." *History and Theory* 36, no. 3 (1997): 392–405.
Gunnell, John G. "Time and Interpretation: Understanding Concepts and Conceptual Change." *History of Political Thought* 29, no. 4 (1998): 641–58.
Handler, Richard. "Cultural Theory in History Today." *American Historical Review* 107, no. 5 (2002): 1512–20.
Harlan, David. "Intellectual History and the Return of Literature." *American Historical Review* 94, no. 3 (1989): 581–609.
Howarth, David. "An Archaeology of Political Discourse? Evaluating Michel Foucault's Explanation and Critique of Ideology." *Political Studies* 50, no. 1 (2002): 117–35.
———. *Discourse*. Buckingham: Open University Press, 2000.
———, Aletta J. Norval, and Yannis Stavrakakis, eds. *Discourse Theory and Political Analysis: Identities, Hegemonies and Social Change*. Manchester, U.K.: Manchester University Press, 2000.
Ireland, Craig. "The Appeal to Experience and its Consequences. Variations on a Persistent Thompsonian Theme." *Cultural Critique* 52 (2002): 86–107.
Joyce, Patrick. "History and Post-Modernism." *Past and Present* 133 (1991): 204–209.
———. "The People's English: Language and Class in England, c. 1840–1920." Pp. 154–90 in *Language, Self, and Society: A Social History of Language*, edited by Peter Burke and Roy Porter. Cambridge, U.K.: Polity Press, 1991.
———. *Visions of the People: Industrial England and the Question of Class, 1848–1914*. Cambridge: Cambridge University Press, 1991.
———. "A People and a Class: Industrial Workers and the Social Order in Nineteenth-Century England." Pp. 199–217 in *Social Orders and Social Classes in Europe since 1500: Studies in Social Stratification*, edited by M. L. Bush. London: Longman, 1992.

——. "The Imaginary Discontents of Social History: A Note of Response to Mayfield and Thorne, and Lawrence and Taylor." *Social History* 18, no. 1 (1993): 81–85.
——. *Democratic Subjects: The Self and the Social in Nineteenth-Century England.* Cambridge: Cambridge University Press, 1994.
——, ed. *Class.* Cambridge: Cambridge University Press, 1995.
——. "The End of Social History?" *Social History* 20, no. 1 (1995): 73–91.
——. "The Constitution and the Narrative Structure of Victorian Politics." Pp. 179–203 in James Vernon, ed., 1996.
——. "The Return of History: Postmodernism and the Politics of Academic History in Britain." *Past and Present* 158 (1998): 207–35.
——. "The Politics of the Liberal Archive." *History of the Human Sciences* 12, no. 2 (1999): 35–49.
——, ed. *The Social in Question: New Bearings in History and the Social Sciences.* London: Routledge, 2002.
Kane, Anne E. "Theorizing Meaning Construction in Social Movements: Symbolic Structures and Interpretation during the Irish Land War, 1879–1882." *Sociological Theory* 15, no. 3 (1997): 249–76.
——. "Cultural Analysis in Historical Sociology: The Analytic and Concrete Forms of the Autonomy of Culture." *Sociological Theory* 9, no. 1 (1991): 53–69. Also pp. 73–87 in *The New American Cultural Sociology*, edited by Philip Smith. Cambridge: Cambridge University Press, 1998.
——. "Reconstructing Culture in Historical Explanation: Narratives as Cultural Structure and Practice." *History and Theory* 39, no. 3 (2000): 311–30.
——. "Narratives of Nationalism: Constructing Irish National Identity during the Land War, 1879–82." *National Identities* 2, no. 3 (2000): 245–64.
——. "The Fall of Feudalism in Ireland: A Guide for Cultural Analysis of the Irish Land War." *New Hibernia Review* 5, no. 1 (2001): 136–41.
Kirk, Neville. "In Defense of Class. A critique of Recent Revisionist Writing upon the Nineteenth-Century English Working Class." *International Review of Social History* 28 (1987): 2–42.
——. "History, Language, Ideas, and Post-Modernism: A Materialist View." *Social History* 19, no. 2 (1994): 221–40.
——, ed. *Social Class and Marxism. Defences and Challenges.* Aldershot: Scolar Press, 1996.
Kirk, Neville, and John Belchem, eds. *Languages of Labour.* Aldershot: Ashgate, 1997.
Laclau, Ernesto. "The Death and Resurrection of the Theory of Ideology." *Journal of Political Ideologies* 1, no. 3 (1996): 201–21.
Laclau, Ernesto, and Chantal Mouffe, *Hegemony and Socialist Strategy: Towards a Radical Democratic Politics.* London, Verso, 1985. Reprinted with a new preface (2001).
Lockman, Zachary. "Imagining the Working Class: Culture, Nationalism, and Class Formation in Egypt, 1899–1914." *Poetics Today* 15, no. 2 (1994): 157–90.
—— "'Worker' and 'Working Class' in pre-1914 Egypt: A Rereading." Pp. 71–109 in *Workers and Working Classes in the Middle East: Struggles, Histories, Historiographies*, edited by in Zachary Lockman. Albany, N.Y.: State University of New York Press, 1994.

Martin, James. "The Political Logic of Discourse: A Neo-Gramscian View." *History of European Ideas* 28, no. 1 (2000): 21–31.

Mayfield, David. "Language and Social History." *Social History* 16, no. 3 (1991): 353–58.

McConachie, Bruce. "Doing Things with Image Schemas: The Cognitive Turn in Theatre Studies and the Problem of Experience for Historian." *Theatre Journal* 53, no. 4 (2001): 569–94.

McDonald, Terrence J., ed. *The Historic Turn in the Human Sciences.* Ann Arbor: University of Michigan Press, 1996.

Newton, Judith. "Family Fortunes: New History and 'New Historicism.'" *Radical History Review* 43 (1989): 5–22.

Palmer, Bryan D. "Response to Joan Scott," *International Labor and Working-Class History* 31 (1987): 14–23.

———. *Descent into Discourse: The Reification of Language and the Writing of Social History.* Philadelphia: Temple University Press, 1990.

———. "Critical Theory, Historical Materialism, and the Ostensible End of Marxism: The Poverty of Theory Revisited." *International Review of Social History* 38 (1993): 133–62.

Poovey, Mary. "Speaking of the Body: Mid-Victorian Constructions of Female Desire." Pp. 29–46 in *Body Politics: Women and the Discourses of Science*, edited by Mary Jacobus, Evelyn Fox Keller, and Sally Shuttleworth. New York: Routledge, 1990.

———. "Figures of Arithmetic, Figures of Speech: The Discourse of Statistics in the 1830s." *Critical Inquiry* 19, no. 2 (1993): 256–76.

———. "The Social Constitution of 'Class': Toward a History of Classificatory Thinking." Pp. 15–56 in *Rethinking Class: Literary Studies and Social Formations*, edited by Wai Chee Dimock and Michael T. Gilmore. New York: Columbia University Press, 1994.

———. *Making a Social Body: British Cultural Formation, 1830–1864.* Chicago and London: The University of Chicago Press, 1995.

———. *A History of the Modern Fact. Problems of Knowledge in the Sciences of Wealth and Society.* Chicago and London: The University of Chicago Press, 1998.

———. "For Everything Else, There's. . . ." *Social Research* 68, no. 2 (2001): 397–426.

———. "The Liberal Civil Subject and the Social in Eighteenth-Century British Moral Philosophy." *Public Culture* 14, no. 1 (2002): 125–45. Also pp. 44–61 in Patrick Joyce, ed., 2002.

Price, Richard. "Languages of Revisionism: Historians and Popular Politics in Nineteenth-Century Britain." *Journal of Social History* (fall 1996): 229–51.

Purvis, Trevor, and Alan Hunt. "Discourse, Ideology, Discourse, Ideology, Discourse, Ideology. . . ." *British Journal of Sociology* 44, no. 3 (1993): 473–99.

Rabinbach, Anson. *The Human Motor. Energy, Fatigue and the Origins of Modernity.* Berkeley and Los Angeles: University of California Press, 1990.

———. "Rationalism and Utopia as Language of Nature: A Note." *International Labor and Working-Class History* 31 (1987): 30–36.

Reid, Donald. "The Night of the Proletarians. Deconstruction and Social History." *Radical History Review* 28–30 (1984): 445–463.

——. "Reflections on Labor History and Language." Pp. 39–54 in *Rethinking Labor History: Essays on Discourse and Class Analysis*, edited by Lenard R. Berlanstein. Urbana and Chicago: University of Illinois Press, 1993.

——. "In the Name of the Father: A Language of Labour Relations in Nineteenth-Century France." *History Workshop* 38 (1994): 1–22.

Sawyer, R. Keith. "A Discourse on Discourse: An Archaeological History of an Intellectual Concept." *Cultural Studies* 16, no. 3 (2002): 433–56.

Schöttler, Peter. "Historians and Discourse Analysis." *History Workshop Journal* 27 (1989): 37–65.

——. "Mentalities, Ideologies, Discourses: On the 'Third Level' as a Theme in Social-Historical Research." Pp. 72–115 in *The History of Everyday Life: Reconstructing Historical Experiences and Ways of Life*, edited by Alf Lüdtke. Princeton, N.J.: Princeton University Press, 1995.

Scott, Joan W. "History and Difference." *Daedalus* 116, no. 4 (1987): 93–118.

——. "On Language, Gender, and Working-Class History." *International Labor and Working-Class History* 31 (1987): 1–13.

——. "A Reply to Criticism." *International Labor and Working-Class History* 32 (1987): 39–45.

——. "Deconstructing Equality-versus-Difference: or, The Uses of Poststructuralist Theory for Feminism." *Feminist Studies* 14, no. 1 (1988): 33–50.

——. "History in Crisis? The Others' Side of the Story." *American Historical Review* 94, no. 3 (1989): 680–92.

——. Review of *Heroes of Their Own Lives: The Politics and History of Family Violence*, by Linda Gordon. *Signs* 16 (1990): 848–52.

——. "Women's History." Pp. 42–66 in *New Perspectives on Historical Writing*, edited by Peter Burke. Cambridge, U.K.: Polity Press, 1991.

——. "The Evidence of Experience." *Critical Inquiry* 17 (1991): 773–97. Reprinted, in a shorter version, as "Experience." Pp. 22–40 in *Feminists Theorize the Political*, edited by Judith Butler and Joan W. Scott (London: Routledge, 1992).

——. "The Tip of the Volcano." *Comparative Studies in Society and History* 35, no. 3 (1993): 438–43.

——. "Rewriting the History of Feminism." *Western Humanities* 48, 3 (1994): 238-51.

——. "Universalism and the History of Feminism." *Differences* 7, no. 1 (1995): 1–14.

——. "Introduction." Pp. 1–13 in *Feminism and History*, edited by Joan W. Scott. New York: Oxford University Press, 1996.

——. *Only Paradoxes to Offer: French Feminists and the Rights of Man*. Cambridge, Mass.: Harvard University Press, 1996.

——. "Border Patrol." *French Historical Studies* 21, no. 3 (1998): 383–97.

——. *Gender and the Politics of History*. New York: Columbia University Press, 1988. There is a revised edition with a new preface and a further chapter (1999).

——. "Fantasy Echo: History and the Construction of Identity." *Cultural Inquiry* 27, no. 2 (2001): 284–304.

Sewell, William H. "*Corporations Républicaines*: The Revolutionary Idiom of Parisian Workers in 1848." *Comparative Studies in Society and History* 21 (1979): 195–203.

——. "Property, Labor, and the Emergence of Socialism in France, 1789–1848." Pp. 45–63 in *Consciousness and Class Experience in Nineteenth-Century Europe*, edited by John M. Merriman. New York: Holmes and Meier Publishers, 1979.

———. *Work and revolution in France: The Language of Labor from the Old Regime to 1848.* New York: Cambridge University Press, 1980.

———. "La confraternité des prolétaires: conscience de classe sous la Monarchie de Juillet," *Annales, ESC* 36, no. 4 (1981): 650–71.

———. "Ideologies and Social Revolutions: Reflections on the French Case." *Journal of Modern History* 57 (1985): 57–85.

———. "Artisans, Factory Workers, and the Formation of the French Working Class, 1789–1848." Pp. 45–70 in *Working Class Formation: Nineteenth Century Patterns in Western Europe and the United States,* edited by Ira Katznelson and Aristide Zolberg. Princeton, N.J.: Princeton University Press, 1986.

———. "Uneven Development, the Autonomy of Politics, and the Dockworkers of Nineteentn-Century Marseille." *American Historical Review* 93, no. 3 (1988): 604–37.

———. "Collective Violence and Collective Loyalties in France: Why the French Revolution Made a Difference." *Politics and Society* 18, no. 4 (1990): 527–52.

———. "How Classes are Made: Critical Reflections on E. P. Thompson's Theory of Working-Class Formation." Pp. 50–77 in *E. P. Thompson: Critical Perspectives,* edited by Harvey J. Kaye and Keith McLelland. London: Polity Press, 1990.

———. Review of *Gender and the Politics of History,* by Joan W. Scott. *History and Theory* 29, no. 1 (1990): 71–82.

———. "The Sans-Culotte Rhetoric of Subsistence." Pp. 249–69 in *The French Revolution and the Creation of Modern Political Culture,* Vol. 4: *The Terror,* edited by Keith M. Baker. Oxford: Pergamon, 1994.

———. "The Concept(s) of Culture." Pp. 35–61 in Bonnell, Victoria E., and Lynn Hunt, eds., 1999.

———. "Whatever Happened to the 'Social' in Social History?" Pp. 209–26 in *Schools of Thought: Twenty-Five Years of Interpretive Social Science,* edited by Joan W. Scott and Debra Keates. Princeton, N.J.: Princeton University Press, 2001.

Somers, Margaret R. "Workers of the World, Compare!" *Contemporary Sociology* 18 (1989): 325–29.

———. "Narrativity, Narrative Identity, and Social Action: Rethinking English Working-Class Formation." *Social Science History* 16, no. 4 (1992): 591–630.

———. "What's Political or Cultural about Political Culture and the Public Sphere? Toward an Historical Sociology of Concept Formation." *Sociological Theory* 13, no. 2 (1995): 113–44.

———. "Narrating and Naturalizing Civil Society and Citizenship Theory: The Place of Political Culture and the Public Sphere." *Sociological Theory* 13, no. 3 (1995): 229–74.

———. "Class Formation and Capitalism. A Second Look at a Classic." *European Journal of Sociology* 37, no. 1 (1996): 180–202.

———. "La ciudadanía y el lugar de la esfera pública: un enfoque histórico." Pp. 217–34 in *Ciudadanía: justicia social, identidad y participación,* edited by Soledad García and Steven Lukes. Madrid: Siglo XXI, 1999.

———. "The Privatization of Citizenship: How to Unthink a Knowledge Culture." Pp. 121–61 in Bonnell, Victoria E., and Lynn Hunt, eds., 1999.

Somers, Margaret R., and Gloria D. Gibson. "Reaclaiming the Epistemological 'Other': Narrative and the Social Constitution of Identity." Pp. 37–99 in *Social*

Theory and the Politics of Identity, edited by Craig Calhoun. Cambridge, Mass: Blackwell, 1994.

Stansell, Christine. "A Reply to Joan Scott." *International Review and Working-Class History* 31 (1987): 24–29.

Steinberg, Marc W. "Culturally Speaking: Finding a Commons between Post-structuralism and the Thompsonian Perspective." *Social History* 21, no. 2 (1996): 193–214.

——. "'The Labor of the Country Is the Wealth of the Country': Class Identity, Consciousness, and the Role of Discourse in the Making of the English Working Class." *International Labor and Working-Class History* 49 (1996): 1–25.

——. "'A Way of Struggle': Reformations and Affirmation of E. P. Thompson's Class Analysis in the Light of Postmodern Theories of Language." *British Journal of Sociology* 48, no. 3 (1997): 471–92.

Stone-Mediatore, Shari. "Chantra Mohanty and the Revaluing of 'Experience.'" *Hypatia* 13, no. 2 (1998): 116–33.

Suny, Ronald Grigor. "Back and Beyond: Reversing the Cultural Turn?" *American Historical Review* 107, no. 5 (2002): 1476–99.

Sweeney, Dennis. "Work, Race and the Transformation of Industrial Culture in Wilhelmine Germany." *Social History* 23, no. 1 (1998): 31–62.

——. "Corporatist Discourse and Heavy Industry in Wilhelmine Germany: Factory Culture and Employer Politics in the Saar." *Comparative Studies in Society and History* 43, no. 44 (2001): 701–34.

Taylor, Charles. "Modern Social Imaginaries." *Public Culture* 14, no. 1 (2002): 91–124.

Taylor, Miles. "The Linguistic Turns in British Social History." *Bolletino del XIX Secolo* 4 (1995): 5–13.

Thompson, James. "After the Fall: Class and Political Language in Britain, 1780–1900." *Historical Journal* 39, no. 3 (1996): 785–806.

Toews, John E. "Intellectual History after the Linguistic Turn: The Autonomy of Meaning and the Irreducibility of Experience." *American Historical Review* 92, no. 4 (1987): 879–907.

Valverde, Mariana. "Poststructuralist Gender Historians: Are We Those Names?" *Labour/Le Travail* 25 (1990): 227–36.

——. "The Rhetoric of Reform: Tropes and the Moral Subject." *International Journal of the Sociology of Law* 16 (1990): 61–73.

——. "The Dialectic of the Familiar and the Unfamiliar: 'The Jungle' in Early Slum Travel Writing." *Sociology* 30, no. 3 (1996): 493–509.

——. "Identity and the Law in the United States." *Feminist Studies* 25, no. 2 (1999): 345–61.

——. "Some Remarks on the Rise and Fall of Discourse Analysis." *Histoire Sociale/Social History* 33, no. 65 (2000): 59–77.

Vernon, James. *Politics and the People: A Study in English Political Culture, c. 1815–1867*. Cambridge: Cambridge University Press, 1993.

——. "Who's Afraid of the "Linguistic Turn"? The Politics of Social History and its Discontents." *Social History* 19, no. 1 (1994): 81–97.

——. "Border Crossing: Cornwall and the English (imagi)nation." Pp. 153–72 in *Imagining Nations*, edited by Geoffrey Cubit. Manchester, U.K.: Manchester University Press, 1998.

———. "'For Some Queer Reason': The Trials and Tribulations of Colonel Barker's Masquerade in Interwar Britain." *Signs* 26, no. 1 (2000): 37–62.

———. "What Is a Cultural History of Politics?" *History Workshop Journal* 52 (2001): 261–65.

———, ed. *Re-reading the Constitution. New Narratives in the Political History of England's Long Nineteenth Century.* Cambridge: Cambridge University Press, 1996.

Weir, Lorna. "The Wanderings of the Linguistic Turn in Anglophone Historical Writing." *Journal of Historical Sociology* 6, no. 2 (1993): 227–45.

Zammito, John H. "Reading 'Experience': The Debate in Intellectual History among Scott, Toews, and LaCapra." Pp. 279–311 in *Reclaiming Identity. Realist Theory and the Predicament of Postmodernism,* edited by Paula M. L. Moya and Michael R. Hames-García. Berkeley and Los Angeles: University of California Press, 2000.

Index

Sonenscher, Michael, 13
Spiegel, Gabrielle M., 130n25
Stansell, Christine, 42, 48
Steinberg, Marc W., 118, 124
subject. *See* identity
subjectivity, 29–30
Suny, Ronald Grigor, 147n1
Sweeney, Dennis, 146n33

Taylor, Charles, 24
Taylor, Miles, 18

Thompson, Edward P., 7–8, 18, 34, 47,
  52, 124
Toews, John E., 28, 125
total history, 3, 5

Valverde, Mariana, 134n21, 138n3
Vernon, James, xix, 23, 75, 115, 119

Walkowitz, Judith, 13
Williams, Raymond, 14

About the Author

Miguel A. Cabrera is Professor of Modern History at the University of La Laguna (Spain). He is the author of "Linguistic Turn or Return to Subjectivism? In Search of an Alternative to Social History" (*Social History*, 1999) and "On Language, Culture, and Social Action" (*History and Theory*, 2001).